IT'S NOT EASY WEARING GREEN

You Can't Make This Stuff Up!

Joel D. Glover

It's Not Easy Wearing Green
(You Can't Make This Stuff Up)

Copyright © 2019 Joel D. Glover

All rights reserved. No part of this book may be reproduced or transmitted in any form or by any means without written permission from the author.

ISBN: 978-0-9600469-2-8 (Paperback)
ISBN: 978-0-9600469-3-5 (ePub)
Also available for Kindle

Book design and layout: Lighthouse24

DEDICATION

IN MANY REGARDS it wasn't easy wearing green. I had not grown up hating the game warden, but I soon learned a lot of folks did. Looking back, I realize my time on the job was made much easier by the fact that veteran wardens took me under their wing. Many of the stories in this book are episodes I shared with Hershel Patterson. Hershel had been a game warden for nearly twenty years when I was hired. He graciously shared his experience with me, allowing me to avoid many pitfalls. I felt we worked well as a team. He taught me a lot, and he has told me I taught him a little bit. That is satisfying. It is hard to believe as I write this Hershel has been retired for twenty-one years. We still talk every week, and from time to time reminisce about the "good ole days." I appreciate his service as an officer when it really wasn't easy wearing green. He and many others fought the early wildlife wars, which resulted in the healthy wildlife populations we enjoy today. I treasure his friendship, and I dedicate this book to him.

CONTENTS

Preface 9
Introduction 11
Disclaimer 13
"They Shot My House" 15
A Dog Named Elvis 25
A Plastic Tarp 33
The Flu and Night Hunters Too (Cold, Wet, and Muddy) 35
You Gotta Have a Sack 41
Things Happen Fast 46
A Trophy Is in the Eye of the Beholder 49
The Corn Started Flying 52
Big Slimy (Bad Company Corrupts Good Morals) 56
Just Yesterday 68
Chivalry Is Not Dead, or Is It? 74
Big-Footed Baiter (I'm Telling You It's Baited!) 76
The Stew in the Back Seat 82
Arrest Him! 86
Come on out Bruce 90
Go Back and Do It Again 94

Cover Me Rick 98
Deaf Man Hunting 104
Do You Want to Try for a Thousand? 109
Death Scribble 111
Falling in Your Lap 115
Good Communication 119
Funeral Security.. 121
Hang On, I'm Going to Hit You 128
Have You Seen Jake Jackson? 130
Protecting the Bald Eagle 136
Holly Springs Road 139
I Ain't Gonna Hurt My Back!....................................... 144
How Many Tickets Do You Want? 147
I Had to Shoot It 152
J.G. Wentworth.. 158
I Have the Only Permit 162
Women! 167
I'm Crazy.. 170
If That Gun Could Talk.. 175
Keep Your Hand out of Your Pocket.......................... 180
You Know the Kind 193
Kotex Shooter 197
Like Marsh MaDillon.. 200
Littering! 205
No Headlights in Texas 210
I'm a National Guard Colonel! 212

Look Daddy	216
No First Class for You	219
Right Place, Right Time	224
Not What They Wanted (Sorry about Your Gun)	229
You Can Camp Out with the Sheriff	232
A Dog Named Cedrick	241
On Three Wheels	243
Severe Handicap	246
Sitting on the Corn	250
Something No Other Game Warden Had Ever Done!	254
They Took Off!	265
The Defendant Will Speak with You Now (Thanks, Grandpa)	267
Do You Believe in God?	274
Vole Control	281
You Sprayed the Kids!	283
Turkey Whipping	289
Vaccinating the Raccoons	292
Welcome to Coosa County Court	296
Mister, Ya Deer Is Ruint	300
You Are a Lot Nicer Than the Last Guy	303
Murder in Richville	309
Bumper Jack	313
It's Not Easy Wearing Green	318
Another Divine Appointment	321
Epilogue	329

PREFACE

WHEN I ASKED a guy if he had any ID and he said, "'bout what?" I realized I was in for a wild ride. It was by the grace of God I survived thirty-two years in wildlife law enforcement, and I thank and praise Him. While I loved being a wildlife biologist and conservation officer, the title of this book is true. It's not easy wearing green. Please don't think I'm complaining. After all, I sort of chose this line of work. Although I had no idea what all it entailed, I jumped into it with both feet and loved the majority of it.

Granted, being hated by a bunch of folks, who don't even know you, due to your job was sometimes a bummer. Having friends quickly change the subject when you walked up was annoying. Working both day and night, without being compensated for many of the hours, was sometimes a pain. However, for the most part, I did that voluntarily. While I devoted and donated a lot of time to my career, my self-directed schedule allowed me to attend Little League games, band concerts, high school football games, and church regularly. I will admit there were few free weekends during the hunting season.

Another reason it wasn't easy wearing green was because I was over two hundred miles from my family. That is hard. Conservation Officer Hershel Patterson told me if I would stay in Coosa County for two years, I wouldn't want to leave it. He was right in that I grew to love Coosa County. Thankfully, the folks at

Rockford Baptist Church became our extended family. However, it was a long way from Mother and Dad.

It wasn't easy wearing green (or blue) when law enforcement officers started becoming targets of scorn, disdain, and protests. I wish those who are so quick to condemn would walk a mile in our shoes. I know there are bad apples in policing just like in every other walk of life; however, they aren't the norm. I was fortunate that for the vast majority of my career I did not fear being shot when I stopped to put gas in my vehicle. Unfortunately, it's not as easy to say that today.

It wasn't easy wearing green when politics and money began affecting wildlife policy more than what was good for the resource. People, especially politicians, don't seem to understand that *everything* is rooted in our natural resources. That being the case, it probably wouldn't hurt to listen to resource professionals, not cronies who stand to profit, when making decisions about natural resources.

Looking back, I know that God was with me through it all. I praise Him for holding me in His hand. I know my stay here is just temporary. I'm thankful for the many mentors, friends, and coworkers he placed in my path. As always, I praise Him for my family, who supported me all the way.

INTRODUCTION

THIS BOOK IS basically a continuation of my last book, *Parables from Poachers*. While working on that book, I consulted with probably the most well-known author of game warden books, Terry Grosz. I had written Terry a letter revealing to him our somewhat similar lives. We both had obtained multiple college degrees in wildlife. He started his career in Colusa County (California) and I began mine in Coosa County (Alabama). We both married school teachers, and we both had two sons. Suffice it to say we had a few things in common. I talked with Terry on several occasions, and he graciously provided advice to my miserable carcass. I must admit, although I had read that phrase in several of his stories, it took me back when he referred to me that way on the phone. He assured me it was important that I write my stories to help new officers who would glean techniques and tricks to assist them in their careers. He told me he wanted me to send him four copies of my book once it was published, and I assured him I would.

After I received my books, I was working to get them sent to folks who had told me they wanted one. I had placed four books in a box when I realized I had misplaced Terry's address. I decided I could find it online, so I googled Terry Grosz and learned he had passed away a few days earlier. My heart was broken. I had so wanted for him to see my finished product, but it wasn't to be. It had never crossed my mind that this might happen, but it should have.

After reading my book, some of my family commented that I had lived a charmed life. I know they were referring to my having survived some dangerous encounters; however, we would all do well to remember tomorrow isn't guaranteed for anyone.

As I write this, the officer who I often refer to as my best pupil, Lt. Jerry Fincher, is mourning the loss of his mother, who passed away this morning. I am at the age where many of my family and friends are stepping into eternity. Just this week, there have been five people drown in Alabama. Many of these were in the prime of their lives. There is a statistic I have quoted several times, and that is that one out of every one person dies. Folks, we will all spend eternity somewhere. The choice is yours. It's a choice I encourage you to make today. Choose wisely. Choose Jesus.

God bless you.

DISCLAIMER

THE STORIES YOU ARE ABOUT TO READ ARE TRUE, but the names have been changed because some of these folks probably would not want to see their names attached to some of the stuff they did. On the off chance that you read something in here and it sounds familiar or sounds like something one of your friends might do, it might have been them. I don't know who all your friends are!

These stories represent my best recollections. There could be a possible error, but I doubt it. I do not mean to embarrass or malign anyone.

I will tell you this. After my first book came out, I had a fellow tell me that after he read one of the stories he told his wife that the main character in the story was her father. It was! So much for changing the names. You can't make this stuff up! Enjoy!

"THEY SHOT MY HOUSE"

THE MAN WAS OBVIOUSLY UPSET. However, after learning what had just transpired, I considered him to be extremely calm. I told him to go back in his home and let me handle things. I backed my truck beside his house and began my vigil. It wouldn't last long.

As one of very few law enforcement officers in our rural county, it was not at all unusual for me to respond to a variety of calls having nothing to do with game or fish. During my career, I responded to everything from a discipline problem at the elementary school to a murder. In addition, we often assisted at automobile accidents and house fires. Responding to people in need was simply being a part of the community, and being a part of the community led to many arrests.

Thanksgiving night found me enjoying an evening at home. Even though it was an official state holiday, we were never really off. Try as I might to be off, it was inevitable I would receive numerous calls on holidays. Some calls were reporting illegal activity, while others were simply asking questions, such as "Where can I buy a license today?" Many times, I had young folks tell me they wanted to be a game warden. I would always ask them why, and the normal answer was because they loved to hunt. I would then tell them they needed to understand, when everyone else was hunting, I was working. This was normally especially true on holidays.

Although I was trying to enjoy the holiday, I was monitoring the sheriff's office (SO) radio. About 9:00 p.m., I heard the call go out concerning a house fire in Rockford. In our rural county, all fire protection was provided by volunteer fire departments. Rockford had a volunteer fire department, and volunteers were normally contacted by telephone or by the Coosa County Sheriff Department radio. My scanner came to life with the dispatcher soliciting volunteers to assist with the structure fire. I wasn't actually a fireman and therefore didn't respond. However, after a few minutes and another call for assistance, it was obvious they were still in need of more help. Therefore, I got in my truck and started toward town. As I reached Highway 22 at the end of my half-mile-long driveway, the dispatcher came over the radio and said they did not need any more assistance. Therefore, I turned around and headed back to the house. I got out of the truck and was about to step up on the porch when I heard a distant shot.

A skill all conservation enforcement officers (CEOs) should do their best to perfect is the pinpointing of shots. Being able to pinpoint the location of a shot was often the difference in whether or not you caught an illegal hunter. I thought I had a good idea where this shot had come from, so I jumped in my state truck and took off toward the location, which was approximately two miles from my home. In my experience, two miles was a pretty long distance to hear a shot under good conditions.

Of course, pinpointing shots wasn't an exact science; you hoped you were at least in the general vicinity. As I neared the area where I suspected the shot had originated from, I noticed a commotion in the front yard of a house and figured this was the spot. I pulled up to find the entire extended family in the front yard, along with a freshly killed spike buck. I exited my truck and was immediately approached by the homeowner, who exclaimed, "They shot my house!" The old man held out his hand, not as if to shake mine but as if to give me something. I held out my hand, and he dropped what appeared to be a double-aught buckshot pellet into it. He explained the projectile had come through the exterior wall of his home and knocked a picture off the wall in his den.

As he was describing what had occurred, his adult son grabbed the deer by the antlers and began to drag it away. I called out to him and told him to leave the deer where it was. "Why?" he asked in a somewhat belligerent tone.

"Because they will probably come back for it, and I'll catch them," was my reply. I asked the landowner to have everybody go back in the house and turn the lights out. Although they obviously didn't think the shooter would be back, they complied. I backed my truck up the driveway and hid as best I could beside the house and began my wait. You never knew whether the shooter would return in five minutes, the next day, or not at all.

I called CEO Hershel Patterson and told him what had taken place. I informed him I was hidden beside the house and hoped to catch the folks if they came back. He explained he was answering a complaint in the Marble Valley area of the county but to call him if I needed him. Marble Valley was about as far as one could go and still be in Coosa County, which meant he was at least an hour away from my location. It was not at all unusual for that to be the case. When you had two or even three officers attempting to cover 652 square miles, backup was often a luxury that didn't exist. I was accustomed to working without backup; however, that didn't mean I enjoyed it!

I had been sitting in the dark for about ten minutes when I noticed the landowner coming around the end of the house. He walked up to the passenger side of my truck and asked if he could sit with me. I told him he could. He sat down in the truck and asked if I thought the people would return. I told him they knew they had killed the deer and would probably come back to retrieve it. He said he couldn't believe someone would shoot into his house. He went on to say two of his grandchildren had been sleeping on the front porch in sleeping bags and the buckshot had gone directly over their heads. I realized just how serious this situation was.

Think about it. Your children and grandchildren have come to your house for Thanksgiving. You've enjoyed a great Thanksgiving meal and fun with the children. It is a mild night, and the kids have asked if they can sleep outside on the screened-in front porch, a "campout," if you will. Surely there is no harm in that, so you prepare a pallet for them, and they snuggle down into their sleeping bags. Minutes later, an idiot comes along, and a shotgun blast splits the night. A projectile comes through the exterior of your home and knocks a picture off the wall. It takes you a few seconds to realize what has just happened. You then rush to the porch and find the projectile had missed the children by a mere four feet. I would say that's enough to get grandpa in a fighting mood, not to mention grandma!

Many people do not understand one of the most dangerous aspects of someone shooting from the road is they do not know what lies beyond their target. This is especially true in the dark. During my career, I knew of several houses that were shot into by night hunters. Not to mention the vehicles, outbuildings, and livestock.

About thirty minutes had passed with no activity. The landowner once again asked if I really thought the shooter would return for the deer. As I contemplated answering him with "No, I just wanted to spend the remainder of my holiday sitting in my truck beside your house," I observed a slow-moving vehicle nearing our location and told the man I thought the hunters were arriving right now. As we watched, the vehicle pulled to the side of the road. Two men jumped out and grabbed the deer and stuffed it in the rear hatch of the car. As the car began to pull away, I started the truck and told the landowner to fasten his seat belt. I wasn't sure what was going to happen, but I did not have a good feeling. I think that came from the fact I was driving a low-bid Dodge pickup with a 318-cubic-inch engine, and the violators were in a Z28 Chevrolet Camaro sports car!

Knowing the Camaro would easily outrun my pickup; I decided to leave my headlights off until I got close to the vehicle. This was before our department passed the policy preventing us from driving with our headlights off. I was standing on the gas and we were quickly closing the gap on the sports car. Once I was directly behind the vehicle, I pulled on my headlights and activated my blue lights. To my surprise, the car immediately pulled to the right side of the road. My first fear had been relieved since there didn't appear there would be a chase.

I radioed the tag number and my location to the jail and told the landowner to sit tight. I opened my door, and standing behind it, I yelled at the driver to turn the car off. The driver immediately turned the car off. His next move definitely got my attention. After turning off the ignition, he removed the keys and threw them out the window into the road. This was something I had only seen occur on television, but it told me one of two things. This guy either watched a lot of police shows or this wasn't his first rodeo!

Noting there were four subjects in the vehicle, I again radioed the jail and requested they send me a backup unit. I knew in our rural county backup might be there in five minutes or an hour, but at least they knew where I was and would be coming, and they had to be closer than Hershel was! I gave a loud verbal command for all the occupants to put their hands on the ceiling. Dealing with multiple suspects in the dark is always a dicey situation. I cautiously approached the car.

I eased up on the driver's side and illuminated the interior of the car with my Maglite flashlight as best I could. "Where's your gun?" I asked.

"We don't have one," was the driver's reply.

As I was still looking for the gun, in my peripheral vision I observed a vehicle pulling up behind my truck. Hoping it was a deputy, I backed away from the car and toward my truck. Expecting to see a deputy's car, I looked behind my truck and there saw a man, who was unknown to me, standing beside his pickup and holding the biggest pistol I had ever seen.

Before I had time to decide whether to draw my gun or run for cover, the man said, "I'm here to help you."

Although I did feel some relief, I thought, "This is quite the predicament. I've got a carload of outlaws in front of me and helpful Dirty Harry behind me." Evidently this whole episode was more than the landowner could take, seeing how he was nowhere to be found! I told the guy behind my truck, who turned out to be a neighbor who had heard the call on the scanner, I had things under control and to just stay where he was and let me handle it.

Keeping one eye on the Good Samaritan, I slowly returned to the violators. I once again asked where their gun was, and they once again denied having one. I instructed everyone to keep their hands up against the roof of the car and for the driver to exit the vehicle and come back to me. He slowly climbed out of the car and walked back to me. I instructed him to place his hands on the hood of my truck. With one eye on the car and one on my "helper," I moved in and handcuffed the young man.

Although I felt I had the three-ring circus somewhat in hand, I was so thankful to see the patrol car pull up and Deputy Dan Bearden climbing out. I quickly explained the neighbor with the hog leg of a pistol was backing me up while I was taking the driver out of the car. We thanked the neighbor and told him we would take it from here. We got the remaining three occupants out of the car.

The four-man crew was very diverse. The front seat passenger was sixty-four years old and the grandfather of the twenty-year-old driver. In the rear seat was a forty-one-year-old and a local fifteen-year-old, who I later learned was serving as their guide.

With everyone out of the vehicle, I searched for a weapon but could not come up with one. I retrieved the driver and took him to the front of his vehicle and advised him of his rights. I asked him to tell me what had taken place. He stated they had been driving down the road and saw the deer and decided to stop and pick it up. I knew that wasn't the case, and I sensed he didn't have much confidence in his answer. Further questioning revealed he was from Jasper, which was over one hundred miles from our current location. I asked why he was in this area, and he stammered around a bit and decided they had been looking for a place to hunt.

"At night?" I asked. He wasn't sure how to answer that. I asked him how he was going to find a place to hunt in the dark. He was trying to think quick but was struggling. He stated they were looking for signs on trees. With him on the ropes, I was asking questions rapid fire. When I asked what kind of signs, he replied he was looking for University of Alabama signs. I advised him there was no University of Alabama land in this county that was open to hunting. As he tried to come up with another answer, I gave him my best "I know you're lying" look. I asked if he wanted to try another story.

He gave me a pitiful look and replied, "No."

I again asked where his gun was, and he said he had taken it back to the hotel in Alexander City. Alexander City was about sixteen miles to the east and the closest town with a hotel.

Feeling I had gained considerable ground by having him admit he had possessed a firearm earlier, I decided to push harder. Again, utilizing my best "you're guilty as sin" look and tone, I asked who had done the shooting. He hesitated before he replied his grandfather had shot the deer with a double-barrel shotgun. I told him I appreciated him telling me the truth and informed him he was under arrest and I would be taking all of them to jail.

While waiting on me to finish questioning Junior, Grandpa Clarence had become quite upset over being detained for, as he put it, "no reason." I asked if he would like to tell me what had happened, and he gruffly replied nothing had happened. This type of blatant denial coupled with his belligerent demand that he be released didn't take long to get on my last nerve. He informed me I had held them long enough and he was ready to go. I told him he was going all right, going to jail!

"For what?" he snorted, and I snarled back, "For night hunting and shooting into a house."

"We didn't shoot into no house," was his surly retort. I told him whether he wanted to admit it or not, he was going to jail for it. The old man uttered those words that never sit well with a law enforcement officer: "I'm not going to jail." Less than one minute later, he was being placed in the back seat of a patrol car, and about five minutes after that, he was being escorted through the heavy metal door of the "Rockford Ramada," my pet name for the Coosa County jail.

After getting the paperwork started at the jail, I loaded the young driver in my truck, and we headed to the hotel in Alexander City. It was an interesting ride. Alabama Highway 22 leads directly from the Coosa County jail to Alexander City. The road traverses the entire county, east to west. Although it is a state highway and regularly traveled, during the winter the deer treat it as if it's theirs. As we made our way east, there were deer standing around every curve. Each time my young prisoner would spot a deer, he would get all excited like a kid in a candy store.

We arrived at the hotel and I confiscated four long guns and told the hotel clerk the occupants had found other accommodations for the night. The return trip was just like the other, with the young fellow pointing and hollering each time we saw a deer. I sort of regretted having to inform him all of the weapons and his vehicle were all subject to being confiscated. I had to explain that meant they probably would not get them back.

We arrived back in Rockford, and the young violator asked if he could retrieve some turkey and dressing from his car and take it in the jail. I explained to him he could not take it in, but seeing how it was 3:00 a.m., they would be having breakfast soon. He asked if they would take their order for breakfast. It was at that point I knew throwing the keys out the window of his car was something this guy had seen on television because it was obvious he had not been to jail before. We went into the jail, and I pointed out the sign that read, "This isn't Burger King where they do things your way, this is the county jail and you will do things our way." I told him they would let him know what was for breakfast.

Seeing how the crew was on a joint venture, each one was charged with hunting at night, hunting from a public road, and hunting by aid of a vehicle. The shooter was also charged with reckless endangerment. In court, the men pled guilty to the charges and paid the landowner restitution to repair his home and to avoid a lawsuit. The juvenile was found to be a child in need of supervision and was also assessed some fines. The total fines, costs, and restitution amounted to $10,400.

This case disproved at least three commonly held notions. One, night hunting is done by kids. Although there were a couple of "kids" involved, the shooter was a sixty-four-year-old grandfather. Two, nobody is hurt by night hunting. Had the buckshot been four feet lower, it likely would have hit the two grandchildren camping out in sleeping bags on the front porch. Double-aught buckshot has nine pellets in each shot shell. They were very fortunate that the deer took the majority of the load. Three, night hunters usually drive four-wheel-drive trucks with loud exhaust. I had the opportunity to catch hundreds of night hunters, and I caught as many in cars as I did in trucks. As a matter of fact, folks were caught night hunting using everything from motorcycles to tractor trailers!

Although the defendants paid some heavy fines, it was nothing close to what it could have been if one of the grandchildren had stood up and looked at the car sitting in the road as the shot was fired!

One last important point. The landowner did not call and report the shot to anyone. Even after someone shot through his house. If I had not heard the shot, in all likelihood nothing ever would have been done. Come on folks, report violators. Your life could depend on it.

A DOG NAMED ELVIS

I HAD HEARD SOME OUTLANDISH STORIES in my time, but I had to admit this woman had a vivid imagination. While her story was filled with interesting details, the freshly killed deer in her truck at four o'clock in the morning trumped all of her excuses.

One of the best aspects of my job was the freedom it afforded. Although we were to work forty hours each week, for the most part we set our own schedule. I once heard retired Enforcement Chief Tim Cosby say we should give the state the best forty hours we could, meaning we needed to work when we could be the most productive. Therefore, work time might be at 4:00 a.m. or midnight or on some days from 4:00 a.m. until midnight. During the hunting season, it wasn't difficult to find a time to work; it was difficult to find a time not to work!

January 31, the last day of gun deer season before they later extended it until February 10, I found myself lying in bed looking at the clock. Unable to sleep and remembering I had made several arrests on the last day and night of the season in the past, I decided to get out and prowl around. At about 3:45 in the morning, I was in my green game warden truck, contemplating where I should go. As I neared the end of my driveway, the decision was made for me when I heard the Coosa County sheriff's dispatcher calling the

Coosa County conservation enforcement officer on the radio. I could tell by the inflection in the dispatcher's voice she was attempting to reconnect with him, and I assumed he must be out on a vehicle. I radioed the dispatcher and asked for the last known location for the officer. She stated he was out on a vehicle on Highway 231, south of Coosa County Road 10. She added she had tried to reach him several times but had not received an answer. I headed toward the location, blue lights flashing.

As I flew down the road, I continued to try to reach the officer on both the truck radio and my handheld unit. Each time he didn't answer, I pressed the accelerator a little farther. Although the young man had been working for a couple of years, I knew that even the most experienced officer could quickly get into trouble at four o'clock in the morning in the middle of nowhere. Although Highway 231 was a major thoroughfare, you could almost count on one hand the number of vehicles traveling it after midnight. That was before a casino was built twenty-five miles south in Wetumpka. That development changed the traffic pattern substantially and not in a good way!

The Coosa County Road 14 sign was just a blur as I flew past it. Although I had been in high-speed chases previously, I was traveling at a very high rate of speed for a low-bid four-wheel-drive pickup. As I came over the rise in the road, I spotted the flashing blue lights ahead. As I slid up to the officer's truck, which was behind the suspect's vehicle, I was relieved to see not one but both of the county officers were on the scene and okay. I also observed a doe deer lying on the ground behind the truck and a man and woman standing on the passenger side.

After they got over the surprise of seeing me arrive on the scene unsolicited, the pair related to me a nearby resident had observed a vehicle spotlighting their pastures along Highway 231 and called in the complaint, complete with vehicle description and tag number. When the officers arrived, they spotted the slow-moving black extended-cab pickup truck with a camper shell, which matched the description. They stopped the vehicle and, seeing wet blood on the tailgate, found a doe deer in a cooler in the bed of the truck. They found a pistol in the front passenger's side floorboard, along with a spotlight. The driver told them the deer had been run over and when he was loading it in the truck, his girlfriend's dog had gotten out, and she was back down the road looking for the dog.

Although they were a little leery about the story, one of the officers went back down the road and sure enough found a woman on the side of the road and brought her back to the truck. I asked if they had questioned the pair, and he said they had not. I walked to the suspect's truck and looked under and behind the seat for another weapon. I had caught people night hunting for deer with a pistol in the past; however, it was not that common. In my experience, deer being shot at in the dark with a pistol was by people who made a snap decision. Those who are intentionally night hunting for deer normally use a high-powered rifle or a shotgun. However, whatever weapon is used, it is all illegal.

I approached the couple and asked if they had any other weapons in the vehicle, and they said they did not. I moved to the rear of the vehicle and opened the camper shell and lowered the bloody tailgate. In plain view was a Walmart bag that I could see contained a box of rifle cartridges. I slid the bag toward me and, without removing its contents, I turned and gave the male suspect a knowing look.

Developing a good "I know you're lying" look is essential for a law enforcement officer. While it definitely doesn't work on every outlaw, I've had it work on a bunch of them. Although I did not say a single word, the fellow suddenly remembered he did have a rifle in the bed of the truck. We retrieved the high-powered rifle, and I secured it in my vehicle. We separated the pair for further questioning.

You never know who may be a violator. Many people erroneously believe people who break the game and fish laws and regulations are either kids or rednecks. While that is often true, they definitely aren't the only ones. As I began to talk with the male "suspect" I learned he was an occupational therapist and a captain in the naval reserve. I asked the man to move to my truck where I read him the Miranda warning from the card I always kept in my wallet. Noting he was seventy-five miles from home, I asked what he was doing in Coosa County at four in the morning. He replied they were just out riding around.

I found it almost comical how he answered the question with the attitude that it was perfectly normal for someone to be here in the middle of nowhere at four in the morning with a dead deer, rifle, pistol, and spotlight. We moved on. I asked how he had obtained the deer, and things began to get interesting. The suspect stated he observed someone in a dark-colored Ford Explorer as they shot the deer. As he observed, the driver of the Explorer sped away, leaving the deer in the field. He stopped where the vehicle had been and saw the white belly of a deer in the field alongside the road. He got out and retrieved the deer and placed it in the cooler in the bed of his truck. I asked what he planned to do with the deer. He thought for a minute and said he was going to put it on ice and get it processed. I asked if he had any ice, and he replied he did not. I asked if he knew where there were any processors in the area, and he again said he did not.

I have said many times, questioning an individual is very much an art. Over time you learn how to read people and what to say or ask and when to say or ask it. A technique that worked well for me many times was when you had received an answer that the suspect knew was pretty shaky, just to let it hang in the air for a moment. I would often act as if I was contemplating the answer for a minute and would then just shake my head as if somewhat disgusted. I found that remaining silent after they had given me what they thought was a good answer would often rattle their cage. I gave this guy about a minute of silence and ended the interview.

I escorted him back to his truck and brought the female subject, a licensed practical nurse, back to the front of my vehicle. I did not know I was about to hear one of the wildest tales of my career. I read the woman the Miranda warning. She stated she understood her rights and requested that I illuminate my face with my flashlight so she could read my lips since she was hard of hearing. A unique request I had never heard before. So, with my light shining in my face, I began the questioning by asking her what she was doing in Coosa County at four in the morning. She immediately answered they were lost. She went on to explain they were looking for her sister's house in Eclectic, a town in another county about thirty miles from our current location. She explained she needed to keep her sister's children so she could go to work. I noted this answer was much different than the one I had received from the male suspect and moved on. I reasoned he had forgotten they were looking for the woman's sister's house when they were just out riding around.

I asked the woman how they had ended up with a deer in their vehicle, and she started on a diatribe unlike any I had ever heard. She said she and the male subject had been playing car tag with a dark-colored Ford Explorer as they drove south on Highway 231. The vehicles had passed each other several times. As they were coming down the road, she heard a very loud gunshot. I asked if she heard it from inside the truck, and she replied she did because she had the window down due to her asthma. I asked if she could see a vehicle when she heard the shot, and she replied she could not. I found this interesting in that the area where the deer had been shot was on the end of a straight stretch of road with visibility of about one-half mile. I know my jaw was slack upon learning a woman who needed me to shine my light in my face so she could read my lips from a distance of three feet could hear a gunshot from a half mile away!

She went on to say after hearing the shot they had come upon a dark-colored Ford Explorer in the road with a black man standing behind it with all of his stuff in the road. I asked what kind of "stuff," and she said she didn't know. As they approached the vehicle, the man quickly loaded his "stuff" in the dark-colored Ford Explorer and hurriedly drove away. She said her boyfriend said he was going to "show them" by getting the deer they had shot. He got out to retrieve the deer, and she got out with her dog to use the bathroom.

I mistakenly thought she was referring to the dog using the bathroom; however, she continued her story, saying while she was squatted on the side of the road, the dark-colored Ford Explorer came back by and the black man hollered and yelled at her. Her boyfriend, "being macho," took off after the dark-colored Ford Explorer, leaving her on the side of the road. She said her dog, a Pomeranian named Elvis Presley, which had been shaved except for a mane so it would resemble a lion (you can't make this up), had run into the field, and she was looking for him when the officers came and got her.

I looked at the woman in disgust and told her I had been doing this for a long time, and her story was the biggest load of crap I had ever heard. She looked at me in mock disbelief and said, "That's what happened." Not believing their story, we provided the pair with a handful of paperwork and allowed them to go on their way. The fact that they left without stating they wanted to keep looking for their dog gave me the feeling the dog likely did not exist. Think about it, would you leave your Pomeranian named Elvis with a mane like a lion on the side of the road in the middle of nowhere? I didn't think so!

I'm sure you noticed that while the woman was very confident concerning her story, the one thing she really knew was the description of the vehicle. While it is good for a witness to get a good description of a vehicle, when a defendant is that adamant about the vehicle that played a major role in their ordeal, it serves to make me a little skeptical. Since both suspects had given the description, I did not know whether or not the vehicle really existed or if they had had the opportunity to get that segment of their story together prior to questioning.

Since we were now not far from daylight, we decided to stay in the area and see what the light of day would reveal. It would be irresponsible to leave a lion dog on the loose! We found where the deer had been shot in the field and dragged to the road. We also found where a second deer had been shot. We followed the blood trail that led out of the field and through some adjacent woods. At one point we jumped the deer, which appeared to be a six- or eight-point buck. We looked for the deer for three hours but were unable to locate it. We also failed to locate a dog that had been shaved so it resembled a lion.

When the couple appeared in district court to answer the charges of hunting at night, hunting from a public road, hunting by aid of a vehicle, and hunting without a permit, we were in for another surprise. When the cases were called, the male subject requested his cases be continued to give him time to hire an attorney. Since it had only been two weeks since the man was apprehended, the judge granted the request. I assumed the female subject would make the same request; however, she stated she would proceed without an attorney and would like to plead guilty to all charges. She went on to say she was the one who had shot the deer, and there was no need to prosecute her boyfriend. The judge accepted her plea and sentenced her to the maximum fine and costs in each case ($3,376) and revoked her hunting privileges for three years. While I guess chivalry goes both ways and is admirable, I had the feeling it would not help in this situation.

The next month, the male half once again appeared in court and was found guilty on all charges. He did receive a slight break from the judge who only charged him $2,407 and revoked his hunting privileges for three years.

Shockingly we never received a report of a Pomeranian dog that looked like a lion being spotted in the south end of the county. Go figure!

Although we did not need him to testify, the witness who had observed the vehicle and heard the shots was in court that day. In the courthouse parking lot, I thanked him for being observant and calling us when the event was happening. Although it wasn't the first time they had experienced problems with night hunters, and he had every right to protect his property, I reminded him many of these folks could be dangerous, and he needed to be cautious. He thanked me for our efforts as he was getting into his dark-colored Ford Explorer!

A night of hunting deer in Coosa County = $5,783.00

Losing your Pomeranian shaved to look like a lion and named Elvis Presley = priceless.

You can't make this stuff up!

While the folks in this incident tried to develop a good story, the truth came out in the end. This will be the same for everyone. The Bible says everything will come to light. We all have secrets, and we all have sinned and come short of the glory of God. However, Jesus gave his life so we could be cleansed. You can accept the free pardon of sin Jesus offers. Today is the best time.

A PLASTIC TARP

AFTER YEARS OF TAKING REPORTS of black panthers, hyenas, little yellow marshmallow people, and a black bear that turned out to be a mule (yes, those are all true), I would sometimes begin to think we had the market cornered on tall tales and low IQs. I was wrong. My friend Sheriff's Deputy Shane House says if you have any doubt about the dumbing down of America, just try to direct some traffic. Just recently I was helping at a two-vehicle accident. We were stopping traffic and providing directions for how to get around the accident. In the roadway were one of the crashed vehicles, two fire trucks, two ambulances, four police vehicles, several volunteer firemen vehicles, and about twenty people. To say the road was blocked was a gross understatement.

As the drivers rolled up, I would ask their destination and provide them with directions. After a bit of a lull, a driver pulled up and I asked where he was trying to get to, and he replied, "Work." This was a bit frustrating but nothing I hadn't experienced before.

I asked, "Where do you work?" and he replied, "At the plant." Since I was sure those answers made sense to that guy, I hoped my answer to him would as well. I told him he couldn't get to work from here, and he would need to go back home and start again! Listening to these folks' answers reminded me of the story

I heard about someone who had called the fire department to report a house fire. The dispatcher was not familiar with the address the caller gave and asked, "How do we get to the house?"

The caller responded, "Don't y'all still have the big red truck?" When I heard that I thought it was a joke, but now I'm not so sure.

I would think everyone likes to see someone who is good at their craft, no matter what it may be. When someone is a consummate professional, it's impressive. One vocation that has reached perfection is the reporters who are required to find the most uneducated doofus redneck to interview after the tornado has hit the trailer park. How they find some of these folks is beyond me. Now, as many of my stories indicate, I have dealt with a lot of doofuses and more than my share of rednecks; however, I have not encountered the people these reporters are able to find.

My good friend Dr. Jim Armstrong relayed to me one of the best I ever heard. He said a man was being interviewed following a hurricane that had come on shore and ravaged the shoreline. The interviewer no doubt looked long and hard to find this fellow. Jim reported the man looked into the camera and stated, "They told us we should evaporate, but I stayed here—but next time I'm gonna evaporate!" You can't make that up!

I eventually learned everyone who worked with the public on a regular basis had their share of stories. One day I had stopped in a local auto body repair shop and was talking with the owner and his shop foreman about a possible repair when I realized they got their share of dimwits. They explained a woman had come in and reported her car had been significantly damaged, and she wanted them to give her a repair estimate. While this was something that happened multiple times each day, what came next was a little unusual. When they asked what type of coverage she had on the vehicle, she replied, "A plastic tarp."

You can't make that stuff up!

THE FLU AND NIGHT HUNTERS TOO!
(COLD, WET, AND MUDDY)

ANYTIME THE PHONE RANG during hunting season, my first thought was it was probably a hunting complaint. This belief was strengthened by the fact that during many of the early years of my career, almost every call was a complaint, at least during the deer season. One stormy night, the phone rang. When I answered, my partner Hershel Patterson said, "This is Hershel." Although I literally talked to Hershel on a near daily basis, it was a good thing he identified himself. He sounded awful. He said he was very sick, which appeared to be an understatement, but he had just received a call saying someone had shot a deer on Alabama Highway 259, and he was on his way to pick me up. Not only did the idea of sitting in the car with someone who was deathly ill make me uneasy, the fact it was pouring rain and about thirty-eight degrees made it even worse. However, thirty minutes later I was in the passenger's seat heading toward the complaint.

Highway 259, which was also known as Fish Pond Road, is eleven miles long and runs north to south on the extreme eastern side of Coosa County. Early in my career it was a perpetual night hunting hot spot. As a matter of fact, it was where I caught my first night hunters six days after being hired!

Hershel told me the complainant had said someone had shot and killed a deer in front of his house and had driven off without picking the deer up. Our plan was to get there and be waiting when the violator returned for the deer. We radioed Coosa County Deputy Brett Oakes and told him what we had and asked if he would set up down the road from us and help contain the vehicle we hoped would return soon.

There were at least two schools of thought among road riding night hunters. Some would shoot a deer, immediately load it up, and leave the area. This probably was the best way not to be apprehended however it had some disadvantages. Often times a deer did not die instantly when shot. Therefore, the shooter would sometimes have a fight on their hands when they reached the animal. It is not good for a deer to come back to life once you have loaded it in your truck or, worse yet, after you have closed it up in the trunk of your car. In addition, using this method, you leave the scene with a freshly killed deer and a weapon, which is pretty incriminating if you get stopped. The other alternative was to shoot the deer, mark the spot, and come back and pick it up later. Some would come back in a few minutes and some the next day. This gave the area a chance to calm down in the event someone heard the shot and also provided the shooter the opportunity to "get rid of" their weapon. This way, if he was to be stopped, he could claim they simply saw the deer, thought it was a roadkill, and picked it up. Of course, we would not believe that, but I guess it made sense to try it. Obviously, this group was implementing the latter method.

We arrived on the scene, and, luckily, we quickly located the deer. Having to spend a lot of time in the road looking for a deer increased the chance that the shooter might return, spot you, and just keep driving. Hershel knew of a hiding spot about 150 yards up the road, so we headed that way. If you ever need to know where there is a road that is accessible yet well hidden, ask your local conservation officer. Quickly finding a hiding place is often essential for a game warden. Just like in this case, officers often need a secluded place from which they can monitor the road. At other times, we need a place to hide a vehicle while we search a nearby property for people or bait or both. We know some places.

Every time I heard the line in the old Roger Miller song that said "knows every lock that ain't locked when no one's around," it made me think of us. We usually knew which gate was open and which was locked, and if it was locked, we normally either had the code or key, whichever it took. I had three hundred keys on my ring! Needless to say, you didn't carry that around in your pants pocket.

The dim road we entered unfortunately had a swell in it, and although we were able to back over the hump, the Ford Crown Victoria would not climb back over. Try as he might, Hershel could not get the car to pull the hill. I can tell you from experience, you don't want to have your vehicle stuck when someone shoots in front of you! Not wanting to be stuck when the violator came back, we knew we had to get the car over the rise. You guessed it; soon there was a fat young game warden protégé behind the car, pushing on the rear bumper. Luckily, my pushing combined with Hershel's driving was enough to get the car over the hump. Of course, now I was soaking wet and covered with mud from head to toe. I figured if being in the car with Hershel didn't make me sick, being soaking wet in the cold night would. My odds weren't looking very good.

Shortly after getting the car unstuck we saw headlights approaching from the south. I moved out to the edge of the road to try and identify the vehicle; however, the rain was pouring, and I couldn't see anything but the headlights. However, I did see the vehicle had stopped, and I heard what I thought had to be either a deer being thrown in the bed of the truck or a tailgate being shut and then a door slamming.

I ran back to the car and told Hershel I was ninety percent sure they had picked the deer up. We radioed Brett and told him to come toward us as we were stopping the vehicle. The pickup passed our location, and, spinning the whole way, we pulled out behind it and activated our blue lights. Adding to the danger, we noticed the vehicle had dark-tinted windows, which kept us from knowing how many occupants were inside. Dark-tinted windows exponentially raise the danger level for law enforcement officers. If I had had a tint meter, I probably would have spent a lot of time in the Montgomery office explaining why I had written folks so many tickets!

The truck came to a stop in the highway. I approached the passenger side as Hershel came up on the driver's side. I yelled for the occupants to open the door, but it didn't happen. This was a tense time. Not being able to see into a vehicle you feel sure contains a weapon and whose occupants have just committed a crime that will likely cost them a few thousand dollars doesn't put one at ease. I tried the door handle and found it was locked. I again yelled for them to open the door. By this time, Deputy Oakes had joined me on the passenger side of the truck.

Like so much of law enforcement, it was time for a quick decision. Had it not been raining and I could have been totally sure these folks had picked up the deer, I likely would not have hesitated to allow the deputy to bust out the truck window with his baton as he was ready to do. While that may sound extreme, you must keep in mind these folks have committed a crime using a firearm, and we're two feet from them yet cannot see what they are doing. Luckily it did not come to that.

As we contemplated our next move, the passenger rolled the window down about three inches and asked, "What do you want?" I had never had this happen before, and it did not sit very well with me or Brett, as I was covered in mud and we were standing in the pouring rain. These folks had a car behind them and one in front of them, each with blue lights flashing, and they evidently didn't know what was happening!

Immediately after Brett loudly told me he was going to bust the window out, the door flew open and a teenaged-looking boy quickly jumped from the truck. Brett grabbed the boy and put him on the side of the truck while I looked in the cab of the truck for a weapon. I did not find a weapon, but I did find another passenger, and I removed him from the truck. While pulling him out, I realized the first passenger was giving Brett some trouble. He would not stay on the side of the truck and kept yelling at Brett, "Hit me, hit me, I'm just 17, hit me!" The way he was acting, I wasn't sure whether or not Brett was going to grant his wish. Brett spun him around and got a set of cuffs on him while I handcuffed the other passenger and Hershel hooked up the driver.

The mouthy passenger kept ranting and raving and now was demanding to know what this was all about. I shined my flashlight in the bed of the truck to illuminate the deer and say, "That's what this is about," but I quickly had to swallow those words as I realized there was no deer in the bed of the truck! Feeling a little sick to my stomach, I was afraid this guy might have a legitimate question.

We moved the three suspects to the nonhighway side of Hershel's car, and Hershel whispered to me, between coughs and wheezes, "Where's the deer?" I told him I was sure they had loaded it up, and he said, "Find it!" I returned to the truck and looked again but still found nothing. It was not as if the bed of the truck was empty; it contained a dog box. Dog boxes in pickup trucks were common at the time. Folks routinely hunted deer, quail, rabbits, and raccoons with dogs. The boxes came in different configurations. While some were merely a top that covered the bed of the truck with the dogs being held underneath, others were actually a box with a bottom in it that simply sat in the bed of the truck. That was the type I was looking at. The box normally was about half as long as the truck bed, leaving some area between the box and the truck cab. I felt sure the deer would be lying between the box and the cab, but there was nothing there.

Mr. Mouth was still ranting, and I had a sickening feeling we might soon be releasing these guys. I was covered in mud, I was soaking wet, and I had been exposed to a killer flu and for what? I replayed in my mind what had occurred. The truck had stopped at the precise point where the deer had been laying. Someone had gotten out in a blinding rainstorm. I had heard something landing in the back of the truck, and I had heard a door slam. It had to be there. Then it hit me. I yanked down the tailgate of the truck and there, stuffed inside the dog box, was the doe deer. I could not remember a time in my young career when I was more elated.

We put the trio in Brett's car, and he transported them to the Coosa County jail. It turned out, despite what Mr. Hit Me claimed, they were all over eighteen years old and therefore got to spend the night in the big boy jail.

YOU GOTTA HAVE A SACK

I DID NOT KNOW it was a mandatory prerequisite that a conservation enforcement officer (CEO) keep a sack in his vehicle, but it was a lesson I would not forget. I normally always enjoyed working with the older CEO's. They always had some good stories, and there were usually some pearls of wisdom embedded in there somewhere. One such occasion occurred when I prepared to attend court in neighboring Clay County. Veteran CEO Lee Bonner gave me some words of wisdom I held on to for the remainder of my career.

Working a deer hunt on a wildlife management area (WMA) was an every-weekend affair during the first seventeen years of my career. The WMAs provided public hunting opportunities and were located throughout the state. When I began work, a four-dollar deer and turkey license in addition to your regular state hunting license and a free permit gave sportsmen the opportunity to hunt on approximately six hundred thousand acres across the state. I took my first deer on a WMA hunt. It was a great asset for folks like myself who did not have deer around my home and did not own any property to hunt on if there had been deer around.

The deer hunts on the WMA were normally for bucks only and sometimes were either-sex hunts. While working a buck-only deer hunt on the Hollins Wildlife Management Area, I was at the check station when a fellow brought in an approximately four-month-old male deer commonly referred to as a button buck. A button buck was a male deer that was young enough that their antlers were still below the hide. In Alabama, a deer was considered a legal buck when it had hardened antlers above the natural hair line. The antlers on this guy's deer had yet to come through the skin, and therefore it was considered an antlerless deer. I explained this to the fellow, and he stated he could see the knots on the head of the deer and therefore knew it was a male when he shot it. I again explained the law and asked for his driver's license.

While writing the man a ticket, I kept thinking his name sounded familiar. His last name was the same as the sheriff in the adjacent county, but I didn't think that was where I had seen it. I finished with the ticket and informed him I would be keeping the deer as evidence. The defendant left, and I removed the head from the deer and carried the remainder of the deer to a needy family that lived nearby. That was back when you could still do logical, sensible things like that. Don't get me started on that.

On the way home, try as I might, I could not remember where I had seen the fellow's name. The next week I had to return to Clay County to sign a warrant on the guy. For on-view violations, we would place individuals under arrest and then fill out a bail bond and have them sign it. The bond amount varied depending on the charge. A WMA violation was normally a $300 bond. We would explain the bond to the violator, telling them it was basically a promissory note saying they would either handle the charge prior to court or would appear in court on the specified date. If they failed to appear, a warrant would be sworn for them, and they would be picked up and held until the next court date. We would then at our earliest opportunity go to the circuit clerk's office and turn in the bond and sign an arrest warrant for the individual.

While signing the warrant, it finally came to me where I had seen the name previously. A couple of weeks earlier I had been working a hunt on the Coosa WMA. While working with CEO Hershel Patterson, I had gone through a stack of failure-to-appear warrants he kept over his visor. Many of the warrants were several years old; however, until the court recalled them, they were valid. I now remembered one of those many warrants was for the individual I had arrested days earlier. I met with Hershel and obtained the warrant with plans to serve it on the upcoming court date.

The next month, prior to the 1:00 p.m. court time, wildlife biologist Gene Carver and I met with CEO Lee Bonner for lunch. As we were leaving the restaurant, we were discussing the cases set for court and I decided to ask Lee if he had a paper sack I could put my evidence deer head in to take it into the courtroom. I had frozen the head in a plastic bag; however, the plastic was now beginning to sweat, and I felt it would be better if I could put the plastic bag inside a paper sack. Little did I know that what seemed to me to be a simple request was going to prompt a lesson in proper equipment for conservation officers.

As we walked to Lee's car, I asked if he might have a sack I could use to place the evidence in. Lee looked at me and asked, "You don't have a sack?" I replied I didn't. He just stood there staring at me and then, in almost an incredulous tone, asked, "You don't have a sack?"

I really did not understand what the big deal was about asking for a paper sack, but it evidently was a big deal to Lee. I explained to him I did have the deer head in a plastic bag, but I had thought it would be good if I had a paper sack to put it in.

He stared at me and said, "You should always have a sack."

Now I knew Lee Bonner was straight by the book when it came to wildlife law enforcement; however, I sure didn't remember the officer's handbook saying anything about always having a paper sack. I did keep a supply of plastic ziplock bags for the collection and storage of bait evidence, but I could tell this was more involved than that.

I was actually getting a little aggravated with all of the sack talk, and I told Lee I would just use the plastic bag I had. Lee went to his car, opened the trunk and pulled out a large paper sack. He handed me the bag and said, "You should always have a sack." I'm sure the look on my face told him I didn't really understand the vast importance of the sack and prompted him to ask, "Do you know why?"

Although I felt it was blatantly obvious by now I did not know why, I replied I had not known that. It was then I learned a very valuable lesson about being a conservation officer. Lee explained you should always have a sack because you never knew when you are going to come across someone who has some corn or beans or fruit or pecans and he or she will say, *I'd give you some of this, if I had a sack.* "So, you should always have a sack!"

With the mystery of the sack solved, I put the deer head in the sack, and we headed off to court. The case was called, and the defendant pled not guilty, so we had a trial. The defendant explained to the judge how he knew it was a male deer when he shot it, and I explained that according to the law it was not a legal buck. I informed the judge I had the head if he wanted to view it. Reluctantly he said for me to show it to him.

Judge George Simpson ran a very formal courtroom, and it's just a wonder my next comment didn't result in my being held in contempt. As I placed the bag on the judge's bench, I made the comment, "It would have probably been better if I had frozen the head." At that, the judge jumped back as if it might bite him. I couldn't help but giggle. I told him the head was frozen and was double bagged. Judge Simpson eyed me with a look that said he thought my comment was funny but not to ever try anything like that again. I fully understood, although nothing was spoken. The judge said he didn't want to see any more of the head than was necessary. I showed him the top of the deer head and he found the defendant guilty. After the judge announced the amount of the fine and court costs, I informed him and the defendant I had a failure-to-appear warrant for the defendant. I placed the man under arrest, allowed him to go to the clerk's office and pay his fine and costs, and we headed to the Coosa County jail.

I got the fellow booked into the Rockford Ramada, my pet name for the only housing available in Rockford, the jail, and headed for home. At home I went to the kitchen and retrieved a paper sack and put it in my truck. I kept a sack in my vehicle for the remainder of my career because "you should always have a sack!" Thanks Lee.

Unfortunately, Lee passed away in 2017. There were many officers who attended his funeral. After eulogies given by CEO Sgt. Andy Howell and wildlife biologist Gene Carver, other officers were given the opportunity to share about Lee. I told this story. I told them it had been my pleasure to have had the opportunity to work with and learn from Lee. I always found it interesting that he was a game warden a year before I was born. He was of the generation who provided the protection necessary for us to have the healthy wildlife populations we have enjoyed for many years. He was a no-nonsense kind of guy who earned the respect he received. It was my good fortune to have known him. Rest in peace.

THINGS HAPPEN FAST

ANYONE WHO HAS READ many of my stories probably knows my favorite and most productive place to work was at the old skating rink site in Weogufka in west central Coosa County Alabama. It makes sense to me that your favorite spot would be the place that was usually productive. Much of conservation law enforcement encompasses many hours spent sitting and waiting for someone to come along and do something. I wish I had a dollar for every hour I had sat in the middle of nowhere and didn't see anybody. It often seemed the only way to get someone to come along was to crank up and pull out into the road. About the time your rear wheels hit the road, the person you were waiting on would come easing toward you. This was infuriating; however, you learned to live with it since it happened so often. However, there was always good with the bad, and sometimes everything seemed to go just right. January 22 was just such a day.

In response to complaints, wildlife biologist Gene Carver and I sat up a road hunting detail on Coosa County Road 56. Although we placed our pursuit vehicle behind the old skating rink, we did not put the deer in our normal spot. We decided to try a new spot approximately three hundred yards east of the old faithful woods road where we had caught so many. I was afraid the old place might be too well known and thought the new spot might just prove successful. It was also a bit of an experiment.

The new location was in a power line right-of-way and just off the edge of the yard of an old house. Although no one lived in the house, there was a car in the driveway, and the grass was kept cut to give the appearance that someone did live there. The decoy was stationed less than fifty yards from the house. I had learned through experience many folks hunting from the road gave little or no thought to what was near or beyond their target. This was a detail in the broad daylight, and I wanted to see whether or not the close proximity of the house would prove to be a deterrent for the illegal activity.

I had carried the fake deer through the woods and put it in place in the power line right-of-way. I moved to my observation point and checked my watch. It read 9:55 a.m. Gene and I had theorized hunters would be leaving the woods and driving the roads about this time. We did not know how prophetic we were.

One thing this location did not have was the good hiding location like the old spot. The plan was for me to hunker down in some brush in an area that had had all of the timber cut a few months earlier. Although the area was basically open, there were sufficient stump sprouts and logging slash enough to hide my oversized carcass. Approximately five minutes after deploying the decoy, I was still busy making my nest in some logging debris when a dark blue Chevrolet pickup truck traveling westbound slowed to a stop. As I observed from behind a stump approximately twenty-five yards away, the driver of the vehicle placed a 30-30 Marlin rifle (he was close enough I could make out the make of the firearm) out the window and fired one shot, striking the deer decoy in the left side of its chest. When the deer did not go down, the shooter took off, although I'm sure he knew he was had. Although I had jumped out and stopped several violators on foot during my career, since we were a fair distance apart and there were no side roads the vehicle could turn off on, I decided to radio Gene and told him the driver of the blue pickup had shot and was headed his way. The driver continued west and was quickly stopped and arrested by Gene, who prepared bonds for hunting from a public road, hunting without a permit, and hunting by aid of a vehicle.

It turned out the shooter was the son of a nearby landowner whose hunting club was only a couple of miles farther down the road. Always good to have your neighbors helping you out! That was not the shortest I ever had to wait for someone to shoot the decoy, but it didn't miss it by much.

As I stated earlier, the decoy was placed less than fifty yards from a house. This once again proved that violators will shoot deer wherever they spot them. This was a fact many people, including some judges and prosecutors, unfortunately did not realize.

Looking back, I was so fortunate that my first district court judge had experienced night hunters shooting just outside of his house and had a father who enjoyed hunting. The judge had a true disdain for those who would illegally dip into Mother Nature's pantry. And woe be unto anyone charged with cruelty to a domestic animal. I think some of those are still in jail!

Just like in this story, life often happens fast. So, does death. The Bible tells us to be alert and be ready.

A TROPHY IS IN THE EYE OF THE BEHOLDER

THE BUCK STOOD STILL AS A STONE. He seemed to stare as the shooter exited his vehicle. It was as though he was mesmerized by the glint of light reflecting off the riflescope. He did not move when the bullet ripped through his chest, blowing Styrofoam out the other side!

I did my best not to work on Sunday. Maybe I should say I tried not to schedule any work on Sunday. However, sometimes the work came and found me. Early on in Coosa County I made some good friends who remain so until this day. Clyde Earnest, Allen Foster, and, later, Charles Zeitvogel co-owned 350 acres in north central Coosa County. All of these men were very gracious, allowing me to utilize their property to take both of my sons hunting and fishing. In my position, you received several offers to hunt and fish; however, you had to be very discreet about which offers to accept. Unfortunately, many offers came with strings attached. I very much appreciated the ones that didn't.

One year, as the deer season was in full swing, Allen reported to me he was hearing some shooting fairly regularly along Ridge Road every Sunday morning. Coosa County Road 111, the Ridge Road as it was known locally, ran through their property.

Although normally a rough dirt road, the thoroughfare received a lot of traffic, especially during the hunting season. I told him I would check into it. The best way for a violator to get caught is to set up a regular pattern. I suspected the reported activity might be one individual since it was indeed regular.

I contacted Conservation Enforcement Officer Hershel Patterson and wildlife biologist Gene Carver and informed them of the complaint and set up a decoy detail. Based on the information provided, I asked them to meet me on Ridge Road around 8:30 Sunday morning. Fortunately, there was a good place to set up the decoy; however, there was not a corresponding hiding place from which you could see the deer. We decided I would set in the woods, watching the dummy deer, while Hershel and Gene covered each end of the road.

Sunday morning was not unlike a lot of mornings when I had a detail lined up in that I had not slept very well. I had breakfast with my family and traveled to Ridge Road. I unloaded the deer and placed him in the spot I had chosen earlier. I thought the setup looked good but was afraid the deer might blend in with the surroundings so well it might not be seen. This was a common problem. I had seen many known road hunters roll past a decoy that just seemed to melt into the woods. There was a fine line between having the deer conspicuous enough that it was seen yet natural enough it would get shot. The decoy was not there to lure a shot from a hunter but to facilitate an opportunity for the violator looking to break the law. I completed the setup and drove to where I had planned to meet the others and leave my vehicle.

Soon Hershel and Gene arrived. I told them I had already deployed the deer but was a little concerned that it might be hard to see. No sooner had those words came out of my mouth than a rifle shot split the early morning calm. I jumped in my truck and quickly made my way to the deer. There I saw a young man standing beside a pickup parked in the roadway. The fellow appeared to be in his midtwenties. He wore a sour yet sheepish look on his face. As I pulled up to him, he gently laid his rifle on the hood of his truck.

There was little need for discussion as I approached. I asked for his driver's license. He removed it from his wallet and handed it to me and commented about how real that deer looked. As I wrote his citations he continued to make small talk, telling me he had killed a doe earlier on his club and had decided to ride the road and see if he could find a buck. As I readied the bonds for his signature, he again commented how good the deer looked. At this point, I began to wonder if another deer had stepped in front of our ragged decoy with the pitiful little three-point rack. The violator signed the tickets and looked at me and said, "Yeah, all I could see was that rack on my wall!" Now I knew he had shot something other than our deer. I told him I would have to keep the deer he shot, but he could always frame his ticket and hang it on the wall. He laughed, got in his truck and drove away. I looked at the puny looking decoy he had shot and realized a trophy is in the eye of the beholder.

What does your trophy look like? Is it your wife, kids, boat, truck, checking account, or buck on the wall? Anything you put before God is your God. God is a jealous God. He tells us not to have any gods other than him. It's not easy, but it is essential.

THE CORN STARTED FLYING

Most arrests made by conservation enforcement officers (CEOs) are "on view," which means the violation occurs in the presence of the officer. Even with this being true, the general public would probably be surprised to know many of these violators, although caught in the act, still proclaim their innocence. Whether they have just shot at a decoy or are sitting directly over a pile of corn, many will plead their cases to the nth degree. During the 2005–6 deer season, Talladega County CEO Jerry Fincher encountered an individual whose argument got cut short.

Checking an area where an attractant or bait has been placed is not as simple as it may sound. Many times it is simple, in that there is a shooting house or a ladder stand set up within fifty yards of the bait and positioned so anyone in the stand would be looking directly at the bait. Obviously, when that was the situation, we would ease into the area and see if someone was in the stand. If they were, things were normally handled rather quickly, and we moved on. The tricky part was when you felt certain someone was hunting the area, but they were not in the stand you had located.

It was not at all uncommon to find a violator somewhere other than you expected. Therefore, whenever you were near the baited area, you had to keep your head on a swivel, searching high and low. I've caught baiters as high as thirty-five feet in a tree and lying in a depression in the ground. You just never knew.

Early in the deer season, CEO Fincher had located a five-gallon corn feeder with a spinner attached to the bottom suspended in a tree in rural Talladega County and had been monitoring the area on a regular basis. As Jerry eased into the area once again, he spotted a hunter sitting on the ground approximately fifty yards from the feeder. Jerry engaged the man, asked to see his high-powered rifle, and asked for his hunting license. The officer pointed toward the feeder and asked the man if it belonged to him. Not answering the question, the man responded that the feeder was empty and the battery that operated the spinner was dead. Law enforcement officers are very familiar with folks who utilize the technique of giving unsolicited information instead of answering a direct question.

Having checked the feeder only a couple of days earlier and knowing it held corn, Jerry suggested they go over and look at it. As they approached, the hunter restated his claim that the feeder was empty and the battery was dead. Many times, I have had someone sitting watching a feeder tell me the battery on the feeder was dead, thereby implying there is no corn being thrown from the feeder. While their argument may be correct, they often forget gravity is always at work. Many people seem to be of the opinion that if the feeder no longer has a working battery, the area is no longer baited. Almost every time there is a bucket holding corn hanging from a tree, some of the corn will find its way to the ground. Therefore, the person is still in violation even though the feeder may not actually be "working."

As the pair approached the hanging feeder, to prove his point the man reached and grabbed the bucket, pulling it toward him to show the officer everything was on the up and up. Just as he said,

"See, it isn't working," the feeder came to life and sprayed both men with corn. Talk about messing up your argument. There wasn't a whole lot of talking after that!

I can't count how many times someone lied to me or tried to fool me. There really is no way to know since I'm sure they were successful many times. Most law enforcement officers wise up pretty quickly to the schemes and lies people throw at them. This is probably true in part because it happens so much. It was one of the most difficult things for me to get used to.

It still amazes me the way that people automatically lie to try to get out of anything. While online, I came across an explanation for this activity. The researcher stated that many people instinctively lie because telling the truth feels like giving up control. It went on to say the folks tell lies in an effort to control a situation in order to get the reaction or outcome they desire. Another idea is that people will lie because of their lack of respect for or, in many cases, utter disdain for authority. I can tell you there is very little respect for authority today, and that is more of a problem than people realize. The reason I say that is that God is the ultimate authority figure. I know for a fact many people have lied to me, fooled me, and had total disregard for the authority I possessed. For the most part, that did not amount to a hill of beans. But when anyone fails to acknowledge the authority of God, they are treading on thin ice.

The Bible speaks to this plainly in Galatians 6:7. To me, it's one of the most powerful verses in the Bible. It reads, be not deceived, God is not mocked. You will reap what you sow. We are really good at deceiving ourselves and sometimes others, but we cannot deceive God. While we may talk a good game, God knows our heart. He knows us at our core, and he says we will reap what we sow. What are we sowing?

Whether someone does not want to give up control, they want

to dictate the ultimate outcome, or they have no respect for authority, they will one day realize God is sovereign.

There is an old adage that says, "Fool me once, shame on you; fool me twice, shame on me." If you do not believe that God is all powerful, if you do not believe that you can't fool Him, then you have successfully fooled yourself. The day is coming when *every* knee will bow and *every* tongue will confess that Jesus Christ is Lord. Be not deceived; it's going to happen. **Choose today whether you will have eternal life in Christ or whether you will reject Him and forever endure the wrath of God. Your answer to Him is something you totally control!** Don't be like the guy in this story. Do something now before it hits you right in the face.

BIG SLIMY

(BAD COMPANY CORRUPTS GOOD MORALS)

PRIOR TO THE GOOD COMMUNICATIONS we have available today, the old police radio was quite different. You had to learn how to listen to the radio since there was so much traffic on it that did not apply to you. Over time you would learn to listen to the clutter and be able to pull out anything you needed to hear. Early in my career in Coosa County, sorting through radio traffic was compounded by the fact that the county road crew shared the frequency with the county sheriff's office (SO). Believe me when I tell you that made for some interesting listening. One of the things taught at the police academy was proper radio etiquette. The first rule concerning the radio was you listened before you started talking. Since different incidents could be occurring at the same time, you needed to be sure you didn't pick up the microphone and start talking in the middle of someone's pursuit or hot call. Since the county road workers did not receive this training, it wasn't unusual for someone to come on the radio and ask their buddy to bring them some diesel fuel right in the middle of an officer calling in shots fired. It often got interesting. Luckily, the sheriff's office eventually got their own frequency.

BIG SLIMY (BAD COMPANY CORRUPTS GOOD MORALS)

Before I complain too much about communications, I recall Hershel telling me about how early in his career his supervisor had put him out on an island in the river and told him if you see something illegal, shoot your pistol. Yeah, I could have had it worse!

Around lunch on the second day of December, I heard the county sheriff's investigator on the radio stating a subject was still in the woods. Since we were in deer season, it crossed my mind this could be something we needed to be involved with. I called the SO and asked for the details on the call. As I suspected, it was a hunting-from-the-road-and-without-a-permit incident. I advised them I was en route to the location. During this time, we had one conservation enforcement officer (CEO) in the county, and although I was responsible for a thirty-eight-thousand-acre wildlife management area and for private lands wildlife management in twelve counties, I was the closest thing he had to a partner.

The call was in the Diamond Graphite area of the county. A little-known fact is that Coosa County is one of the few areas in the United States that has a belt of high-quality graphite traversing the entire county. In the 1920s, there were graphite mines across the county. One was known as the Diamond Graphite mine. Although there is little trace of the mine today, the area is still commonly referred to as Diamond Graphite. Interestingly, about five years ago, a company once again became interested in the graphite in the county and has been doing a significant amount of testing of the quality of the material. One of the predominant testing areas is on the Coosa Wildlife Management Area, where I worked for seventeen years.

Arriving at Diamond Mountain Hunting Club, I was met by the club president, Jim. Jim related to me he had heard someone shoot from the road, a busy US highway, at the large kudzu patch just north of the clubhouse. He said a large buck had been spotted in the kudzu patch several times, and he feared someone had shot it. Anyone who isn't familiar with kudzu may have a difficult time imagining what I'm talking about. Kudzu is an Asian trailing vine that is extremely aggressive. It has been measured growing as much as a foot a day. In the 1930s and 40s the Soil Conservation Service actually recommended that landowners plant kudzu to prevent soil erosion. It was effective, but, as is often the case, there are unexpected and undesirable consequences when exotic species are introduced. The result has been tremendous expanses of kudzu throughout the south. The kudzu patch along Highway 231 on the Diamond Mountain Hunting Club was approximately fifteen acres in size.

The president said, upon hearing the shot, he immediately went to the area and observed a young man standing in the kudzu approximately one hundred yards off the road. He called to the man who came to him. When he asked the man what he was doing, he replied he was looking for a place to use the bathroom. When asked what he was doing so far from the road, he replied he did not want to be seen. If I had a dollar for every time some outlaw I had found on the side of the road had told me they were just going to the bathroom, I would have a lot of dollars. Interestingly, this Einstein added he wasn't deer hunting or anything. Jim said he told him to go across the road if he needed to use the bathroom. He said the fellow had crossed the road and had never returned.

Unbeknownst to him, Jim had just encountered a perpetual wildlife law violator. I asked if the fellow had a weapon, and he replied he did not. I asked him to give me a description of the subject, and he said he was probably twenty-five to thirty years old, about five feet nine inches tall, and 160 pounds, with dark hair. He added, "He told me his name was Randy Jarvis." I could not believe what Jim had just said. Although I knew it would not be the first time an outlaw had given another outlaw's name, I felt deep inside that wasn't the case.

I was somewhat familiar with Randy Jarvis in that Talladega County CEO Jerry Fincher had apprehended him a month earlier hunting deer at night. I knew, if it indeed was Randy, at least we would be able to find him, and I had in the back of my mind that the multitude of charges he was already facing might help me in this case. I asked Jim what else the man had offered, and he said he had indicated he had been to the SO earlier in the day to give a statement about a stolen four-wheeler. I asked the club president if he had found it strange that the fellow did not have a vehicle. He gave me a curious look and said he hadn't really thought about it. On a hunch, I asked him if he had observed an old green Ford Bronco (a vehicle formerly used as a game warden vehicle) while he had been standing on the side of the road, and he said he had. The Bronco belonged to Randy Jarvis's father-in-law, Larry Gaines (aka Big Slimy).

I had called Coosa County CEO Shannon Calfee as soon as I realized we needed to respond to the call. He soon arrived at the kudzu patch, and I brought him up to speed on what we knew and told him we needed to find the deer they had shot. I told him where Randy had been standing in the kudzu patch and said that would be a good place to start. Fortunately, Shannon was young and energetic and took off into the kudzu. I stayed at the truck and continued to take information from the witness and coordinated an effort to find the culprit, although I feared Big Slimy had already picked him up. I must admit the old TV show *Wild Kingdom* came to my mind. I felt like I was Marlon Perkins instructing Jim to seek out the wild animal while I observed from a safe vantage point. I digress.

In a few minutes, my radio beeped. I saw it was Shannon calling. I answered, and he excitedly said, "I found it."

I too was excited and asked, "Is it a buck?"

His reply was definitely nothing I had anticipated. He replied, "It's a turkey."

That possibility had not crossed my mind. I told him to bring it back. He soon returned with the bird. I took a couple of photographs and placed the large gobbler in my vehicle. I would later carry the bird home and freeze it.

I called CEO Jerry Fincher and told him what had occurred and that I wanted to find and question Randy Jarvis as soon as possible. He told me he had his contact information. I asked whether or not he had appeared in court in Sylacauga yet, and he said he had not.

In short order, we arranged an interview with Randy. Prior to the interview, I obtained warrants for hunting in closed season and hunting without a permit. Mr. Jarvis arrived at the jail, and we went into a small interior interview room. There is something about that big metal door slamming behind you that sets the tone for an interview. I began by advising him of his rights. I asked him to tell me everything that had occurred on the day he was confronted in the kudzu patch. He was very cooperative. He stated his father-in-law, Larry Gaines, had brought him to the Coosa SO to give a statement concerning a stolen four-wheeler. He indicated they left the jail about 11:30 a.m. and headed north on Highway 231 toward Sylacauga. About ten minutes up the road, the pair ended up in an argument, and Larry stopped the vehicle and made him get out. That's when he was confronted by the hunting club president and had decided he needed to get out of there, so he had walked home. After hearing his statement, I knew he wasn't being as cooperative as I had thought.

I gave him my best "your lies disgust me" look and said, "That's it?" He nodded his head yes. I asked him if he thought I would have had him come all the way down here to tell me that.

He replied, "That's what happened," and I replied, "No it's not." He looked at me with a smirk that was probably meant to irritate me, and it did an outstanding job.

I regained my composure and told him he needed to know I had already obtained warrants for him for hunting in closed season and hunting without a permit. The smirk had now totally left his face. I went on to tell him I was contemplating obtaining warrants for hunting from the road and hunting by the aid of a vehicle. "I didn't do that," was his reply.

I asked how he felt it would look when I showed up at his upcoming court appearance in Sylacauga with a fistful of warrants for him. Although it probably would not have made any difference, he evidently didn't know that. Although he tried to keep his "everything's cool" look on his face, I could tell his mind was spinning, trying to decide what to do. I knew I had him on the ropes, and it was time to pour it on. I asked if he knew that when someone was out on bond and committed additional crimes that they normally weren't eligible for bond on the new charges. I let that hang in the air for a minute.

I could see the distress on his face, and I sensed it was time to play my trump card. I said District Court Judge Teel was going to enjoy seeing him and his father-in-law in court again. He knew he had not been in Coosa County court before, but I knew he knew Larry had been there several times, and the judge did not like him one bit. I was hoping Randy did not know that the Judge Teel now on the bench was the brother of the Judge Teel who had heard all of the previous cases. I took it as a good sign when Randy asked, "If I tell you the truth, how can you help me?" I told him I wasn't really there to help him, but that honesty was always the best policy and that I currently only had two warrants for him and was not sure whether or not I would obtain any more. We sat in silence for about a minute as he contemplated his few options.

Pretty soon he looked at me and said he would tell me what happened. I had my pen in my hand as he began to tell the tale. He said on their way home from the jail, when they reached the kudzu patch in an area known locally as Diamond Graphite, Larry spotted a turkey gobbler. Randy said they went up the road and turned around and came back. He said Larry stopped in the middle of the highway and shot the turkey with a 30-06 rifle. They turned around in the hunting club drive and came back. Larry told Randy to get out and get the turkey. So, Randy exited the vehicle, and Larry drove off. Shortly after that, the club president arrived and confronted the young man standing in the kudzu patch alongside the US highway.

He went on to tell me he had not shot anything and was just trying to pick up the turkey. I asked what Larry had said when they got back together, and he said he had told him to use the story he had told me earlier. I wrote out a statement containing everything he had said. I told him to read it and, if it was the truth, I wanted him to sign it. He read and signed it. I brought out the two warrants I had for him and served them on him. Although I should not have let him sign his own bond since he was already currently on bond, seeing how he had come clean I cut him some slack. I told him when the court date was and that he needed to appear on that day and be ready to testify. He gave an affirmative nod and left the jail.

Armed with his statement, a statement from the club president, and the timeline being corroborated by the sheriff's office interview, I obtained warrants for Larry Gaines. The warrants were for hunting without a permit, hunting from the public road, hunting by aid of a vehicle, and hunting in closed season. I soon contacted Larry and asked him to meet me at the jail.

Larry arrived at the jail, and I escorted him into the interview room. I advised him of his rights and asked him to tell me what had occurred. He told me he had brought Randy to the SO to give a statement and, when they were returning home, they had got into an argument, and he had put him out of the truck. He said he did not know what he had done after that. That was the end of his statement. I knew Larry would not be near as easy as Randy had been. Larry was a convicted felon and had several previous game and fish violations. He knew the right to remain silent was his friend. I told Larry I felt there was a lot he was leaving out of his statement. He only shrugged. I told him I had talked with the Diamond Mountain Club president, and he had told me he heard a shot just before he observed an old game warden Bronco turning around in their driveway. Larry replied that a lot of people shot up that way. I asked why was he traveling south and turning around in their drive when he had been going north and was past the clubhouse when he put Randy out of the truck? He evidently had not anticipated the question and it took him a minute to come up with an answer. He said he had decided to come back and pick the boy up but had not seen him. I stated my contention that he had shot a turkey and was turning around to go and retrieve it. He said, "You can't prove that." It was not lost on me that he did not say he hadn't done it!

I said, "I've got an eyewitness."

He squinted his eyes and looked at me and said, "If you are talking about that lying %&*# son-in-law of mine, I can tell you not to believe anything he says." He went on to say, "What that boy needs is a bullet right between his eyes."

I must admit I had not anticipated that statement and wasn't exactly sure how to respond. I told Larry that based on the totality of the circumstances I had obtained warrants for his arrest. I showed him the warrants and allowed him to sign bonds and be on his way. Although it was nothing that could be used against him, I found it really interesting that on his way out of the jail, Larry stopped by to speak with the sheriff and asked him if he could serve as a trustee if he ended up in jail! Sounded like a question from a guilty man to me.

I was pretty nervous as the court date approached. Using a codefendant as a prosecuting witness was never a safe bet. As usual I had put this case together by myself, as the assistant district attorney (ADA) didn't normally bother himself with such trivial matters. To be quite honest, I had not consulted the ADA for fear he might say we didn't have enough to pursue the cases. I knew our case was not the strongest I had ever brought, but I felt we might be able to win it. My uneasy feeling got worse when I realized Randy Jarvis was not present in the courtroom. As the judge was making his way through the docket, I crossed my fingers hoping the witness would show up.

Soon, Larry Gaines's cases were called, and we both stepped up to the judge's bench. He pled not guilty to all charges, and we were sworn in. The judge told me to tell him what had occurred. I proceeded to tell the entire ordeal, taking my time, hoping the witness would appear. I informed the judge I had a witness to everything, but he was currently not in the courtroom. I told him I had another witness who would corroborate the visit to the SO on the day of the incident and the timeline and another who would testify to seeing the defendant's vehicle just after hearing the shot being fired. The judge asked the defendant if he had any questions to ask me. He looked at me and asked if I had seen him do anything, and I said I had not. The man had been in court enough to know that I could only arrest him for a misdemeanor violation if it had occurred in my presence. I quickly pointed out I had obtained the warrants for his arrest based on the results of my comprehensive investigation and the totality of the circumstances. As the judge sat silently contemplating what to do, the courtroom door opened and in walked Randy Jarvis.

BIG SLIMY (BAD COMPANY CORRUPTS GOOD MORALS)

"The other witness is here," I nearly shouted at the judge.

The judge called the witness to the bench. The judge had Randy swear to tell the truth and then instructed him to tell what had occurred. My hopes fell hard when Randy said, "I really don't remember." Knowing this wasn't good, I spoke up and told the judge I had a sworn written statement from the witness outlining the events that had taken place. I asked if I could question the witness. The judge looked over at the ADA and, seeing he wasn't paying any attention, turned to me and dejectedly said, "Go ahead."

I asked the witness if he had been at the SO on the date in question and if Larry Gaines had driven him to and from the appointment in an old green Bronco. He replied he had. I asked if he had talked with the president of Diamond Mountain Hunting Club at the kudzu patch on the side of Highway 231 that day. He again replied, "Yes." I continued and asked if it was not true that Larry had shot a turkey from the truck and had put him out to retrieve it. He hesitated and then stated he could not remember. When asked if he remembered giving me a statement about what had happened that day, he stated he did. I asked the judge if I could place his statement into evidence since it detailed everything that had occurred.

The judge took the statement and briefly perused it. He dismissed the witness and then addressed the defendant. As I held my breath, the judge said, "Mr. Gaines, the court finds you guilty." I wanted to shout. The judge levied fines and court costs totaling $2,046. Mr. Gaines stated he didn't have the money to pay the fines, and he was placed in the jury box to await transport to the jail.

Interestingly, it was now time for the court to hear the cases against Randy Jarvis, aka Mr. Forgetful. Randy approached the bench, and, in spite of having given a statement admitting his guilt, he pled not guilty. I raised my hand and swore to tell the truth. I told the judge these charges were from the same incident we had just discussed in the Gaines cases. I went over the details of the case with the judge, emphasizing Randy's role in what had occurred. I told him Randy had been caught on the property by the club president who was present and would testify. The judge asked Randy if he had any questions for me, and he stated he did not. I asked if I could question the defendant.

With permission granted, I asked Randy why he would plead not guilty after giving me a statement where he admitted his guilt. He replied that he had not shot anything. I responded he had told me he was in the kudzu patch attempting to retrieve a turkey.

He replied, "Yeah, but I didn't shoot the turkey."

"Then who shot it?" I asked in my most accusatory tone.

"Larry did," was his indignant reply.

"Larry Gaines?" I asked.

"Yes," he answered.

I immediately asked, "Is this the same Larry Gaines you could not remember in your earlier testimony?" He did not answer. I turned to the judge and said, "Your honor, I submit that this defendant has a problem telling the truth, and I think he is guilty of the crimes charged."

To my surprise and elation, the judge said, "I agree." Randy was convicted and fined $898.

I must admit I got by with a lot in this case. I appreciated the judge giving me the opportunity to ask the defendants some questions, and I felt their lack of adequate answers sealed their fate. These were obviously perpetual violators, and I feel justice was definitely served in this case.

I took the turkey to retired CEO Byron Smith, owner of Conservation Decoy Company, and he created a fine decoy out of it. It was my earnest desire to catch Big Slimy shooting the decoy, thereby catching him killing the same turkey twice. Now that would be a story! (As I was editing this story, Big Slimy was again arrested for hunting by the aid of bait and not wearing hunter orange!)

It wasn't at all unusual for us to encounter folks whose memory failed them when it came to remembering what they had done or who they had done it with. Sometimes it was as if they had no memory at all, especially if admitting to knowing the identity of a counterpart would adversely affect them. It often reminded me of the disciple Peter. Although Peter pledged his unyielding allegiance to Jesus, Jesus told him he would deny Him three times before the next morning. Peter said there was no way that would happen, and yet it did. The Bible says when Peter realized what he had done he wept bitterly. What about you? Have you ever had someone deceive you, lie to you, or disappoint you in some other way? That is difficult to take. Are you like Peter in that you have let Jesus down? What could be worse than promising Jesus that you would love Him and would never deny Him and then find yourself doing just that? What could cause that? Like with Randy in this story, it could be the bad influence of others. We are all vulnerable to temptation. The Bible says bad company corrupts good morals. The folks around Peter aided in his fall.

Peter failed miserably, yet the Lord forgave him. In fact, He said he was the Rock upon which he would build His church. It's not too late. The Savior is waiting. He can make things right. And He never forgets!

JUST YESTERDAY

ONE OF THE MOST IMPORTANT SKILLS for a conservation enforcement officer (CEO) to develop is fortunately one of the simplest. It is imperative that a CEO learns to be observant. Simply paying attention, while driving down the road, resulted in numerous cases during my career. One memorable case began while traveling along Alabama Highway 22, the state highway that split Coosa County from east to west. Traveling west toward the Coosa Wildlife Management Area, I noticed some brand new five-gallon tripod feeders in various stages of assembly in the front yard of a house I believed belonged to a hunting club. Although it was not illegal to feed wildlife, it was illegal to hunt where feeding was taking place. When I spotted these devices, although I didn't know the folks who had purchased them, I had my doubts that they had been purchased simply to feed the animals.

Obviously, it took a lot of legwork to convert feeders in the yard to arrests for hunting by the aid of bait. The first step was determining whose and how much land the hunting club was hunting on. Then it was time to put in the legwork of walking the woods and locating the feeders. In this case, it took some digging to figure out where the group was hunting since the bulk of their property was a mile from the clubhouse. With the property located, next came the walk.

Looking for bait ranged from total frustration to total elation. Many times, I received information concerning the location of bait, and unfortunately the informant would add that dreaded phrase, "You can't miss it!" Believe me when I say bait is often easy to miss. On numerous occasions I have had to contact an informant and request further directions. Depending on what "bait" was being used and how it was being deployed, it sometimes was the equivalent of looking for a needle in a haystack. Other times it would stand out like a sore thumb. This case was somewhere between those two extremes.

A pretty long walk revealed the location of several feeders and the somewhat unusual fact that some of them were filled with scratch feed. During this time, we had a fall turkey season, and my suspicion was someone in the club was interested in killing a turkey over the feed. We monitored the feeders for the entire deer season and failed to find anyone hunting in the vicinity. Contrary to what you might think, this was not uncommon. It was always interesting to see the look on the face of a new officer when I told him some bait cases were worked for several seasons before anyone was apprehended.

Another necessary skill for a CEO is the possession of a good memory and/or the ability to take and keep good notes. I found later in my career that a combination of these assets was best. Prior to the next season, our county CEO, Shannon Calfee, and I walked the property and once again located feeders filled with corn and more. In addition to finding the feeders, we also found the hunters had now invested in some ladder stands that were set up overlooking the feeders. We took this as an obvious sign they would definitely hunt over the feeders this year. With opening day fast approaching, we decided this would be our first stop on opening morning. Just to be certain, Shannon checked the area again two days before opening day. I could hear the urgency in his voice as he called me on the radio. He prefaced his news with the statement, "You ain't gonna believe this." Then, in a voice that was a mix between disbelief and dread, he said, "The feeders are gone."

This was definitely not what I wanted to hear, and my one-word question/reply was "Gone?"

"Gone," was his one-word answer.

Hoping to salvage something, I asked if there was still corn on the ground, to which he replied, "Yes, some."

The rule in Alabama on hunting by the aid of bait was all feed must be gone ten days prior to any hunting taking place. Since we were within two days of the season, anyone hunting in the area for the next ten days would technically be in violation. Although I had won many convictions on this type of evidence, it was a lot easier when the corn was still there.

I must admit this revelation had really dashed my hopes, and opening morning found me not at all confident in catching anyone on the property. I felt as though over a year's worth of work had now been wasted. This thought was confirmed when I pulled up to the gate on the property on opening morning and noticed there were no vehicles there. I began running everything through my head, trying to pinpoint when we had been seen checking the property. This was always a very real possibility, and the result would often be exactly what we were experiencing.

Disgusted, I began to back away from the gate when I noticed what appeared to be fresh four-wheeler tracks in the damp dirt. I exited my truck, climbed over the fence, and followed the tracks into the woods. Approximately fifty yards into the woods, I found two four-wheelers. I realized I had once again taken a seat on the game warden roller coaster. One minute was frustration and the next elation. I wasn't elated yet, but I was better than I had been.

The discovery of the four-wheelers prompted me to go and check the closest stand. As I eased up to the stand that had previously been overlooking one of the feeders, I noticed it was unoccupied. The roller coaster ride continued. As I got a little closer, I noticed there was a camouflage coat in the stand that had not been there previously. Talk about a roller coaster, I was feeling like I was at Six Flags over Georgia! This whole ordeal was filled with ups and downs. Looking into the small field where the feeder had been, I received quite a shock. There, where the five-gallon feeder had been previously, was a bright blue thirty-gallon feeder. I could not believe it. Further investigation revealed the feeder was full of corn, and the ground was covered with corn as well. I hurriedly made my way back toward my truck. I radioed my partner and told him to come to my location. While waiting on him, I moved my truck so it could not be seen by anyone on the property.

Shannon soon arrived, and I told him about the four-wheelers and asked if he had checked the closest stand when he looked at the area a couple of days earlier. He dejectedly said he had checked it. I asked if it had a camo coat on it.

"No," he replied in a cautiously optimistic tone.

I hesitated for effect and asked, "Did it have a big blue feeder full of corn in front of it?"

I could tell Shannon felt I was messing with him when he chuckled and said "no" once again.

I wasn't chuckling when I quickly shot back, "Well it does now!"

"You're kidding," was his quick reply.

"Nope, it's baited to the gills," I said.

He replied, "Let's go."

We decided to split up and search the property. I soon came across a climbing tree stand sitting on the ground in the middle of the main trail on the property. I was doing my best to spot someone in the area but was having little luck. I would much rather have found the people in the stands than to have to continually keep watching over my shoulder as I slipped through the woods. It is hard to describe the feeling you have knowing you are in the woods attempting to locate folks who are armed to the teeth and who know if you find them it will be expensive. You hope the price they will have to pay isn't enough to cause them to do something stupid.

I eased along the trail and soon came out into another opening and there observed another big blue feeder. As I was looking at the feeder, some movement caught my eye, and I observed a camo-clad man with a rifle walking into the other side of the opening. He quickly saw me, and I motioned for him to come to me. Since the property was obviously baited, I didn't know whether the fellow would come to me or run the other way. Luckily, he walked to me, and I took his rifle and unloaded it. I asked how many folks were hunting the property, and he said there were two others.

Shannon soon showed up with another forlorn looking fellow in tow. I asked where the third fellow was, and they told me he was in the stand closest to the road, the stand I had already checked. I pointed at the feeder and informed the two hunters the area was baited and they were under arrest.

Now I've got to tell you I have heard a lot of excuses, and some have been very outlandish. However, what I was about to hear was a new one on me. One of the defendants said in a matter-of-fact tone, "Wait a minute. We just put this out yesterday!"

Although I had to stifle a laugh, I told the violator it really didn't matter when the bait had been put there, just that it was there now. On our way out, we once again checked the stand closest to the road, and, sure enough, there sat poacher number three looking at the feeder.

With the trio rounded up, we moved to the hunt club headquarters to handle the paperwork. There we found a truck loaded with over a thousand pounds of corn. They were no doubt prepared for a long season.

Later, the violator's father/father-in-law joined our church. We became friends and today serve together in the sheriff's reserve unit. However, this case was like all the others, in that they never forgot it, and neither did I.

CHIVALRY IS NOT DEAD, OR IS IT?

I GUESS HE WAS HER KNIGHT IN ARMOR; however, it wasn't very shiny, and he sure could have used some polish!

For over seventeen years, I was the area biologist on the Coosa Wildlife Management Area (WMA) a thirty-eight-thousand-acre hunting area in Coosa County in east central Alabama. The duties on a WMA are many and varied. One of those duties was the enforcement of state laws and regulations. Therefore, I tried to always be observant.

The WMA was located about seventeen miles from my home in Rockford, and I made that drive thousands of times. One day as I crossed the bridge over Hatchet Creek, I noticed a vehicle in the campground along the creek, so I pulled in to check things out. This was our only campground situated along a navigable stream, and it received a pretty good amount of use. As I headed toward the vehicle, two individuals came into view. A young man and woman were seated in lawn chairs with four rods and reels stuck in the ground in front of them. This was a common method folks used to have multiple lines in the water, hopefully increasing their chance for success. The technique presented a problem for law enforcement officers.

I approached the pair and greeted them while noticing they did have lines in the water and were in fact fishing. I asked how they were doing, and they responded they were good. The male was very talkative and informed me they had just gotten married on the previous day. I congratulated them and asked if they were having any luck fishing. The man's jovial mood immediately changed, and he quickly responded he wasn't fishing. I asked what he was doing, and he replied he was just sitting there. This was the problem. Since no one had a rod and reel in their hand, it was difficult to ascertain who was actually fishing. It was obvious having two rods and reels with lines in the water directly in front of two people indicated both folks were fishing; however, I couldn't swear in court I had seen these folks actually fishing. It was evident someone was, but who?

I asked the woman if all of the fishing equipment belonged to her. She looked at her new husband; however, he would not meet her disgusted gaze. She reluctantly claimed she was the one fishing.

"With all four rods?" I asked.

"I guess so," she replied.

I looked back at the man and asked if he agreed with that, and he again responded he wasn't fishing. I asked the woman if she had a fishing license, and she said she did not. I requested her identification and issued her a citation for fishing without a license. I finished the ticket and explained the bond to her. I looked at the man and said, "It is good to see chivalry is not dead." The look on his face was exactly what I had anticipated. He had no idea what I was talking about.

About a year later, I had occasion to be in court in a neighboring county and again encountered the pair. They were still together and were even dressed alike. They each wore an orange jumpsuit and leg shackles! You can't make this stuff up!

BIG-FOOTED BAITER
(I'M TELLING YOU IT'S BAITED!)

THE LANDOWNER WAS ADAMANT. He knew his neighbor was baiting turkeys, and he wanted something done about it. After scouring the property a second time, I had to again report to the man there was nothing there. I only thought he had been adamant before. I could tell by the urgency in his voice he "knew" there was something there, and he begged me to find it. He was right, and I learned a good lesson.

"You can't miss it." I guess most are familiar with what often happens when someone giving directions uses that phrase. I heard that line many times when someone was telling about where someone was hunting over bait. Very often I've had "there's corn all over the place" turn into a few kernels, and I've had a few kernels turn into the mother lode. Locating bait was often a moving target since it literally could be here today and gone tomorrow.

Around the turn of the century, boy does that make me sound old, a fellow I knew fairly well contacted me and told me I should probably look at his neighbor's property for bait. We were in the spring turkey season, and the ardent turkey hunter was quite upset that he could hear turkeys gobbling on the neighbor's property every morning but none were on his place. This was a very common complaint during turkey season, and it did warrant a look at the property holding the birds.

For many hunters in the south, the wild turkey is the ultimate game bird. I have hunted turkeys across the country and have found the eastern subspecies of the wild turkey to be the most difficult to take of the five species in North America. Many turkey hunters in Alabama, myself included, do their best to hunt almost every day of the season. We are blessed with a long season that stretches from mid-March to the end of April in most of the state. In addition, we enjoy a large bag limit. The pursuit of the monarch of the woods is the ultimate experience in the woods for me and several others in Coosa County. With this being the case, you can imagine the aggravation felt when one believes somebody is illegally enticing turkeys on the adjacent property. The caller was upset and was depending on me to fix the situation.

The property this guy was worried about was on the Wayside Road in the south end of Coosa County. Like most of the county, the area was sparsely populated. I was familiar with the place and made my way down there a couple of days after getting the call. The property had a great network of four-wheeler trails, making it relatively easy to look at. The tract wasn't very large, and it took a couple of hours to give it a thorough look. Although the place had plenty of turkey sign, I found no evidence of bait.

A few days later, the complainant called and asked what I had found. When I told him the place was clean, he could not believe it. His adamant stance concerning the place being baited led me to believe he didn't just assume there was bait on the property, he had likely seen bait on the property. It was not unusual for folks to check things out on their own before contacting us. The hunter sort of begged and sort of demanded I give the place another look. I told him it would be a couple of days before I would be able to get back to the property.

I again made the trek to the south end of the county and walked the entire property. Once again it was clean. A few days passed, and I received another call from the now irate hunter. He told me he was certain there was bait out on the property. I informed him I had been over the entire property twice, and there was no corn there. He assured me there was corn on the property, "right now." Although he did not say so, I felt certain he had seen the corn. I told him I would check it out.

I contacted game warden Hershel Patterson and told him I had received another call about the property and felt I needed to look at it again and asked him to accompany me. Hershel commented it sounded like this guy had been on the property, and I told him that was my feeling as well. Hershel said he would meet me after lunch, and we would check the place out.

Checking turkey bait required you be very alert since unlike deer hunters, who normally hunted in the early morning and late evening, a turkey baiter might be on bait at any time of the day. In addition, the violator would be fully camouflaged and somewhat hidden. Not seeing any vehicles at the camp house, Hershel and I entered the property. I explained the layout of the trails and fields and he went left and I went right. It was obvious from boot prints and ATV tracks; a person or persons had been on the property earlier in the day. It also was almost immediately obvious that whoever had been on the place had baited it heavily! Following the trails, we concluded someone had laid a bag of corn on the rack of the four-wheeler, cut the corner off the bag(s), and driven over the roads and fields, leaving a golden trail that anyone could follow.

Hershel and I met and compared notes while leaving the area.

Since this was Thursday afternoon, we decided Saturday morning would be a good time to catch the culprit(s). Since the corn was scattered all over the property, we considered the entire place to be baited and only needed to find the hunters to make the case. However, finding a camo-clad hunter wasn't the easiest thing to do!

As we drove back to Rockford, we discussed a few possibilities. First was the question of whether or not the caller had something against the landowner and could have in fact placed the bait on the area in an attempt to get them caught. While this wasn't unheard of, fortunately it was rare in our experience. In addition, we both knew the complainant and felt he was above anything so underhanded. We surmised, as an avid turkey hunter, he was upset that the neighbor had drawn all the turkeys to their property illegally. We felt certain that, upset enough, he had gone and checked the property out. We didn't know that for a fact but felt it was a good possibility. It would not be the first time someone had done something like that. While that wasn't kosher, we didn't try to probe too deeply. If the neighbor had been on the property, that would possibly constitute a trespass violation, which wasn't something we enforced. If they had gone hunting on the property without permission, then we would address that.

We arrived early Saturday morning, having decided the best way to find these guys would be to watch them as they entered the property. Knowing which road they took to start with would no doubt allow us to locate them more quickly. Often, we could locate a turkey hunter as he either tried to locate the turkey using a locator call or as he called to the gobbler using hen calls. We had a good hiding spot across the road from the camp house and were there waiting well before sunrise. Shortly after our arrival, a vehicle pulled into the property, and two individuals got out. Just as Hershel and I had done two days earlier, one hunter went left and one went right, and, unbeknownst to them, we were right behind them.

Since hunters found in a baited area often denied knowledge of any wrongdoing, we always looked for something to tie them to the bait. In this instance, we knew an ATV had been used to put the corn on the property, and there was a four-wheeler in the shed by the camp house. However, we had also noticed one other pertinent thing, and that was the huge size of some of the boot tracks on the property. Hershel and I surmised it had to be at least a size fourteen! This also loomed in the back of my mind as I made my way through the dark looking for Sasquatch! I shouldn't say that, seeing how my youngest son now wears a size seventeen!

Within thirty minutes, Hershel and I were back at the vehicle each with a hunter in tow. Things had pretty much gone as planned except for one major thing. **There was not a kernel of corn on the property!** Not one kernel where less than forty-eight hours earlier there had been one hundred pounds! This development caused us to work things a little differently than if the fellows had been standing in the corn.

Back at the truck, the guys were trying to act innocent, although I'm sure they didn't think our presence was a mere coincidence. We told the pair the reason we were there was because the property had been baited with corn. Taking a guess, I looked at the smaller of the two and asked, "Is that your four-wheeler in the shed that was used to put the corn out?"

He wanted to protest but knew if we had found the four-wheeler we had probably also found the empty corn sacks, so he simply nodded his head. We wrote each man a citation for hunting by the aid of bait. I explained the property would be considered baited for ten days and then could be hunted again. The men said they understood and apologized for having put the bait out.

BIG-FOOTED BAITER (I'M TELLING YOU IT'S BAITED!)

As we turned to leave, I looked at the big guy and asked, "By the way, what size boot do you wear?"

He looked a little puzzled and replied, "Fourteen."

THE STEW IN THE BACK SEAT

As I neared the Coosa River bridge on Alabama Highway 22, I was surprised (this was back when I was still surprised by stuff) to see a young man standing beside a car, pointing a rifle into the woods. While this would not have been unusual during the hunting season, it was the end of August, and the daytime high temperatures were hovering around one hundred degrees. Since it was only 10:30 a.m., the temperature was only about eighty-eight with the humidity about the same. Not even the wildlife moves much in this type of weather. As a matter of fact, I had just passed a dog chasing a rabbit, and they were both walking! However, if there is something out there, there is likely someone willing to try to shoot it.

I executed a U-turn and pulled in behind the vehicle. The "shooter" was a young guy, maybe eighteen or nineteen years old. Holding the rifle, he turned and looked at me and said, "This gun won't even shoot." A few things were at work here. Where most police officers, when faced with an armed subject, would come out with their gun drawn and shouting commands, we were used to subjects being armed. While this familiarity probably made us less cautious than we should have been, someone possessing a firearm was not necessarily a red flag for us. However, it was a priority for us to gain control of the firearm.

THE STEW IN THE BACK SEAT

I cautiously approached the young man and took the rifle from him. He told me he wasn't trying to shoot anything, and I asked what he was doing. "Just looking," was his response.

I was thinking it was interesting he needed to hold a rifle (that "won't even shoot") and look down the sights (iron sights—no scope) to see something. Although I was still relatively new to the law enforcement game, I wasn't that new. As I carried the rifle and placed it in my truck, I checked it and found it wasn't loaded.

I had noticed there were three more people in the car, so I approached to gather some identification from the occupants and the nonshooter. When I got to the driver's door, the smell of alcoholic beverage nearly knocked me down. Although the vehicle was pulled off of the roadway, it was on the right-of-way, it was running, and the woman behind the wheel was subject to being arrested for driving under the influence if she was indeed intoxicated. Although the smell was undeniable, I was having a little trouble convincing myself this woman might be drunk, seeing how it wasn't even lunchtime, and surely no one would be out drinking and driving in the morning. I was for some reason under the impression that type of activity was reserved for nighttime. Hey, I said I was still young and naïve.

Keeping an eye on the other three, I opened the driver's door and asked the woman to step out. While I was familiar with several field sobriety tests, I had learned one of the best indications of whether or not someone was drunk was observing them as they exited their vehicle. As this woman climbed out, she displayed classic drunken posture. At first, it was as if her leg was asleep and didn't want to hold her up. Her right hand was desperately trying to find a handhold on the door as she fell back against it. Having somewhat successfully made it to her feet, she now straightened up and started a determined stagger toward the rear of the car. It wasn't a dignified stagger but more of a loosely coordinated stumble that relied heavily on the side of the car to remain upright.

When she finally reached the rear of the vehicle, I asked her how much she had had to drink, and she replied, "None." She added she had been eating some of the stew they had in the back seat. I informed her I could smell the odor of alcoholic beverage about her person, and I was going to have to take her to jail and test her. She protested she had not had anything to drink. Her slurred speech didn't help to convince me. The other three people were now out of the car and pleading her case. Although I didn't feel threatened, I knew this could get out of hand quickly. I told them I was going to take her to the jail and test her, and if she wasn't over the limit, I would bring her back. This was not a distraction technique; it was actually the procedure at the time. The fellow who had the rifle earlier said, "Well you will have to bring her back because she hasn't had a drop to drink." I assured him if that was true, I would bring her back.

I placed the woman in the front seat of my truck, since everyone frowned on us hauling folks in the bed of the pickup (don't ask how I know that), and we headed to the jail. Since I wasn't certified to operate the Intoxilyzer 5000, the instrument that measured the alcoholic content of someone's blood, I radioed the jail and requested a certified operator. At this time, the legal blood alcohol content was .10. I felt certain she would check, but, as with many drunks, she seemed to sober up a lot during the twenty-minute ride to the jail. I was sure hoping I would not have to return her to her vehicle.

We arrived at the jail and entered the little room that housed the Intoxilyzer machine. The operator went through all the preliminaries and instructions and told the lady to blow in the tube. This was often when the wheels would come off. Many folks felt they could "beat" the test by either placing their tongue over the mouth piece or providing less than a sufficient sample in some other manner. Fortunately, since this woman had not had anything to drink, she did not hesitate to provide a good sample. I held my breath and waited for the reading to show on the screen. The machine beeped and started printing the readout. When I looked at the display and it read .21, I let out a big breath of my own. At 11:00 a.m. on a weekday she was double the legal limit. As I left the jail, I couldn't help but think Wow, that was some stew they had in the back seat.

You can't make this stuff up!

The woman in this story was adamant that she had not had a drop to drink. She was sure, yet she was wrong. We all have been wrong from time to time. However, there are things we cannot afford to be wrong about. I've heard preachers during the invitation time of a service ask the question "Do you know that you know that you know that you know you are saved?" It is a question we must be sure of. Where we will spend eternity hangs in the balance. If you don't know for sure you are saved, today is the day to make sure. Jesus is ready and waiting.

ARREST HIM!

Everybody has obligations, and failure to meet them often has repercussions. Some repercussions are uncomfortable, while others result in steel bracelets and bars.

District court in our rural county regularly never failed to provide an interesting array of charges and characters. Everything from traffic tickets to preliminary hearings on felony cases came before the district judge. Included in that mixture were a multitude of misdemeanors and violations, which included our wildlife laws and regulations. The size of the docket varied. Since we only had district court once a month, it wasn't unusual to have a hundred criminal cases and sometimes three hundred traffic violations set to come before the judge. Of course, just because there were a couple of hundred names on the docket, on average we would have sixty or eighty folks in attendance, not counting officers or attorneys. Many individuals would fail to appear for court. There were many reasons why that might happen. Some folks would be incarcerated in another county and therefore couldn't attend. Others would simply decide not to show up. In most instances, this would result in the judge issuing a failure to appear warrant for their arrest. Failing to appear set several things in motion, and all of them were costly.

ARREST HIM!

The names of the defendants were in alphabetical order on the court docket. Somehow it seemed the people I arrested always had a last name that started with a letter near the end of the alphabet. Therefore, I got to observe a lot of cases while waiting on mine to be called. As the judge made his way through the list, depending on the case, he might hear it right then or set it for trial later in the day. As you can imagine, the day could get long. Normally about an hour or so in the judge would call a recess. During that time, folks could go to the bathroom, confer with attorneys, and so forth. Although the court was officially in recess, there was normally a lot going on.

Following a recess, the judge returned, and I could tell he wasn't in a good mood. Think about it. You are dealing with hundreds of cases. The majority of the people who have shown up for court are armed with some hard luck story. Several will tell you how the officer was mistaken. Some of their ad-libbed lines were well rehearsed lies, while many did their best to make something up on the spot. I'm certain that got old quick!

As I stood off to the side of the judge's bench, he took his docket in hand and called the next name on the sheet. As a middle-aged man approached the bench, I could tell by the judge's demeanor something was amiss. I guess since I was standing nearby, he locked eyes with me, held up a piece of paper, and pointing at the man now standing before him said, "He has a warrant for his arrest. Arrest him."

Although I definitely had not anticipated this, I turned to the man and taking his arm said, "You're under arrest."

As I was placing handcuffs on the man with a bewildered look on his face, the judge told me to take the fellow to jail and tell the intake officer he would be over later to give them some instructions. I took the man by the arm and led him out of the courtroom, down the stairs, and out of the courthouse. Unlike in some counties, our jail was not connected to the courthouse. It was about two blocks west of the courthouse. Since the distance between the two was short, the normal practice was to walk those ordered to jail across the parking lot and past the post office to the county jail.

Seeing how I was not familiar with the man and knew he wasn't someone we had charged with a game and fish violation, as we walked across the parking lot I asked the man what this was all about, and he replied he had no idea. I didn't necessarily believe that, seeing how he had not offered any resistance nor voiced any protest. A normal person who did not know why they were being placed under arrest would normally at the very least ask a few questions.

You may be wondering how I could arrest someone when I didn't know what the charge was or any details. The answer to that is arrest warrants normally say something to the effect of any certified officer is instructed to arrest this individual. That is plain enough. The law also says we need only have knowledge that an active warrant exists in order to effect an arrest. A judge with a warrant in his hand was more than sufficient for this guy to be put in jail.

We soon arrived at the jail, and I advised the jailer this man was under arrest. I knew he would ask the usual question, and he did. "What are the charges?"

"I can't tell you," was my reply. That answer received the unfriendly look I had expected. Court dates were not a good day to be in the jail as they were busy booking people in, explaining how to get people out and hearing how everyone was innocent. I knew not to belabor the point and informed the jailer the judge had told me to arrest the man and bring him to jail and he would be over later with the details. That explanation did not sit very well; however, he knew, like I did, you did what the judge said.

ARREST HIM!

I had the man sit down on a steel stool in the booking area and removed my handcuffs from his wrist. I then cuffed him to the steel rail attached to the wall, and I returned to the courthouse. I found the judge standing in the clerk's office, and I told him the man was in jail. He advised me the man needed to get comfortable, seeing how the judge had earlier issued a warrant for him based on his owing $83,000 in back child support. I couldn't help but think that in order to get that far behind on child support this guy had missed more than a few payments. Seeing how the guy had told me he had no idea what the problem was, I reasoned that paying his child support must have just slipped his mind! Evidently several times!

You can't make this stuff up!

Obviously, the man in this story was either very forgetful or not very observant. I can't tell you how many times I have informed someone there was a warrant for their arrest only to have them claim they had no knowledge of it or what it might have stemmed from. This almost always proved to be false. Although they doggedly claimed to be innocent, it normally didn't turn out that way.

I can tell you now there is a judgment coming, and we will definitely be found guilty because we are guilty. All have sinned and come short of the glory of God. But the gift of God is eternal life through Jesus Christ. Don't allow eternity to sneak up on you. It's coming. Where will you spend it? The choice is yours.

COME ON OUT BRUCE

I HAD DUTIFULLY CHASED the violator to the best of my ability. The briar thicket we ran through had likely never before seen a human. As I stood wiping blood from my neck and hands, I at least had the satisfaction that the violator was now hemmed in between me and my partner, who had rolled up on the scene. My excitement quickly turned to dismay. Using exaggerated hand gestures, I attempted to relate to my partner he needed to stop his vehicle. Totally ignoring me, he pulled right up to me. I would find out later, as was often the case, the veteran officer knew something I didn't.

I'm certain almost everyone has heard the old adage "Experience is the best teacher," and I can testify that is true in the area of conservation law enforcement. Fortunately, I was placed in a county with two experienced conservation enforcement officers (CEOs) who, although leery to start with, eventually began to share their vast knowledge with me. This sharing of wisdom did not begin automatically. I was not necessarily received with open arms upon my arrival. Although the officers did work with me, they were skeptical to begin with. My assistant chief had told me the relationship between the wildlife section and the enforcement section wasn't good in the county (I would later find out it wasn't good anywhere). It seemed my predecessor, although charged with law enforcement responsibility, did not like arresting anyone and didn't want anyone else arresting anyone on the thirty-eight-thousand-acre wildlife management area he was responsible for. This was of course in sharp contrast to the view of the officers in the county and therefore a large rift had developed. The assistant chief told me it would be my job to pull things together. Therefore, I contacted the officers my first day on the job and advised them I wanted to accompany them in order to learn the county and the job. Although I had no previous law enforcement experience or training, during my first week on the job I assisted on three night hunting arrests!

I distinctly remember CEO Hershel Patterson telling me him and his partner, CEO Earl Brown, would teach me more in three months than I had learned in college in the last six years. I was a bit skeptical about that, seeing how I had just earned two college degrees. However, it wasn't long until I began to understand he knew what he was talking about. Of course, he had been a game warden since I was six years old!

One thing I realized rather quickly was although I could learn a lot in a hurry, there was no shortcut or substitute for learning the county and the people. This was about to become very clear to my young self.

As was often the case in the Alabama gun deer season, it was warm and sunny. Too warm for deer hunting, I thought; however, Hershel and I were in his patrol car, riding along a rural county road in the Hanover community of central Coosa County, looking for hunters. As we came around a curve in the gravel road, we came face to face with what first reminded me of a scene from the movie *Deliverance*! There, standing in the middle of the public road, was a large, bearded man wearing bib overalls and no shirt. Cradled in his arms was what appeared to be a lever-action 30-30 rifle.

As Hershel slid the car to a stop, the fellow hit the woods at a full run. I immediately threw open my door and took off after the subject. Unfortunately, we were soon running through one of the worst briar thickets I had ever been in. I could not see the man in front of me, but could easily hear him fighting through the rough terrain. After a couple of minutes that seemed like half an hour, I was still following the subject, while at the same time wiping the blood the briars had coaxed from my neck and face. As I followed the noise, I soon heard gravel crunching and realized I was about to come out on another gravel road. Through the maze of limbs and briars, I could see it was Hershel driving down the road. I painfully made my way into the road and motioned for Hershel to stop the car and pointed into the woods at the last place I had heard the suspect. Hershel paid me no attention and drove right to my location.

As he got out of the car, I whispered to him the guy was still close by in the woods. He looked at me with a knowing smile and turned around and hollered, "Come on out Bruce!" At first, I didn't understand what was going on. Hershel again hollered, "Come on out Bruce!" and as I stood there daubing at the blood oozing from several parts of my body, a bloody "Bruce" came walking out into the road, rifle in hand. Hershel approached Bruce and took his rifle. As I sat in the car tending to my wounds, Hershel wrote Bruce tickets for hunting from the road, hunting without hunter orange, and no hunting license. Bruce signed the tickets and we were on our way.

As we drove away, Hershel looked at me and grinned. I asked him why he didn't tell me he could just call the guy out of the woods. He said, "I wanted to give you a chance to catch him."

Hershel explained he had realized as we ran off into the thicket the violator was a member of a local family whose members he had dealt with numerous times. He figured the fellow would cut through to the other road since it led to his house. Therefore, he drove around to cut us off and make the apprehension. As I steadily wiped at the blood on my neck, face, and arms, I told him I really preferred the call-out method and requested we try that first the next time. That wouldn't be the last lesson I would learn during my CEO education.

I must admit we weren't able to utilize the call-out method very often. I can understand it. Bruce was guilty, and he knew it. Therefore, he felt the best thing to do was run and hide. This may work for a little while; however, there is a day coming when all running will stop. Every knee will bow, and every tongue will confess. You can count on it. Don't wait until it's everlasting too late.

GO BACK AND DO IT AGAIN

EARLY IN MY CAREER, the opening day of dove season was one of the busiest days of the year for conservation enforcement officers (CEO). I guess it was due in part to the fact it was the first season to open in the fall, and folks had been itching to get out and do some shooting. In the south, a lot of folks would make a grand production out of the day by shooting birds in the afternoon and grilling and eating them that evening. For the CEO, it was a busy day spent hurrying from one shoot to the next. For a large percentage of dove hunters, opening day was their entire season, as they did not go again for the rest of the year.

It was rare that the first day of the season wasn't hot and sticky. Many folks felt it was imperative they drink several cold beers during the day and into the evening. Believe me when I tell you having the game warden show up wasn't the highlight of anyone's day.

Since Coosa County had basically no agriculture and therefore very few doves, I normally went south to neighboring Elmore County and assisted our officers there. My friend and mentor CEO Byron Smith worked Elmore County and normally had several baited areas ready to be worked on opening day.

When the birds started flying, temptation was strong, and many hunters had a hard time waiting for noon, which was the official shooting time on opening day. Although you could occasionally catch someone shooting early, the birds usually didn't get to flying well until later in the afternoon. Therefore, we would typically start checking hunters around two or three in the afternoon. Of course, this sometimes changed, depending on the amount of bait on the field and the suspected number of shooters.

Byron was very good at making near air-tight baiting cases. He knew all the tricks violators would employ to "sweeten" their fields. On many occasions, he would have photographs or video of people spreading bait on fields. Of course, when we arrived on opening day, the feed had been disked under the day before, leaving the appearance of a planted field. The baiting law we worked under at that time stated all feed must be removed ten days prior to any hunting taking place. Even if the plan was to disk the bait under making it unavailable to the birds, it must have been done ten days prior to hunting the area. Byron kept a calendar with good notes, seeing how some folks had a hard time counting the days! It was interesting to hear how the violators would vehemently deny the charge and would vow to fight all the way to the Supreme Court if that is what it would take to keep from having their good name tarnished by a #%!& game warden who was trumping up charges against them. No sir, they were not going to take this lying down. After they had duly impressed all of their guests with their dressing down of the game warden, Byron would ask if they would like to see the video of them baiting the field. That usually succeeded in shutting down the most boisterous violator. I have seen some people's faces so red I thought their head might explode!

One hot September opening day, Coosa County CEO Hershel Patterson had headed south to assist in Elmore County. Byron had reported he had located a field that was heavily baited. The people had turned the bait under a couple of days earlier and he felt sure there would be several guns on the field. Byron and Hershel pulled unseen into the edge of the field and parked among the many pickup trucks. They began making their way around the field, checking and taking up licenses. Soon they called all the hunters together. I think most folks who have done much dove hunting know it isn't a good thing when the game warden keeps your license and then gathers everybody together in the center of the field. If any of these folks did not know, they were about to find out!

With the crowd assembled, Byron informed them the field was baited and everyone would be receiving a ticket for hunting by the aid of bait. Of course, the wailing and gnashing of teeth began. Some were worse than others, but the duo soon had everyone ticketed and got in Byron's vehicle and left the field.

Byron drove a couple of hundred yards down the road out of sight of the field and pulled into a dim side road and stopped. He told Hershel he had a feeling some of those good ole boys were still going to try and shoot the birds that had started coming into the fields in droves. He exited the truck and told Hershel to wait for his call and return to the field and get him.

The officer eased into the woods and stealthily made his way back to the field. As he suspected, the boys were gathered around their trucks drinking beer and cussing the game wardens. It wasn't long until one of the crew said he hadn't gone to all the trouble of baiting that field not to get to kill any doves on it. With his courage sufficiently lifted, he announced he was going dove hunting. Several of the others told him they couldn't afford one ticket much less two. However, one friend agreed there were just too many birds not to shoot. Many times, all it takes to commit a violation is a willing accomplice. The pair retrieved their shotguns and started out across the field. They were not far across when two doves came directly over their heads and they unloaded on them. That was all Byron needed to see. He came out of the woods into the edge of the field and summoned the pair to come to him. Although I'm sure they were really unhappy now, evidently they realized the futility of saying anything. Byron completed the paperwork and called Hershel to come and get him.

The plan had worked well for Byron, but for Hershel not so much. Byron's new Ford Bronco was one of the first models that required the brake to be depressed in order to be able to shift the transmission from park. Since Hershel wasn't aware of this, he was pulling on the shifter with all of his might to no avail. He explained to me how he felt certain he was going to pull the lever off the column. He searched the steering column for some hidden lock to no avail. Fortunately, after several frustrating minutes, he inadvertently put his foot on the brake and the shifter easily shifted into drive. When Byron asked what had taken him so long, Hershel replied he wouldn't believe him if he told him.

These fellows received what was coming to them just like we all will. On the Day of Judgment, we will all be judged on everything we have done, good and bad. The Bible says even our idle words will not go unnoticed. Our sins can be forgiven and for our sake we better seek that forgiveness. We will be responsible for ourselves. Like one of the guys in this story, folks often are led down the wrong path by a "friend." There are many ways this occurs; however, in working for over thirty years, I came to realize it was often done so there would be someone else to share the blame. Remember on the day that every knee will bow and every tongue will confess, it will be done individually. You are responsible for you. Choose you this day who you will serve. Decisions matter.

COVER ME RICK

As an area biologist with the Alabama Department of Conservation and Natural Resources, I spent almost every weekend of my first seventeen deer seasons working a hunt on a wildlife management area (WMA). During that time, Alabama had about seven hundred thousand acres in WMAs across the state. There were some areas for small game and some for waterfowl, but most were hunting of all game. In addition, the areas were popular with folks for everything from berry picking to horseback riding to hiking to camping. This being the case, the areas drew all sorts of folks. However, the biggest crowds were those hunting deer. It was a somewhat controlled situation in that all of those participating were required to obtain a permit for each hunt. Eventually, we would move to a season-long permit.

Deer hunts on the Coosa WMA would garner anywhere from 100 to 1,500 people, depending on the type of hunt. The area offered archery hunting, muzzleloader hunting, and rifle/shotgun hunting. Normally during each season, we would have one or two days of either-sex hunting, which drew a large crowd. The first either-sex hunt in the 1970s brought in 2,700 people! Later in my career, we increased the antlerless hunting significantly.

Believe me when I say working a hunt made for a long weekend. The usual routine was to arrive at the WMA check station at 4:30 a.m. Early on in my career, when hunter numbers were high, we would often have hunters waiting on us at 4:30. On days of an either-sex hunt, we would have hunters arrive at 3:30 in the morning to get in line to draw for permits. After we checked the hunters' licenses and issued a permit, we would normally have a lull for two or three hours before harvested deer started being brought in. Things would get busy again until about lunchtime, and there would be another lull. The afternoon was usually pretty slow, and, during this time, we would often patrol the area looking for violators and work the area as needed. We would return to the check station by around three or four in the afternoon and stay until 6:30 p.m. Then we would go home for supper and come back out and work night hunting until midnight or so. We would repeat the same routine the next day. Using this method and counting conservatively, we would work about twenty-eight hours in two days. This schedule really did a number on a forty-hour work week.

One day during a hunt on the Coosa WMA, I was patrolling the area with my supervisor, Rick. Rick began his career as an area biologist on the nearby Hollins WMA. After a few years, he was promoted to supervisor, which was beneficial in some ways, but office location wasn't one of them. The Hollins WMA was comprised primarily of United States Forest Service property, much of which was large hardwood. The majority of the remainder of the area was owned by Kaul Timber Company, which was primarily old growth longleaf pine. The area was very picturesque. In contrast, the office for our district supervisor was in downtown Montgomery, surrounded by asphalt, buildings, vehicles, and sirens. Therefore, whenever he got the opportunity to return to the "field," he normally jumped at it.

We had been patrolling and were on our way back to the check station, traveling north on Coosa County Road 29, which was the eastern boundary of the WMA and stretched the entire length of the area. As we eased along the boundary road, we were met by a primer-gray-colored vehicle, which immediately pulled to the side of the road. Several times during my career I had seen people use this technique when they wanted me to stop and answer a question or listen to a complaint. Therefore, I pulled off the right side of the road, executed a U-turn, and pulled up behind the vehicle. About the time our truck came to a stop, the driver mashed his accelerator to the floor, leaving us in a cloud of blue oil smoke and spraying my truck with dirt and gravel.

I was somewhat surprised by this turn of events; however, seeing how the car did not have a license plate displayed, I immediately began pursuing the vehicle. I radioed the Coosa County sheriff's office (SO) and informed the dispatcher I was 10-100 (in pursuit) southbound on County 29 just south of Mt. Moriah Church, and I would appreciate any assistance they could provide. I didn't really count on getting much help since it was a Saturday afternoon, and at best we would have one unit covering the entire county.

We quickly reached speeds of sixty miles per hour, which was pretty fast on the winding county road. Although I had no trouble keeping up with the vehicle, his driving quickly gave me cause for concern. The driver was taking each curve on the wrong side of the road. After pursuing the car for about a mile, I said to my supervisor, "If he keeps driving like that, he's going to kill somebody." Rick agreed, so I radioed the SO and told them I was ending the pursuit. I advised the vehicle was still traveling south on County 29 approximately three miles north of Kelley's Crossroads, and I was going to trail the vehicle.

Just south of our location was an area known as Double Bridges. Like many areas in rural Alabama, it was a name that had hung on despite the fact there was only one bridge present.

Just south of the bridge was an S curve that had proven to be too much for many drivers during my tenure on the WMA. I felt certain the driver of this vehicle would fail to successfully navigate the curve. I was wrong. We continued south.

Within about one-half mile of Alabama Highway 22 is a rare straight stretch, where you can see for about one-half mile. Rounding the curve, I observed the smoking car as it crossed Highway 22 without ever slowing down. Traveling the speed limit, I followed the trail of smoke.

As we turned onto Coosa County Road 14, I stated to Rick if the guy kept driving the way he had been, we would soon find him in a ditch. At the next intersection, the smoke trail turned north. About one-half mile later, I came around a curve and saw the primed car facing us in the ditch off the right side of the road. I slid to a stop, radioed the SO I had them stopped at Swamp Creek Church, and told my boss to cover me as I headed for the driver's side of the vehicle.

Approaching the car, I learned for the first time the vehicle had more than one occupant. I was somewhat shocked to see a young boy in the front passenger seat. Just as I rounded the rear of the car the driver forced open the door and began climbing out. I graciously assisted him by grabbing him and gently placing him over the trunk of the car. The smell of an alcoholic beverage was strong as I got his hands behind him and quickly applied the handcuffs. While this was happening, I glanced at the passenger to make sure he didn't have a weapon (a kid can kill you as quickly as anybody). That's when I noticed the kid had his hands up and wasn't moving a muscle. I looked toward my truck and spotted my boss, who was standing in front of the car with his pistol at ready gun. If I don't miss my guess, it was probably the only time in his career he had to unholster his weapon on a stop.

As I was handcuffing the driver, he kept grumbling and saying, "Texas gets me first."

I had no idea what that meant, but I replied, "I've got you now."

About that time, a sheriff's deputy arrived on the scene. I asked the miscreant how much he had had to drink, and he replied, "I drank a six pack and smoked a joint!" The deputy, Terry Wilson, who would later become the best sheriff we ever had, said that would work and we placed him in the back seat of the patrol car.

We turned our attention to the passenger, who turned out to be fourteen years old. The boy had received a bump on the head during the wreck (which we had no part off) but was okay. The deputy transported the subject to the jail while we tried to contact someone to come and retrieve the juvenile. I later arrived at the jail and wrote out citations for driving under the influence, no tag, no insurance, attempting to elude, and no driver's license, and signed a warrant on him for reckless endangerment. You would think that many tickets would get someone's attention; however, after viewing his rap sheet, I could see why he wasn't impressed. The ten-page sheet revealed forty-seven previous charges and a current felony warrant out of Texas!

When the court date arrived, the defendant was appointed an attorney, who promptly approached me with an offer. He said, "Since Texas has a warrant on him, why don't we just drop these cases and let them have him. That will get him out of our hair, and everyone will be happy." I told him that might make him and his client happy, but it wouldn't do much for me. The man was convicted on all charges and sentenced to four months in jail.

Four months later, I was shocked during the next district court to again see the man escorted in with the rest of the criminals. Knowing he had finished his time and had been extradited to Texas, I inquired and learned Texas came and got him, took him to Texas, booked him and released him. He promptly returned to Rockford and was arrested for possession of marijuana.

I have told this story several times and had people tell me that someone with that many violations should not be out on the street. I do not disagree with that. However, in order to cut costs and alleviate prison overcrowding, our legislature has made it increasingly difficult to have anyone incarcerated. This is obviously common knowledge among criminals, which has effectively removed the deterrent that jail time once was. In the last few years, I stopped two different individuals who had twenty-two felonies on their record and were out on the street. Aggravating to say the least.

I was thankful that Rick had my back in this incident. Who has your back? Who do you have you can count on? Jesus said, "I will never leave you nor forsake you."

DEAF MAN HUNTING

IN A SPLIT SECOND, which is the time frame for many law enforcement decisions, I had concluded if the fellow standing in the road turned toward me with a gun in direct contradiction to my multiple loud verbal commands, I would shoot him. With my pistol in my hand, I yelled at him for what I considered to be the last time.

Every officer goes through highs and lows when it comes to apprehending violators. Some days everyone you approached was in violation, while other days, you could not buy a case. Some days and nights you might spend without even seeing anybody hunting or fishing. The fruitless days soon fade away, but those days when things went our way, those are the ones we remember. However, even though things may seem to be going our way, that can and does change in a heartbeat.

After catching a dedicated road hunter earlier in the week, we were once again hidden in the woods near the old skating rink site, alongside the Unity Road in Weogufka, Alabama. It seemed as though folks had quit going into the woods to hunt and had decided just to ride along the road looking for a deer to shoot. The technique was an effective way to cover a lot of ground in a short period of time. It was also a recipe for disaster when you had people shooting a high-powered rifle into the woods from a vehicle sitting in a public road. While they might be able to see twenty or even fifty yards into the woods, the projectile from their gun could travel a mile at three thousand feet per second. This practice put anyone and anything in the woods at risk. I have witnessed bullet holes in houses, barns, farm equipment, and livestock. Of course, it was then dead stock!

At approximately 4:50 in the afternoon, three pickup trucks with *Sunrise Logging Company* emblazoned on the door passed the deer decoy we had placed about sixty yards south of Coosa County Road 56. This location had proven to be a favorite for those who would ride the road looking for a deer to shoot. The addition of the fake deer to the landscape often proved to be the straw that broke the camel's back so to speak.

Two of the logging company trucks turned around and came back with the first one easing to a stop in front of the decoy and the other close behind. From my observation site hidden in the woods on the opposite side of the road from the decoy, I observed the passenger getting out of the vehicle. Although I was only thirty yards away, the truck blocked my view of the gun I was sure he possessed.

I felt a shot was imminent, and my senses were on high alert when I heard a muffled pop. I immediately assumed the subject had fired at the deer with a small caliber weapon. I cautiously moved toward the truck on foot, identified myself, and yelled for the driver to cut the truck off. As I attempted to watch both men, the shooter began running toward the second truck. This created an extremely dangerous situation. As I attempted to keep one eye on the subject running and the other eye on the driver of the truck, I hoped my partner, Gene Carver, would soon emerge from his hiding spot and arrive on the scene. Not sure what the running man was up to, I was yelling loud verbal commands of "freeze" and "get down." Unable to see a long gun, I quickly surmised he must have a handgun. This intensified the situation, and I again yelled for him to get down. Keep in mind all of this occurred within a few seconds.

The man continued toward the driver's side of the second truck. Knowing how quickly someone can spin around and fire a handgun, I drew my pistol and pointed it at the man. While the man on the ground was not responding to my loud verbal commands, the men in the second truck were, as they had their hands over their heads. At this time, Gene came out in the road in his truck with blue lights flashing.

Seeing Gene approaching, the man quit running, turned, and saw me pointing my pistol at him and got down in the road. I moved over to him and handcuffed him. With the shooter on the ground, I moved to the driver of the lead truck. I opened the door and took the man out and put him on the hood of the truck. A muzzle loading rifle was in the seat of the pickup, and I found no other weapons. As I patted the man down for weapons, I was watching Gene remove a rifle from the rear truck.

With everything under control, Gene and I began to sort out exactly what had happened. Our shooter had attempted to shoot the deer with the muzzleloader. As was not uncommon with muzzleloaders, the percussion cap on the rifle detonated, the "pop" Gene and I heard, but the powder failed to ignite, and therefore the projectile was not fired. The violator threw the rifle back into the pickup and headed to the second truck to retrieve a high-powered rifle from his uncle Eugene, who was driving the second truck.

As we furthered the investigation, we learned that, due to years of running heavy equipment without hearing protection, the shooter was basically deaf and therefore could not hear me yelling commands at him. The driver of the second vehicle stated he heard me clearly and had proved it by raising his hands over his head.

We advised the shooter of his rights and asked if he possessed a permit for the property, and he replied he did not. Further investigation revealed the muzzleloader used in the incident belonged to the driver of the first truck. We advised the driver of his rights and asked if he possessed a permit for the property, and he advised he did not. Questioning revealed the driver had been arrested previously for the same offense.

We prepared bonds for hunting from the public road, hunting by aid of a vehicle, and hunting without a permit for each subject. Let me clarify the reason we also arrested the driver of the vehicle was not only because the muzzleloader belonged to him but that he controlled the vehicle.

In the Alabama regulations for wildlife and freshwater fisheries, the definition of hunting states, "Hunting includes pursuing, shooting, killing, capturing, and trapping wild animals, wild fowl, wild birds, and all lesser acts, such as disturbing, harrying or worrying, or placing, setting, drawing, or using any device used to take wild animals, wild fowl, wild birds, whether they result in taking or not, *and includes every act of assistance to any person in taking or attempting to take wild animals, wild fowl, or wild birds.*" The driver definitely assisted in the violations by stopping the vehicle and allowing the passenger to attempt to take the deer.

We decided we would not write anyone in the second vehicle a ticket, although we felt they were guilty of aiding and abetting and would have taken part had we not been in sight. We did require the shooter's uncle to sign his bond since he had no identification. With the bonds signed, the group was on their way.

Over the years, Gene and I had learned a lot could be gleaned by conducting a critique of each incident. In looking back at this one, we realized just how fortunate everyone involved was. The shooter was running to the second truck to retrieve a rifle from his uncle so he could again shoot at the decoy. Had he made it to the truck and got the gun, he would have no doubt turned toward me with it, and one or both of us would have likely been shot.

There were several things happening during this stop, as is normally always the case. Law enforcement officers make split-second decisions every day. Unfortunately, these situations sometimes go horribly bad. When that happens, the media and much of the public evaluate the officer's actions without thinking about how it occurred in real time. After months of analysis, people decide what should have been done, having never been in a similar situation. In the event outlined above, had the fellow retrieved the gun and turned toward me with it and I shot him, the headline would have probably read something like "Game Warden Shoots Disabled Man in Street." I say that to ask you to take some of today's startling headlines with a grain of salt. The last thing a law enforcement officer wants to do is shoot someone.

Once again, I was cradled in the Lord's hand, and I thank and praise him for it.

DO YOU WANT TO TRY FOR A THOUSAND?

THE ADJUDICATION OF TRAFFIC OFFENSES before Judge Bobby Teel was rarely boring. The traffic cases were handled at the end of the court day, when the judge's patience was often worn really thin. It didn't help matters that so many of the cited drivers wanted to plead not guilty even though they were obviously in violation. He hated it when that happened.

In the early days, traffic cases were heard on a first-come, first-sentenced basis. The judge would announce for everyone with a traffic ticket to form a line and come to his bench when told. The cases normally consisted of the violator pleading not guilty to speeding and the judge swearing them in and then finding them guilty when they admitted they were exceeding the speed limit, just not as much as the radar had indicated. Every once in a while, an unusual case would come through, such as the day the judge looked at the ticket, called the offender forward, and said, "It says here you were driving down the road with your butt stuck out the window. How do you plead?" You definitely didn't hear something like that every court date!

One day near the end of the court session, a fellow approached the bench not only with a citation but also with a heap of paperwork. I figured this probably wouldn't go well, and I was right. The judge told the man he was charged with operating an overweight vehicle (tractor trailer) and asked how he pled. "Not guilty" was the immediate reply. The three major roadways that traversed the county received a lot of truck traffic. Seeing how Coosa County was 92 percent forested, log trucks made up the lion's share of the traffic, and they kept the roads hot throughout the county.

The truck driver was sworn to tell the truth and then began to plead his case. The man's first mistake, after pleading not guilty, was to lay all of his paperwork on the judge's bench. The judge didn't like that. The truck driver began to explain to the judge how the state trooper and weight crew had not weighed the truck correctly. He went on to detail how not only did they not know how to weigh the truck, but they also had miscalculated the truck's weight and had failed to give him the 10 percent leeway that was customary.

I knew it wasn't going to go well when the judge looked at the man and in a gruff tone asked, "Are you done?" The man indicated he was finished, and the judge promptly pronounced him guilty. He then handed down a $500 fine.

When the driver heard the fine amount, he went ballistic and belligerently stated the clerk's office had told him it would be $148!

The strain of the long court session was now on full display on the judge's face and the vein that was now prominently sticking out on his neck. The judge fired back at the defendant, "It would have been $148 if you would have paid it." Rising to his feet, the judge literally screamed, "Do you want to try for one thousand dollars?"

Realizing he wasn't going to win the fight, the man quickly gathered his papers and went to pay the clerk. Amazingly, the remaining defendants each stepped forward and pled guilty. You can't make this stuff up.

DEATH SCRIBBLE

THE GUY HAD A WEIRD WAY of looking at you. He turned his head sideways and looked out of the corner of his eye. It was peculiar and told me something about him. He was a nut!

Normally my best chance of apprehending someone trying to illegally kill a deer at night was to catch them in the act. However, if I could receive good information from a reliable witness, I had a good chance of making a case. My pet peeve was getting a call in the morning informing me a night hunting incident had occurred the previous night. Therefore, when I answered the phone and the caller stated someone had shot in front of his home early that morning, I prepared to be frustrated. However, as he began to relay the details, a small sliver of hope began to appear.

I was familiar with the caller, Tony. He was the son of a local business man I had known for many years. During my first month in the county, game warden Hershel Patterson had taken me by and introduced me to the business owner. The fellow had been gracious; however, I was taken aback by the fact he referred to me as "Hun." From the get-go the fellow said, "It's nice to meet you Hun," and when we were leaving, after a tour of his garment factory, he said, "Hun, come by any time."

I was a twenty-four-year-old man, and to the best of my knowledge I had never been called "Hun." Once we were back in the car I asked Hershel what all the "Hun" stuff was about. He just laughed and said the fellow had worked with women for forty years and he called everybody Hun. That helped me understand it, but I never forgot it. I digress.

Tony reported that while getting ready to go hunting he noticed a vehicle had stopped in front of his home at approximately 5:00 a.m. As he stepped into his garage to get a better look, the tranquil morning calm was split by the *py-yow* of a rifle shot. Although barefoot, he took off running toward the vehicle. The truck began to roll away; however, he soon caught it and began to beat on the driver's side window. Now if I had just shot in front of someone's house at five in the morning and someone started beating on my window, I think I would have been inclined to have mashed the gas; however, when he hit the window the vehicle came to an abrupt stop.

He demanded identification from the two occupants of the truck. He instructed them to wait while he returned to his house and took down their information. This is when he should have called me. After taking down the information, he returned the license to the driver with a stern warning to never come back and allowed the pair to leave. Shortly thereafter, he realized he had inadvertently kept the license of the passenger. He put the license in the mail to the man later that morning.

I took down the violator's information and asked a few other questions. I conferred with Hershel, and we decided to attempt to set up a meeting with the subjects. We were able to contact them and set a time to meet a couple of days later.

The two men were obviously nervous. We explained we were conducting an investigation of night hunting on County Road 56 in the Diamond Graphite area of Coosa County. They both denied night hunting but did acknowledge being stopped by the landowner. When asked what they were doing there at 5:00 a.m., they explained they were on their way hunting but were not night hunting. I asked if they had seen any other vehicles in the area where the landowner had stopped them, and they stated they had not.

The passenger was the most talkative and was highly upset the landowner had stopped them and took their license and failed to return his. I asked if he had received his license in the mail, and he said he had, but that wasn't all he had received. I had no idea what he might be referring to but had the feeling I was about to find out.

The guy handed me a small scrap of paper with an ink scribble on it. It looked to me to be where someone may have tested a pen to see if it would write by making a couple of quick circles. The fellow stated the scrap of paper had been wrapped around his license in the envelope. The man took a very serious tone and looked at us out of the corner of his eye and asked, "What do you think that means?" I wasn't sure, but I thought I heard the rhythmic thump of a black helicopter in his head. The man obviously believed the scribble had some sinister meaning, like it was a death symbol or something. I resisted a very strong urge to laugh and a strong desire to mess with this guy by gasping, "Oh no, it's a death scribble!"

We explained based on the evidence we had gathered we had obtained warrants for night hunting and placed the men under arrest. The passenger began to explain he would be bringing his psychiatrist to court because he had been "messed up since Vietnam" and had to see his shrink every week. He repeated he got messed up in Da Nang, and he was under a doctor's care. We told him to bring whomever he felt was necessary to court. We prepared the bonds and left.

As we drove back and discussed the case, I was thinking about the comments concerning Vietnam. While I appreciate those who fought there and feel for those who continue to suffer from it, something just didn't feel right. Finally, I realized what was causing the angst. As I looked at the bond, I noticed the man was born in 1959. This would have made him only sixteen at the end of the war. I began to question the truthfulness of his statements.

The cases came to court, and the men were found guilty. There was no psychiatrist present. However, in a departure from his normal hard line, our judge allowed the men to set up a payment plan for their fine. As I recall, they never finished paying it. This was instrumental in helping the judge develop his hard line of "pay or stay" after that.

Interestingly enough, I later learned that claiming to be a veteran and/or a war hero was evidently a common occurrence. Later I assisted in the investigation of someone who claimed to be a navy seal. The investigation revealed not only was he not a seal, he never served in the military at all. Today he carries another title: convicted felon.

Some things are worse than poachers!

Throughout my career I have run across people who try to make themselves out to be something they aren't. Sometimes they are trying to impress you, and sometimes they are trying to get out of something. I have found many people who feel the law doesn't apply to them. Many of them have found out the hard way that it does. Some have had what it took to convince a judge or district attorney to see it their way. A major problem with trying to be something you're not is you often begin to believe it yourself. You may fool yourself and you may fool someone else, but the Bible says be not deceived, God is not mocked. You will reap what you sow!

FALLING IN YOUR LAP

ONE MIGHT ASSUME that apprehending someone shooting at deer from the road would be relatively easy. Well, you should not make such assumptions. During my career, there was no shortage of folks shooting from the road at deer, turkeys, rabbits, road signs, and so forth. Just because it was happening regularly didn't mean the apprehensions came easily.

As you might guess, most, not all, folks tried not to shoot from the road while we were in sight. The difficult part of catching these folks was locating an observation point where we could remain hidden while being able to see a decent segment of the road. This was often the case in Coosa County since we had few fields and the woods came almost up to the road edge in many areas. This meant deer might stand anywhere along the road. We commonly referred to people shooting close to the road as "ditch shooting" since the deer or turkeys were actually in and along the road ditch. One might assume that anywhere in such an area would be a good place to work. I've already warned you about making assumptions! In my experience, areas with fields were often easier to work since folks with the inclination to shoot from the road often concentrated their efforts on the field areas. This by no means meant they would not shoot a deer anywhere they saw one. And I do mean anywhere!

Trying to set up in an area where the woods came up to the right-of-way usually meant you would back up in some hidden trail or fire break in the woods. Unfortunately, in these situations the only place you could see was directly in front of your vehicle. Areas with fields would normally afford us the opportunity to set up where we could see much farther. Of course, if you had too much open area you would sometimes spot folks shooting from the road at such a distance that you could not get to them before they detected you and hightailed it out of the area. We didn't have that problem in our county. Oh, we often had them hightail it out of the area; luckily, we were pretty close on them. In areas with a lot of fields, it was often a guessing game when picking which area to work in. I guess every area had its pros and cons.

Retired Conservation Enforcement Officer (CEO) Hershel Patterson related to me the story of how he and his regular ride along, Jim Crumpton, were working the south end of Coosa County one cold January night. For the most part, each county in Alabama was assigned two CEOs without regard to the size of the county or the amount of work needed. Obviously, during hunting season this staffing was insufficient. In order to cover as much territory as possible, the officers normally did not work together. Working in the middle of nowhere alone with the hope of backup at least an hour away was neither safe nor smart but was often the situation. To try and improve the odds, most officers would recruit someone to ride with them when working night hunting details and such. These folks laid their lives on the line for little more than friendship and adventure.

The pair had reluctantly been in northern Elmore County earlier in the night. Hershel related to me how because there were very few arrests being made in Elmore County, the captain had requested him to go down there and see if he couldn't catch somebody. This was irritating seeing how there was no shortage of night hunters in Coosa County. After a couple of uneventful hours in the adjacent county, Hershel decided to move to a problem area in the southern part of Coosa County. His hopes weren't very high seeing how it was about eighteen degrees and the wind was gusting to thirty miles per hour. A high wind significantly diminished your chances of success when working night hunting since it limited your ability to hear. Hearing a shot or a vehicle can be the difference in whether or not you are able to make an apprehension. However, night hunters try their luck in all kinds of weather.

Hershel had previously received a complaint of someone shooting late at night about halfway through the Wayside Road. Wayside was a sparsely populated road in south-central Coosa County. The only decent place to sit along the road was at Wayside Baptist Church, but it was unfortunately on the south end of the road. Let me tell you, if I had a dollar for every time I had hid behind a church or used a church when giving directions, I would have a lot of dollars. Coosa County, like all of Alabama, was blessed with a lot of churches. Each community would usually have at least one church if not two or three. The churches were often the activity center for the area. Unfortunately, several of them were abandoned as the rural communities diminished.

After much searching, Hershel and Jim found a dim woods road near the area of the complaint and backed their patrol car into the woods. This location was like what I described earlier in that all the duo could see was the thin slice of road directly in front of their vehicle.

Although the wind chill made standing outside of the vehicle, as we normally did, a poor option, they did have their windows partially down to hopefully hear any shot fired in the area despite the high wind.

Miraculously, about twenty minutes into their vigil, the pair did hear a shot; however, the howling wind made it impossible to pinpoint the location. They knew it had to be close for them to be able to hear it. Therefore, they simply sat still hoping the violator would come their way.

The cold was quickly saturating the car, and Hershel decided to crank the engine and warm things up. Just as he reached for the key, they saw the trees along the road light up and knew a vehicle was approaching their location. As the vehicle eased past their vantage point, the brake lights suddenly came on and the truck stopped. A couple of questions quickly crossed their minds, with the main one being, "Is this guy preparing to shoot? And are we in the line of fire?" As they watched, the backup lights lit up, and the truck began backing into the very road the officers were sitting in. As the truck got closer, Hershel decided he had better turn his headlights on so the truck wouldn't crash into his patrol car. He pulled the lights on, and they illuminated the bed of the truck and a dead deer with steam rising off of it! He turned his blue light on, and they got out and apprehended the night hunters.

It is amazing and often humorous the stories a subject can conjure up when they realize they are caught. The vehicle occupants did their best to explain the deer had been killed earlier that day on Butler Wildlife Management Area (WMA). Hershel asked to see the harvest sheet that accompanied all deer harvested on a WMA deer hunt, but the men had misplaced it. He told them it seemed a little odd to him that a deer that had been killed before dark, which was five hours earlier, and that had been riding in the open bed of their truck in subfreezing temperatures for over one hundred miles would still have steam rising from it! Realizing they were caught, the two outlaws simply hung their heads. Hershel retrieved their rifles and then returned to his warm car and started the obligatory paperwork.

I was lucky a lot of times during my career, but I have to say that kind of luck was rare indeed. You can't make this stuff up.

GOOD COMMUNICATION

I HAVE LONG UNDERSTOOD good, clear communication is the key to success in most endeavors. A conservation enforcement officer (CEO) normally is tasked with the protection of wildlife inhabiting hundreds of square miles. With such a large patrol area, it is imperative the CEO develop a good network of information. Good communication is a necessity. Unfortunately, I have witnessed many examples of poor communication. Some of these resulted in missed opportunities for apprehensions, and some resulted in the death of wildlife. Other lapses in communication weren't nearly as serious.

One that struck me as humorous occurred when my partner CEO Hershel Patterson contacted the state credit union. Hershel kept a little money in a savings account with the credit union. One day he called the credit union and asked the teller how much was in his account. She replied that he had $600. He told her to send him five of it. The next day he received a check from the credit union for $5.

Realizing they obviously had not communicated well, he called back and told them he had actually wanted $500 and had received $5. She apologized for the misunderstanding and asked if he wanted her to send him another $495. He replied, "No, just send me five—hundred!" he quickly added.

While I understand the teller did exactly what Hershel had requested, I could not help but wonder just how many people called and asked that they be sent a check for $5.

You can't make this stuff up!

FUNERAL SECURITY

THINGS WERE GETTING PRETTY HEATED. We dutifully assumed a position between the feuding parties. The back-and-forth of insults and innuendo was reaching a fever pitch. I wasn't sure whether the heat in the room was due to the rising temperature or the raging tempers. One might have thought it was loud enough to wake the dead; the body in the casket in the front of the room proved it wasn't.

Anyone in the law enforcement profession will tell you there should be no such thing as routine patrol. Routine patrol, as I was taught at the police academy, is what can get an officer hurt or even killed. Just because you have made a similar stop five hundred times doesn't mean it will be the same this time. You really never know whom you are stopping or what they are thinking. It may be the guy who has just beat his wife to a pulp or the kid who thinks if you find the marijuana in his pocket his world will end. Each stop must be handled carefully. That being said, the truth is everyone falls into a routine at one time or another.

I feel the conservation enforcement officer (CEO) may very well have the hardest time keeping their guard up since we are often expected by our supervisors or administrative heads to get the job done while being cordial good ole boys. This is probably one of several reasons why a conservation officer is many times more likely to be assaulted than other law enforcement officers. I remember when I started work, my partner CEO Hershel Patterson told me several times how when he began his career 10 percent of the officers on the job had been shot. In addition, his former partner had been shot and killed by a nighttime deer hunter. That really puts you at ease—NOT! It got my attention.

Nevertheless, while things often became routine, they were often anything but routine. Such was the case one hot summer day in Coosa County. I had decided to travel to the wildlife management area (WMA) and monitor user activity. The Coosa WMA was comprised of thirty-eight thousand acres on the west side of Coosa County. The area was bordered on the west by the Coosa River, on the south by Alabama Highway 22, County Road 29 on the east, and County Road 15 on the north. Both Hatchet and Weogufka Creeks flowed through the area. There were three legal campgrounds and several illegitimate tent sites.

In the summer, there was no hunting going on, at least there wasn't supposed to be any hunting going on; however, the management area's two hundred miles of open backwoods roads were a huge draw for people to just come and get away from the rat race. Unfortunately, for many folks, getting away from it all included getting drunk, tearing stuff up, throwing out trash, and violating a whole host of regulations. Therefore, from time to time, I would need to patrol the area to try to keep the people at least somewhat honest.

After patrolling the WMA for most of the morning, I decided to go to a nearby country store for a cold drink. If you've never enjoyed the south in the middle of the summer, oh the fun you've missed. It's a stifling sticky kind of hot. We rarely have a dry heat. It is a wet heat. An oppressive, dangerous type of heat. It is often an "I saw a dog chasing a rabbit and they were both walking" kind of heat. You get the picture.

While at the store, I met Coosa County Sheriff Bill Evans, who was also there getting a cold drink and who was more cordial than normal. As I prepared to leave, he asked what I had planned for the afternoon. When I replied, "Not too much," he asked if I would mind assisting his department with a detail. I was always willing to assist the sheriff's office, partly because I normally enjoyed working with them serving a search warrant or working a roadblock or whatever and partly because I wanted them to respond if I ever needed their assistance. I told the sheriff I would be available, and he asked if I could meet him at Salem Church at about 12:30 in the afternoon. I told him I would, and we left the store with me wondering what type of adventure awaited.

I was somewhat familiar with Salem Church and knew that with the exception of one homecoming service each year, the facility was no longer used for services. Therefore, I doubted the church had anything to do with what we were going to do. My guess was it would serve as a staging area for us to prepare to execute a search warrant or go pull up a marijuana patch or something. However, this scenario puzzled me even more. The only three houses within miles of the church belonged to a good friend of mine, his mom and dad, and his sister and brother-in-law. While I was 99 percent sure we would not be searching their houses, I learned early in my career not to put anything past anybody. I have arrested several folks I would not have thought would break the law. The list includes preachers, teachers, engineers, and so on. Therefore, I guess I didn't trust anybody 100 percent; however, the folks living near the church were basically above reproach, and I just couldn't imagine searching their homes.

Thinking back, I had good reason for the uneasy feeling I was experiencing. Only a couple of years earlier, I had been asked by a deputy if I would help him serve a search warrant. I agreed, and we headed to the south part of the county. I asked where we were going, and he replied the location was near the county line. I didn't give it a second thought until the roads we were taking became more and more familiar. I soon realized we were on a beeline to my own hunting club. An old man lived at the club, and soon we were pulling into his driveway. On his porch sat several club members with confused looks on their faces. As I got out of the car, we spoke to one another, and the deputy announced we had a search warrant for the house. As an old adage goes, "I didn't know whether to take a crap or go blind." Saying things were uncomfortable would be a gross understatement.

The deputy told me we were looking for a moonshine still and moonshine. Although I knew the man was well known for making good moonshine, of which rumor had it the sheriff and probate judge were regular customers, I thought that was all in the past. I had been in the house several times and had not seen anything suspicious. Nevertheless, the deputy and I searched the house while the local alcoholic beverage control (ABC) officer and a partner searched the outbuildings around the house. Sure enough, in the kitchen of the house I found a couple of hundred pounds of sugar and a couple of gallons of moonshine. In an outbuilding, the officers found an old copper coil and a milk carton containing over $10,000. The evidence was seized, and arrangements were made for the eighty-plus-year-old man to be charged.

You would think with that experience fresh on my mind, I wouldn't be so quick to agree to assist the next time; however, I took being a law enforcement officer seriously. When they swear you in, you do not say I will uphold the laws of this state when it suits me! Therefore, I headed toward the church, hoping for the best.

The sheriff and a deputy were at the church when I arrived. I noticed a fresh grave had been dug in the cemetery across the county road from the church, and my first thought was, "This probably isn't a good meeting place since they must be going to bury someone here today." I was about to find out I was right on both counts. They were going to bury someone there today and it wasn't going to be a good place to be.

The sheriff began by saying we had a potentially bad situation taking place at the church. He explained there was going to be a funeral and we were going to need to provide security. Although this was early in my career, and I knew I didn't know all of the ends and outs, I had been to several funerals, but I had never seen a funeral out in the middle of nowhere, or anywhere, for that matter, that actually needed security. But I was about to!

My first thought was what person famous or important enough to need security would be attending a funeral out here? I was again out in left field. The sheriff explained the family had not been able to agree as to what the wishes of the deceased were concerning his service or his final resting place. I became aware the deceased had in fact had two families in that after his children were nearly grown, he had divorced his wife, remarried, and had a second family. The two groups obviously didn't get along, and things had gotten so heated one side of the family had vowed to kill the other side either while en route to or at the church! Now things were getting serious. The sheriff shared that one family member had actually threatened to ambush the hearse as it brought the body to the church. The funeral director had caught wind of all of this and, as you can imagine, was more than a little antsy about it. Seeing how I had not received any funeral security training at the police academy and this was some uncharted water, I was glad the sheriff had a plan in place. The plan was to play it by ear and hope for the best. Great plan!

As the bereaved family began to arrive, it was quickly evident there was too much denim and big hair and too many cowboy boots and cigarettes for my liking. Things were every bit as bad as had been anticipated, with the one good exception being no shots had been fired—yet.

Both sides were cussing and threatening each other. As each dirty pickup with a confederate flag in the back window arrived, we would have to check the vehicle and occupants for weapons. This was just too weird. Soon the hearse arrived, escorted by a sheriff's patrol car. The deputy, Terry Wilson, who would later become our sheriff and a good friend, reported there were no problems getting the body to the church. While we all kept a watchful eye, the body was moved inside. We took a position outside the front door of the church; thankfully, things were coming to an end. Or so we thought!

Soon a frantic funeral director came to the door and reported we were needed inside, where a fight was brewing. We headed inside and into the fray. With no air conditioning or even a fan, the musty dust hung in the air in the streaks of sunlight that peeked through the shuttered windows. The temperature was probably around ninety degrees, and the tempers were hotter. When I heard one woman say to the other, "You know this isn't what he wanted," I was thinking I had to agree with that! The other responded, "Yes it is, and how would you even know?" "You know he hated that suit." "That shows what you know, it was his favorite." These types of statements and worse were being hurled back and forth across the aisle, where a sheriff, two deputies, and a wildlife officer stood like militant pallbearers. After threatening there would be no funeral at all if people didn't rein in their emotions, we were finally able to gain a brief break in the action. It was just long enough for a bewildered clergyman to quickly speak a few words over the dearly departed.

Brother Jerry Smith, a fine man of God, was there to conduct the service. He was the epitome of a humble, meek man. Brother

Jerry and I were both members of Rockford Baptist Church. He attended regularly when he wasn't serving as a pastor somewhere else. I was sure Jerry had witnessed some stuff in his life, but I could tell he was as nervous as a cat in a roomful of rocking chairs. It was by far the fastest funeral I had ever attended, and I was proud of it.

Once again, we breathed a sigh of relief, and again it was too soon. Now the feud moved to the graveside, where the fight began over who got to stand where. We were once again forced to take charge and tell the people where they could and could not stand. After the fastest graveside service I had ever witnessed, we informed the people it was time to disperse. They angrily made their way to their vehicles and after vowing to "get even" with each other, they tore out of the parking area.

Now we all again breathed a huge sigh of relief. I must admit in a career chock-full of unbelievable events, this was one of the most unbelievable things I had ever witnessed. Who would have ever thought a day of "routine patrol" would turn into something like this? Routine, I don't think so!

Although this occurred before Jeff Foxworthy made the phrase famous, looking back I can't help but think if you had to have the game warden provide security at your loved one's funeral, you might be a redneck!

While there is no shame in being a redneck, the Bible says you will be known by the fruit you produce. Several times I have heard it said you preach your own funeral. What will be said at yours?

HANG ON, I'M GOING TO HIT YOU

Most conservation enforcement officers (CEOs) are jacks of all trades by necessity. When you wear so many different hats, you must possess many skills. If you've read many of my stories, you've learned the game warden needs to be able to do everything from track an individual through the woods to perform a quick read of body language once someone is encountered. Officers must possess a wide range of skills. One skill I do not possess and have always envied is the ability of many of our officers to masterfully maneuver their boats. Obviously, there are millions of people across the country that can drive a boat; however, believe me when I say that driving a boat and maneuvering a boat into position to check a fisherman are two different things. Pulling alongside a boat with fishing rods protruding on both sides in a high wind with heavy boat traffic isn't an easy thing.

One technique I have witnessed several times is for the officer to pull straight toward the boat to be checked and then shift the boat into reverse. This combined with a turn of the steering wheel, when performed correctly, will result in the boat sidling up alongside the boat you want to check. This technique normally worked well; however, there is always an exception to every rule.

CEO Charles Reames, Ret., related to me that while working fishing on Lake Martin in Tallapoosa County, he approached two bass fishermen who were perched on their fishing stools. Using the technique I described, Charles headed directly for the boat. Unfortunately, when he shifted the transmission into reverse, the prop came off his boat motor. Realizing he now had no way to control his vessel and heading straight for the bass boat, he yelled, "Hang on, I'm going to hit you!" He said the fishermen were still wearing a bewildered look on their faces as they tried to climb out of the bottom of the boat where they had landed when he struck them broadside. Charles said the guys were really good about things and even towed him to the marina. CEOs never knew what was going to happen next. You can't make this stuff up!

HAVE YOU SEEN JAKE JACKSON?

WHILE SERVING TIME for sexual molestation, Jake Jackson, a native of Coosa County, had escaped from prison for the second time. After his first escape, he had followed the same pattern as most escapees and headed for home. He was captured and sent back. Now he was on the lam again. Was he back in Coosa County? We didn't know for sure, but it was a possibility.

An observant landowner can provide a conservation enforcement officer (CEO) more information in ten minutes than the officer can gather in a week on his own. Developing relationships with landowners is critical for officers. These relationships are often built on two important pillars. First, it must be understood the source of the information will remain anonymous. Second, the officer must follow up on the information he receives. These are two basic elements the CEO must consistently adhere to.

I received a call one day in early October from an observant landowner who was concerned about some traffic going past his home into a secluded wooded area in the Mt. Olive community of Coosa County. The landowner gave me a vehicle description and said he had observed two white males making repeated trips into the area. He explained he possessed the hunting rights for the property, and no one other than him or his two sons should be in the area.

I contacted my partner, CEO Hershel Patterson, with the info, and we set a time to check the area out. Bow season did not open until Saturday, so we hoped no one would be in the area. We decided we would check things out around lunchtime since most hunters were more active early and late. As we entered the property, we noticed fresh tracks along the road leading into the area. Reading tracks is an important skill officers need to develop. It is often pertinent to know which way a vehicle was traveling. This is especially true when working a baited area. Although it isn't always possible, it is always an advantage if you know whether or not the suspects are currently in the area. The tracks we observed appeared to be made by a vehicle leaving the area; therefore, we headed in for a look around.

We soon arrived at a campsite. Judging by the size of the pile of wood next to the tent, it appeared someone was either preparing to stay for a long while or thought it was going to turn very cold this October. With no one home, we quickly gave the property a once over. In the fire ring at the camp we observed the remnants of partially burned camo corn sacks. This was the first time I remember finding corn sack remnants; however, checking the campfire ring became a prerequisite when searching properties. Seeing how the archery season for deer would open in three days, we surmised this was probably just a couple of good ole boys who had sweetened an area for bow season. We decided to split up and canvas the area.

Baiting an area in an attempt to kill a deer with a bow and arrow can take many forms. Since we had found the remnants of the corn sacks, we assumed we were looking for corn. Corn put out by folks using a bow and arrow was normally placed in a pile on the ground within twenty yards of a tree stand. Of course, it could be in a PVC pipe attached to a tree or even in a shallow hole in the ground. Just because we thought they were using corn to attract deer, we were always alert for other attractants. These could include soybeans, rice brand, wheat, feed blocks, alfalfa cubes, and another favorite, peanut butter. You never knew what you might find. If an article came out in a hunting magazine saying someone killed a big buck while hunting over a ball of aluminum foil, we would start finding foil in the woods!

It was also important to be on the lookout for tree stands. Most people who hunt with a bow and arrow hunt from a tree stand. The most common tree stands are the ladder stand and the climbing tree stand. While ladder stands are usually fairly easy to spot, the two-piece climbing stand can be hidden effectively. Using the elevated stand allows the hunter better visibility and helps keep the deer from catching their scent. While tree stands are great tools for hunting, they are unfortunately a component in many hunting accidents each year.

After walking the woods for nearly an hour, I returned to our vehicle to find we were no longer alone. As I approached, I saw Hershel was engaged in a conversation with two scraggly looking fellows. One of the guys was about six feet tall and the other was maybe six inches shorter. Both wore faded camouflage jackets and L. L. Bean-type boots, which matched the tracks I had found on the property.

I knew we had in all likelihood blown our chance to apprehend these individuals; however, I did not give up that easily. As I made my way toward the subjects, an idea came to mind. I always taught new officers that they always needed a cover story in the event they were confronted by someone while viewing a property. The cover story wasn't necessarily untrue. However, it was sometimes vague and maybe just a little devious. I quickly came up with a story.

It just so happened a BOLO (Be On the LookOut) had recently been issued for Jake Jackson. Jake was a native of the nearby community of Goodwater and had once again escaped from prison, where he had been serving time for sexual assault. This wasn't his first escape, and in the past he had been recaptured near his hometown. Furthermore, when last captured, he had been in a makeshift camp not unlike the one the subjects were now standing at. By the time I reached the trio, I had the basics of the plan worked out in my head, and all I needed was for Hershel to follow my lead and play along.

I quickly walked up and in a matter-of-fact tone asked Hershel, "Have they seen him?" Hershel stared at me with a confused look on his face, and I asked, "Do they know Jake?"

Before Hershel could respond, one of the subjects looked at me and asked, "Jake who?"

"Jake Jackson," I replied.

The two subjects looked at each other and both stated they did not know the guy. Based on their interest in this subject I was obviously upset about, I decided it was time to lay it on thick. I said it seemed awful funny to me right here, not five miles from his home, we find two suspicious guys, at a campsite just like the one he was caught at last time!

"What do you mean last time?" they asked.

By this time, Hershel was right with me and responded, "The last time he escaped!"

"Escaped from where?" they anxiously asked.

"Prison" I replied. I moved closer until I was violating their personal space and with my most accusatory tone I asked, "Are you sure you don't know Jake Jackson and he hasn't been in this camp?"

This was working great. Both individuals vehemently denied knowing the man or anything about him.

I looked at Hershel and asked, "Do you believe them?"

He hesitated while eyeing them suspiciously and commented that although he had caught one of the guys in the past, he didn't think they would be involved with someone like Jake.

"Okay," I replied, as I was moving toward our vehicle.

Obviously, we had piqued their interest, and now they had a few questions for us. The taller guy looked at me and asked why the guy had been in prison.

"Sexual molestation," I replied in my most uneasy tone.

The next question, I must admit, took me a little by surprise when the second fellow asked, "If we see him, can we shoot him?"

I answered with, "No, you need to leave his apprehension to us, but if you do see anybody you think may be him, you better get to a phone and give us a call."

With that we opened the doors of our vehicle and began getting in. It was all I could do to maintain my composure when one of the subjects said, "Well, if he tries to molest me, I'm gonna shoot him!"

We started the vehicle and began backing out of the area. Once we were out of sight and I was able to stop laughing, I asked Hershel if he thought they had bought it, and he replied we would know Saturday morning. This response answered my next question, which was whether he had located any corn. He went on to tell me he had found two tree stands and corn was all over the place. I told him I had located one stand with a nice pile of corn nearby. We made plans to be in the area early Saturday morning.

Friday night I found it nearly impossible to sleep due to the anticipation of what the morning would hold. I finally reached over and turned off the alarm so it wouldn't go off and disturb my wife, who was sleeping with no trouble at all. I got dressed and went to meet Hershel and try our luck.

We had debated whether or not we felt our ruse was good enough to cover our real interest in the area. I knew it seemed they took it hook, line, and sinker; however, I knew they may have been putting on a ruse of their own. We eased along the road and stopped a couple of hundred yards from the camp. We had waited until about thirty minutes after sunrise in order to give the poachers time to make it to their stands. We stealthily approached the campsite. There we found the suspects' vehicle, but the subjects were nowhere to be seen. We decided to split up and check the locations we had found earlier in the week. I cautiously approached the tree stand only to find no one there. Moving slowly and checking the trees for someone in a climbing tree stand, I started back toward Hershel. As I neared his location, I could hear him telling someone to come down out of the tree. I hurried to his location and found he had already apprehended the first subject and was now ordering the second subject out of a tree where he was perched with a 30-06 rifle.

We escorted both subjects back to their camp and issued them citations for hunting without license, hunting without permission, hunting by the aid of bait and possession of a firearm while bow hunting. In addition, we informed the individuals they needed to dismantle their camp and leave the area. With the paperwork complete, we began the short hike to our vehicle.

As we walked away, one of the individuals called out to us and asked, "Did y'all ever catch that escaped guy?"

"Not yet," we answered and added, "Be sure to call us if you see him."

I had to bite my lip when they dutifully replied, "We will."

PROTECTING THE BALD EAGLE

ONE OF THE BEST COMPONENTS of the conservation enforcement officer (CEO) position is the vast diversity of the calls we received. You literally never knew what might come next. CEO Jerry Fincher called me one afternoon and advised he had just responded to an urgent call of a bald eagle that had been hit by a car. Thankfully, bald eagles are no longer a rare site in Alabama. Bald eagles were definitely in peril when I began work with the Alabama Department of Conservation and Natural Resources Game and Fish Division.

According to the US Fish and Wildlife Service (USFWS), shortly after World War II, DDT was hailed as a new pesticide to control mosquitoes and other insects. However, DDT and its residues washed into nearby waterways, where aquatic plants and fish absorbed it. Bald eagles, in turn, were poisoned with DDT when they ate the contaminated fish. The chemical interfered with the ability of the birds to produce strong eggshells. As a result, their eggs had shells so thin that they often broke during incubation or otherwise failed to hatch. Without reproduction, the species quickly began to decline to very low levels. The DDT contamination combined with illegal shooting and habitat destruction and degradation put the eagle on the fast track to extinction.

Fortunately, the Endangered Species Act afforded the species some habitat protection. The federal government banned the use of DDT, and state and federal agencies initiated conservation practices that enabled the bald eagle to make a remarkable recovery.

In 1985, our department received ten eaglets from Oklahoma. The birds were placed in hacking towers throughout the state. The hacking towers were artificial nests designed so the eaglets could be fed by humans without the eaglet seeing who was feeding it. This was done to keep the birds from imprinting on humans. The birds grew and eventually migrated to the Midwest. However, when they began to reach sexual maturity at four to five years of age, they returned and began to initiate nests, sometimes very near the hacking towers.

The project was a tremendous success, and the population began to grow significantly. The USFWS continues to monitor the population. Today, sightings of bald eagles are fairly common in Alabama.

Arriving on the scene of the reported injured eagle, the officer found traffic stopped in each direction by a woman who was hovering over the injured bird in the roadway. He approached the woman, who was very thankful he had arrived. Although I know the woman thought it was a silly question, Jerry asked her, "What are you doing?" Somewhat bewildered, the woman answered, "I'm protecting this eagle." Jerry then responded, "Ma'am, that's not an eagle, that's a buzzard."

Stunned, the Good Samaritan replied, "It has a bald head." While getting the woman and the bird to the side of the road so the traffic could flow, he explained a feathered head did not lend itself to reaching inside of dead and decaying animals and pulling the entrails out. It was obvious the bird was losing some of its luster with the lady, yet she was persistent. She asked if he would still take the bird to the vet, and he responded by telling her we did not have a buzzard vet, but he would see what he could do.

As it turned out, the buzzard was in bad shape and had to be euthanized. The woman was embarrassed, and the officer had another interesting story. One you just can't make up!

I'm sure you've heard the adage that the road to hell is paved with good intentions. The woman in this story saw what she recognized as a need, and she acted. Her intentions were good. It turned out things weren't exactly as she thought. They rarely are. Yet the point is, she acted. Actions speak louder than words. There are plenty of needs out there; when you see one, act on it.

HOLLY SPRINGS ROAD

As my truck slid uncontrollably toward the defendant with my blue lights flashing, he held his gun to his shoulder and continued firing. I couldn't help but think, "Surely he'll stop shooting once I hit him."

Due to complaints of deer being shot from the road, Conservation Enforcement Officer (CEO) Hershel Patterson, Wildlife Officer Gene Carver, and I decided to set up the deer decoy to try to curtail the illegal activity. The location was ideal. It was on the Holly Springs Road in the extreme north end of Coosa County. At the time, the only structure on the several-mile-long road was Holly Springs Church, and it was literally in the middle of nowhere. One might assume this type of off-the-beaten-path locale would be ideal for violators to ply their trade, and one would be correct.

Although a great location, this area was not unlike most areas in that the most difficult component of the detail was to find a good area to sit and work the decoy. The decoy was our best tool for capturing folks who were bent on shooting at deer from their vehicle as they eased along the county road. The deer decoy was a mounted deer we would deploy in areas where real deer normally stood. Simply by activating a lever on a remote control, we could make the deer turn its head or wag its tail. Many of the road riders could not resist the temptation. Ideally an officer would be able to observe the decoy and the potential violators while sitting in his vehicle so he could respond immediately to whatever occurred.

Unfortunately, this type of prime location rarely occurred in the rolling hills and thickly wooded confines of our county. Unlike many areas, Coosa County had basically no agriculture and therefore very few open fields. The fields that did occur along the roadway were normally littered with cows and therefore weren't the best place to offer something for someone to shoot at! On the Holly Springs Road, we actually found a good location for our truck, but it did not coincide with a good deer location. However, there was a pretty good decoy location just down the road, and since hiding places were so limited, we decided we would have to make it work.

The chosen location for the deer meant a long trek through many virgin briars to set up the decoy. Several minutes and about a pint of blood later, the deer was in position and I was back at the truck. The road test of the deer revealed the set up was quite good. The deer was approximately a hundred yards off the road across a deep ravine. I was sure the road hunters would quickly conclude no game warden in their right mind would cross that ravine to set up a decoy. Of course, as I attempted to stop the bleeding scratches on my arms and face, I was wondering whether or not I was in my right mind!

The road test was a vital part of the decoy set up. If employing the decoy didn't teach you anything else, it did show us how well a deer can blend into the surrounding habitat. Many times, the road test, checking how the deer looked from the roadway where you expected the violators to view it from, would reveal the deer had all but dissolved into the surrounding background. The Holly Springs road test showed that due to deep pine straw and the lay of the land, the deer appeared to be bedded down. I decided this actually looked very natural. Although I could see the road from my hiding spot north of the decoy, it was decided that Gene should sit "on the ground" so he could observe the manikin and the violators and provide the play-by-play of the action over the radio. Hershel was located south of the setup, so we would hopefully be able to apprehend the violators, whichever way they were headed. With everyone in place, we waited for our first prospect. The wait wasn't a long one.

"Got one coming," Gene said over the radio. I gripped the steering wheel in anticipation. Within seconds I heard the familiar *py-yow* as a rifle shot destroyed the morning stillness. "Come on" Gene said. As I cranked the truck and snatched it into drive, a second shot split the morning air. I spun into the road and within seconds was barreling toward the violator's truck. As I approached, I saw the rifle barrel protruding from the driver's window jump. In my mind's eye, I could see the decoy being blown to pieces. Decoys weren't cheap and the department did not provide them. I was closing in on the truck with all of my lights going, and that was saying something.

One of my fellow biologists had in the past referred to me as "Blue Light" Glover. This stemmed from the fact my vehicle was well adorned with lights. When I went to work, I was issued a rotating blue light for the dash. The light was on its last leg. Not only did it barely function, when it did work, its slowly rotating, dim light wasn't easily seen by anyone I was attempting to stop. Therefore, I decided I needed better blue lights. As fate would have it, I soon developed a friendship with the owner of an ambulance service and emergency lighting company who one day, upon seeing my pitiful blue light, felt sorry for me and unsolicited gave me and the two game wardens in the county a blue strobe light for the dash. I loved the light and soon had strobes on the dash, in the grill, in the front bumper and in my back window. Eventually I added a headlight wigwag and strobes in my headlights and taillights. Therefore, when I say I had all my lights going, it means it looked like a blue Christmas tree coming down the road.

In my haste to reach the violator, I had gotten up a pretty good head of steam. Unfortunately, I had failed to take into consideration the fact the road was wet and muddy. This realization came back to me rather quickly, however, as I hit my brakes and began sliding directly at the violator's stopped truck. As my truck slid uncontrollably toward the defendant, he held his gun to his shoulder and continued firing. I couldn't help but think, "He'll stop shooting once I hit him." When I came to a stop, our vehicles were literally bumper to bumper. So much so, in fact, I could not walk between the two trucks. Amazingly, even as I sat literally ten feet from the man with all of my lights blazing, he had yet to realize I was there.

Having a violator develop tunnel vision was not uncommon. Many times, they would be so fixated on the deer they did not notice anything else happening around them. This shooter failed to realize the decoy wasn't a real deer as he fired his fifth shot at the Styrofoam wonder. With his gun now empty and a perplexed look on his face, he lowered his rifle and turned to see me and nearly jumped out of his skin. I did not know someone could jump from the driver's seat and hit their head on the roof, but this guy almost did it. I was glad the man had a good heart because someone with a weak one would not have survived the surprise he received. I hoped I would not learn he had soiled his pants, and luckily I didn't, but I do think he probably peed a little bit!

I quickly realized I could not fit between the bumpers of our trucks and had to go around the rear of my truck. I gave the loud verbal command for the shooter to raise his hands over his head.

HOLLY SPRINGS ROAD

As I made my way toward the shooter, I realized he wasn't the only violator on the scene. Behind his truck was another vehicle and two men who were standing in the road with shotguns. I came up on the driver's side of the shooter's vehicle and reached in and took his now empty rifle. The other violators had evidently decided it would be a good idea to return to their vehicle. While doing my best to keep an eye on my shooter, I ordered the other subjects away from their vehicle.

Gene and Hershel arrived on the scene, and after securing the weapons in my vehicle, we began writing tickets. The shooter was arrested for hunting from the public road and by the aid of his vehicle. The pair standing in the road with their loaded guns pointed at the decoy were charged with hunting from a public road. Surprisingly, all of the subjects had hunting permits for the property. After explaining the bonds to the violators and having them sign them, we told them they were free to leave. Before leaving, the shooter belligerently told me I ought to be out trying to catch the night hunters that were rampant in the area. I told him I would think about it, but I was really enjoying what I was doing right now. He really appreciated that!

We are often really good at pointing out someone else's faults while turning a blind eye to our own. I've had several folks who, while signing a ticket, have felt that was a good time to enlighten me concerning some other nefarious activity that was taking place. Interestingly, when pressed for a name of a suspect or a location where an event was happening, they normally decline to comment any further. We all often like to have the last word. In reality, the final word belongs to Jesus. It will either be well done, my good and faithful servant or depart from me, for I never knew you. Our choice now will make the difference. It will have nothing to do with how we compare to someone else. Think about it.

I AIN'T GONNA HURT MY BACK!

IF YOU ATTEND DISTRICT COURT each month, you will come across some interesting people. You will also learn many of the same people are in court almost every month.

Early on in Coosa County, I had occasion to meet the members of an interesting family. The father was an elderly man we will call Leslie Leakes. Leslie was probably seventy-five years old when I came to Coosa County. He and his family lived in a small house beside Alabama Highway 22 across the road from the Coosa Wildlife Management Area. Evidently, Mrs. Leakes had died years earlier. The son was also named Leslie Leakes. He was a large man with huge wrists that an adrenaline-filled young wildlife biologist could barely get a handcuff on at 3:00 a.m. in the middle of nowhere. (How I know, that is another story!) There were two daughters. One of them was named Leslie Mae Leakes and the other was Mildred Marie. I don't know why this daughter had not been named Leslie something, but she hadn't. At one time or another, I had encounters with each family member. And memorable encounters they were!

As I stood in the courtroom one Wednesday morning, the district court judge called Leslie Mae and Mildred Marie to the bench. He informed Leslie Mae she was charged with criminal mischief and asked how did she plead.

She replied, "Not guilty," in a not so nice tone.

He turned to Mildred Marie and asked why she had signed the warrant against her sister. Mildred explained Leslie Mae had set her chest of drawers outside and chopped it up with an axe. This did not set well with the judge, and he began his characteristic heavy nasal breathing.

Whenever our district court judge began breathing heavily through his nose, it normally always indicated somebody was about to go to jail. With his face turning red, the judge turned to Leslie Mae and asked through clenched teeth, "Did you do that?"

"I did," was her belligerent reply. When the judge inquired why she had done such a thing, "She made me mad," was her short reply.

The judge was now heavily blowing through his nose, which I felt certain meant Leslie Mae was headed to the Rockford Ramada (my pet name for the county jail). He glared at Leslie Mae and asked Mildred Marie how much the chest cost. One hundred dollars was her reply. The judge said, "The court finds you guilty and orders you to pay restitution of $100 and serve ten days in jail."

Leslie Mae cocked her head to the side, placed her hand on her hip and said in a matter-of-fact tone, "I ain't going to no jail!" She then whirled around and exited the courtroom.

You could have checked the judge's heart rate from across the room by watching the veins in his neck, as they were about to explode. He looked at the deputies in the courtroom and snarled, "Get her and take her to jail!"

Coosa County Deputies Dan Bearden and Fred Smoot immediately pursued the slowly fleeing escapee. Leslie Mae went out the back door and down the steps to the sidewalk below. Dan and Fred hustled down behind her and the other officers in the courtroom followed, me included.

Dan Bearden was a big man. While he was only about five feet eight inches tall, he weighed around three hundred pounds. Before you start to think he was just fat, let me assure you while he was fat, he was hard as a pine knot. His hands were huge, and he did not know what it meant to back up from anything. Fred Smoot was probably about six feet three inches tall and around two hundred pounds. Fred had also been a deputy for a long time and commanded respect. Both men were well-seasoned law enforcement professionals; however, they were about to be put to the test.

When Dan and Fred reached Leslie Mae, she promptly laid down on her back on the sidewalk. Seeing how the escapee likely weighed over three hundred pounds, moving her was not going to be easy. This is when things got interesting. As Dan reached and took hold of her arm, Fred decided we would use another approach. He pulled his wooden baton from his belt and drew back in preparation to pommel on Leslie Mae.

Seeing this, Dan yelled at Fred and asked what he was doing. Fred didn't miss a beat when he replied, "I ain't gonna hurt my back dragging her big butt around!" Although Dan was able to dissuade Fred from using the baton, I think Leslie Mae was able to read the writing on the sidewalk and understood it would be in her best interest to get up and walk to the jail and start serving her ten days. You can't make this stuff up.

HOW MANY TICKETS DO YOU WANT?

DURING MY THIRTY-TWO YEARS as a wildlife biologist and officer, I witnessed a lot of things I found hard to explain. Most of the odd occurrences were not weird freaks of nature; rather, they were the weird ways of the people we dealt with. It didn't take me long to figure out people would do anything, and there was often no explaining what they did.

One thing I witnessed several times was what I called the "them too" syndrome. This was a situation where people wanted others to be included in their misfortune, even if it proved costly to them as well. Although the fines typically assessed for violating minor game and fish laws and regulations were normally not exorbitant, when combined with court costs, they could put a dent in one's wallet. As a matter of fact, I often would purposely omit the mention of court costs when violators would inquire about how much their wrongdoing was going to cost them. About halfway through my career, the legislature realized there was something wrong with a picture where the court costs were often four times the amount of the fine. Therefore, they passed legislation stating in conservation regulation cases the court costs could not exceed the amount of the fine. During my tenure, courts costs went up almost 400 percent. This was due to the fact these costs funded numerous activities for many state agencies and other entities.

In an effort to cushion the blow of receiving a ticket, we would sometimes, if the situation warranted it, try to consolidate tickets. This did not happen very often and rarely if ever occurred concerning violations we considered flagrant and/or premeditated, such as hunting without a permit or hunting at night. This technique was most often employed while enforcing the multitude of regulations that applied to the wildlife management area (WMA). The WMA had a whole laundry list of regulations that applied to anyone within its boundaries. Many times, people not familiar with the regulations, and sometimes those very familiar, would be found in violation of a whole passel of them.

I remember one occasion when I came upon a fellow on the Coosa WMA who had brought his son to the area to teach him how to shoot a pistol. Although that was a worthy endeavor, I quickly realized this guy was in violation of at least five WMA regulations. Not only did the man (1) possess a firearm on the WMA without a valid permit, it was (2) an illegal firearm, meaning one not allowed on the WMA; he (3) possessed illegal ammunition; he (4) had been target practicing on the WMA in an area not designated for such; and he (5) had a loaded firearm in his vehicle. I separated the man from his son and explained he was in violation of at least five regulations.

He stated he knew he was on the WMA but did not know there were special rules that applied. I pointed to the nearby bright yellow sign directly in front of him that stated special rules and regulations applied and asked if he had observed the hundreds of yellow signs lining the road he had driven into the area on. He said he hadn't really paid any attention. I told him I was going to issue him a citation for having the loaded gun in the vehicle. He asked what that would cost, and I explained it would be left up to the judge, but it generally ran about ninety dollars. The man belligerently stated he didn't have ninety dollars to throw away on a stupid ticket. For some reason, I did not appreciate his demeanor or opinion. In what he probably considered a belligerent tone, I asked if he had $450 to throw away on five tickets. I think my tone helped him to enter into a brief moment of reflection, after which he wisely decided he would be satisfied with just one ticket.

Although you would probably surmise most people would be happy with the smallest number of tickets possible, on more than one occasion I have attempted to perform a ticket reduction only to have my efforts rejected. One such incident occurred on the Mimosa Point public access area. Public access areas were developed by our fisheries section. They were located along waterways and normally consisted of a boat launch and sometimes some picnic tables. These areas had their own set of rules, which we enforced. These regulations included no camping, no fires, no littering, no off-road vehicles, and no consumption of alcohol, among others. As you might imagine, when you put a boat launch and picnic tables on the lake in the middle of nowhere, it was a magnet for campers and beer drinkers.

The Mimosa Point area was not only an access area but it was also located within the boundaries of the Coosa WMA, which meant it had a double set of regulations in addition to the state laws that applied. As you can guess, multiple violations were the rule rather than the exception.

One night as I pulled into the access area parking lot for a routine check, I immediately spotted a couple of tents. They were pretty easy to spot in the glow of the roaring fire. I pulled up next to the "camp" and exited my truck. More often than not, the folks in such a camp would possess a firearm of some type. With that in mind, I cautiously approached and exchanged greetings with the two men and one woman present. While engaging in some small talk, I was scanning the area for the gun I felt sure they possessed. I did not see a firearm; I did find a two-sided axe. Seeing how no one was too close to the tool, I didn't mention it. I informed the people they were in violation of the rules forbidding overnight camping and fires in an access area. The trio explained they were not aware they were violating the law. I asked if they had noticed the signs on the trees around their "camp" stating the rules that applied, and they stated they had not noticed the signs. I shined my flashlight beam on one the signs on a tree about eight feet from where the folks were standing. They didn't comment. I knew I was going to write them a ticket but was trying to decide how many.

The group had been nice enough, so I decided to try to help them out. I explained they had multiple violations, but if one of the three wanted to claim the campsite, I would issue that person a ticket. The female stated the camp belonged to all three of them. I told her I understood they were all involved, but if one wanted to claim the camp, I would only issue them one ticket. Evidently the men were content with allowing the woman to do the talking. She again stated the camp belonged to all of them. I was finding it difficult to believe these three adults evidently could not grasp the fact we were talking about either three tickets or one. I decided to give it one more try. I told the trio I was either going to write the group one ticket or I would write each person a ticket. For the third time the woman stated it was a joint camp. With that, I instructed all three of the subjects to give me their driver's licenses. I wrote all three individuals a ticket for camping illegally.

Why on earth would somebody elect to pay the full fine and court costs when they could have got out for only one-third of that amount? I have related the facts of this case to several folks, hoping to get a plausible explanation. Many have said the problem was the people involved knew better than to trust one another. They likely felt whoever took the ticket would end up stuck with all the cost. Of course, the way it went, they all ended up stuck with all the cost.

Although hard to understand, one thing the trio in this story did get right was the fact they were all at fault. A lesson we all need to learn, seeing how we are all at fault and just like this group, is we will all pay individually for our sin. There won't be any deals made on judgment day. However, there is a great deal available right now. Actually, it's a deal that is hard to believe. You see, Jesus came to earth, and, while we were yet sinners, He died for our sins. You can accept Jesus and enjoy the forgiveness He offers. As they say, this is a limited time offer, and none of us knows when that time runs out. Think about it.

I HAD TO SHOOT IT

I PAID CLOSE ATTENTION at the police academy when the instructor discussed the spontaneous exclamation. It was one of the few pieces of verbal evidence that could be used against a defendant even though they had not been advised of their rights. It didn't happen often, so when it did, it caught my attention.

At the beginning of my career, the deer decoy was a new, exciting, and very effective tool. Our decoys were made by Conservation Enforcement Officer (CEO) Byron Smith, who, prior to redistricting, was in my district and eventually moved to Elmore County, which was adjacent to Coosa County, where I lived. Therefore, I was able to receive tutelage from the master on how to utilize the decoy. You may be thinking how could someone mess up when using the decoy. The answer to that is easily another whole chapter if not an entire book! The decoy was actually a mounted life-size deer and was an excellent tool when used properly and sparingly. The true value of the decoy was it put the wildlife, or what folks thought was wildlife, the enforcement officer, and the violator at the same place at the same time.

Employing the decoy made it glaringly apparent many people had no qualms about shooting at deer from the public road. I believe when most people think about someone shooting a deer from the road, they primarily think that isn't fair to other hunters or the deer. While that is correct, many folks do not realize the illegal practice is much more serious than that. Not only does this illegal activity take a toll on the resource, it also puts the public at risk. Although we were required to take into consideration what was behind the decoy, the violators never gave that a second thought. This was evident by the multiple occupied houses I have seen shot into. Violators usually only looked at the deer long enough to line up their sights. The thought there may be a house, hunter, farmer, jogger, or anything else beyond their target apparently was of little concern. This was very apparent one Saturday on the Hollins Wildlife Management Area (WMA) in rural Clay County Alabama.

In response to numerous road hunting complaints, the Clay County game wardens had requested some of their cohorts bring one of the new-fangled decoys over and give it a try on the day of a WMA hunt. The deer was set up in a large field about 125 yards off of the paved county road that ran along the northern boundary of the WMA. The road was frequented by WMA users and others, and it didn't take long before the officers had some business.

This detail reinforced the fact violators come in all shapes, sizes, and vehicles. The officers watched as a small pickup eased to a stop in the roadway with the passenger's side facing the decoy. Noting only the driver in the vehicle, the officers were surprised to hear a muffled shot. It was somewhat unusual for someone to shoot from the driver's seat through the passenger-side window; however, you never knew what might happen when the decoy was involved. The shooter's first shot was quickly followed by several more shots. The "catch" vehicle hurriedly made its way to the truck, and the officers were again surprised to find not only was the driver shooting through the open passenger-side window, he was shooting with a 9mm pistol! Normal procedure was to write the violator tickets for hunting from the road, hunting by aid of a vehicle, and hunting without a permit. However, this violator was just full of surprises and notified the officers he actually held a permit to hunt on the property. He was issued the tickets for hunting from the road and by the aid of a vehicle and sent on his way.

Working the decoy often provided some interesting excuses. One of the most interesting "reasons" I ever heard was given during the same Clay County detail. As the officers observed, a small car slowed to a stop. Quickly a loud boom split the tranquil morning. The catch team quickly moved in. Officers found the vehicle held four occupants. It came as a bit of a shock to learn the driver was an Iranian. As you might have guessed, Iranians were few and far between in ultrarural east-central Alabama.

With multiple occupants, it is sometimes difficult to determine who all should be charged. However, in this case, the foreign driver made things somewhat easier when he stated, "They all told me, don't shoot it, don't shoot it, but I told them, all I've ever shot was a camel, I had to shoot it!" The shooter received citations for hunting from a public road, hunting by aid of a vehicle, and hunting without a permit.

The detail was proceeding well, and the decision was made to extend it into the afternoon. I had worked on the WMA that morning and had been monitoring the radio traffic. Needless to say, I was ready to get in on some of the action. I was partnered with a seasoned Clay County game warden in a catch vehicle. It wasn't long until an old, faded red Ford pickup eased to a stop in the public road and the driver cut loose on the manikin. As we headed toward the violator, he released another round at the Styrofoam buck. We pulled up behind the truck and approached the driver. Sitting in the driver's seat was a man that appeared to be about sixty-five years old. He wore eyeglasses with lenses so thick they looked as though they were made from the bottom ends of Coca-Cola bottles (if you can remember when Coke only came in glass bottles). Like many decoy shooters, the man was somewhat embarrassed he had been fooled by the "dummy." Also like many other shooters, he asked the question, "Where did I hit it?" I found the question to be somewhat humorous, taking into consideration the man's advanced age (I thought it was advanced then, funny how things change!), his obviously poor eyesight, the fact the deer was so far from the road, and since he had shot at the deer with a borrowed 30-30 rifle with iron sights!

This decoy setup was a little unusual in that we actually had an officer positioned on the same side of the road as the decoy. Although officer safety normally would not allow this, the layout of the field was such that an officer could be close to the deer and could observe the violators on the road from a safe vantage point. I radioed the officer and told him the guy wanted to know where he had hit the deer. "Where was he aiming?" he replied. I asked the shooter where he had tried to hit the deer, and he replied he had first shot at the white spot on the neck, and when the deer didn't go down, he had shot it behind the shoulder. I relayed the info to our spotter, who answered back with, "That's where he hit it." I must admit this revelation made his claim he had never done anything like this before a little hard to swallow!

Although many of the events of that day were very interesting, after working many decoy details, I realize most of the happenings were not unique. I said "most." As I mentioned earlier, we had an officer in position, watching the violations take place. He had a front-row seat to two incidents that were pretty much unlike any I had observed while working the deer. A vehicle with two occupants came slowly from the south and stopped in the road directly in front of the decoy. Our spotter watched in anticipation as the occupants of the truck ogled the six-point buck, deciding on their next move. He noticed another truck approaching from the north.

Now in my experience, the presence of another vehicle almost always ruined your chances of having someone shoot the decoy. Many times, I have sat for hours on a decoy detail with no traffic only to finally have a likely candidate show up and then be spooked by the approach of another vehicle. It only stands to reason most people don't blatantly break the law with folks watching. However, this was a day of firsts. The second vehicle slid to a stop beside the first truck. The driver jumped out with his rifle. He took steady aim, resting his gun on the dog box on the back of the first truck, and shot the deer! We pulled out and stopped both trucks. It took some convincing for me to believe the occupants of the first vehicle did not know the shooter. I had never witnessed someone shooting with an audience; however, it wouldn't be the last time.

Once again we were set up and waiting when the radio crackled and our spotter said, "He's getting out of the truck." A vehicle had pulled off the side of the road, and the driver had exited the vehicle. Although most road hunters would simply shoot from the vehicle, it wasn't unusual to have one get out and shoot. As we listened for the shot we were sure would come, instead we heard a deer grunting. About that time our observer came over the radio and said, "He's grunting at it." With the grunting failing to get a response from the stuffed buck, the fellow began rattling with a set of antlers. While most officers have had people stop and whistle, blow their horn, and take pictures of the decoy, this was another first for me. And yet, the day wasn't over. While the guy tried to coax the mounted deer closer, another truck pulled up beside the parked vehicle and the driver blasted the decoy!

Keep in mind, all of these incidents occurred in one day. It makes one wonder just how much of this type of activity goes on. There is no doubt in my mind the decoy deer saved the lives of thousands of real deer. This day once again reminded me people will do anything! Believe me; I've watched them do it! Of course, some of them "had to shoot it!"

J.G. WENTWORTH

EVEN THOUGH THE MAN was attempting to flee, I'm sure it would seem to the casual observer that the conservation officer should have jumped in the water to assist the fellow who appeared to be drowning. He was definitely struggling. The officer could tell he was running out of gas as he fought the water. In what was possibly his last desperate plea, he gasped, "Help me." Luckily, the officer was a seasoned professional and was able to handle things with a simple verbal command: "Stand up, you idiot!"

One of the best parts of the job of the conservation enforcement officer (CEO) is the diversity of the duties and knowing that anything can happen at any time. One would probably assume that checking fishing licenses would be a fairly mundane activity, and much of the time it is. However, there are always exceptions. We have had numerous officers assaulted while checking people fishing both from the bank and in boats. You can never let your guard down, whether your subject is young or old, male or female.

Talladega County CEOs Jerry Fincher and Greg Gilliland were in their boat checking fishermen when they experienced one of "those" days. Jerry had maneuvered the boat into a slough, where a young man was fishing from a pier. You may be surprised to learn that many people have the mistaken belief that if you are fishing from a private pier you do not need a fishing license. The pier actually doesn't have anything to do with the license requirement. Whether or not an individual is fishing in public waters is what makes the difference. In Alabama, if you are between the ages of sixteen and sixty-five and you are fishing in public waters, as a general rule, you are required to possess a fishing license. There are exceptions. If you are fishing with a cane pole in the county of your residence, you are not required to have a license.

Since this guy's line was in Logan Martin Lake, Greg asked to see the fellow's license, and he replied he did not have one. Not being his first rodeo, Greg got out of the boat onto the pier and positioned himself between the man and his "escape route" to the dry land. As Greg was writing the man a ticket, Jerry asked dispatch to run a check for warrants. Jerry said once he gave the info to the dispatcher, the man kept watching him with a "Yes, I have a warrant" look on his face.

It is imperative that law enforcement officers learn to read body language. Facial expression often speaks volumes. Sure enough, the dispatcher called back stating the man was wanted in three different jurisdictions. Although the man couldn't hear the radio, he apparently could read Jerry's face. The fellow turned and looked at the officer blocking his escape route. He stood contemplating his next move. It was obvious he was about to bolt. However, the officers were a bit surprised when the man suddenly dove into the water. Although startled, Jerry told Greg to get in the boat and they eased alongside the man who was doing his best to swim to a small island. Obviously, the plan was not well thought out in that the officers were in a boat easing alongside the swimmer and if he reached the island, he would then be on a small island!

The man quickly began to give out and began asking the officers to pull him in the boat. Jerry told the man there was no need for that. Hearing that, the man really began to panic. He was flailing his arms and gasping for air when Jerry told him to stand up. The water was only three feet deep. The man stood up and walked to the island. The officer ordered the man to lie on the ground, which was not a problem seeing how the man was totally exhausted. They asked if he had any weapons and handcuffed him.

Jerry noticed a large bulge in the man's cargo pants pocket. When he asked what was in the pocket the man replied, "Nothing."

Obviously, that wasn't the case. Cargo pants pockets were notorious for holding illegal items, including guns. Jerry pulled open the man's pocket and, to his surprise, found a large wad of hundred-dollar bills. When he asked the man how much money he had, he replied $19,000. The next question was an obvious one, "Where did you get nineteen thousand dollars?"

The man replied, "J.G. Wentworth."

You've likely seen the television commercials for J.G. Wentworth. The company will pay a reduced amount to people who have received a settlement that is being paid over time. The officers counted the money and found it actually totaled $14,800. The man was charged with fishing without a license (FWOL) and attempting to elude and was taken to jail.

A month later, the defendant appeared in court and pled guilty to the FWOL but wanted a trial on the attempting to elude. The judge told him to have a seat and they would have his trial when they finished taking pleas in other cases. When the court called his case, the man was nowhere to be found. Now he had another warrant.

It's not every day you find someone fishing with almost $15,000 in their pocket. I had a sneaking suspicion it wouldn't be in there when he got picked up again. It wasn't! One might think that a fellow with almost $15,000 in his pocket would have pulled out $13 and purchased a license. But, hey, there's no fun in that! You can't make this stuff up.

You have heard it said you can run, but you can't hide. Well, the truth is you can run and you can hide here on earth. But there is coming a day when your running will stop. It can be when you decide to quit running or when Jesus decides you will quit running. You can quit running from God and turn to Him, or you can run until he drops you to your knees. For every knee will bow and every tongue will confess. It's your choice—now anyway.

I HAVE THE ONLY PERMIT

WORKING BAIT WAS A DANGEROUS UNDERTAKING. It often entailed a lot of walking to originally find the bait and a lot more to regularly check the area for hunters. This had to be done without being detected, which wasn't the easiest thing to pull off. For some reason, anyone who saw a game warden in the area felt it was their responsibility to spread the word!

Early in my career I met a local businessman and landowner who owned about 1,300 acres and leased another 3,000 in central Coosa County. The man's son, Jeff, was a big hunter and wanted to be a game warden. He studied criminal justice in college and ended up working an internship with us. During the gun deer season, he accompanied us on an outing that was likely worth several course hours.

During the gun deer season, Conservation Enforcement Officer (CEO) Hershel Patterson and I had received a tip concerning an area that was baited. A check of the area revealed it was indeed baited with mineral blocks and alfalfa cubes. As I have often said, people baited deer with anything they thought might attract them. From peanut butter to lollipops, they tried it all.

Since there was no place near the baited site to hide a vehicle, Hershel decided he would drop Jeff and me out and let us walk in and check the bait. We exited the truck and quickly ran into the woods. It only took one observant citizen to mess you up on bait. As crazy as it sounds, the same people that contacted us about bait in an area would turn around and contact the violator, advising them they had seen us in the area. I can't explain it.

We were soon out of sight of the paved road and were on the woods road that led to the baited food plot. As we quietly made our way along, I began to hear what sounded like a vehicle idling. I held up my hand, and Jeff stopped behind me. I soon realized the noise was in fact a vehicle coming in behind us, and I loudly whispered for Jeff to run.

We dashed off the side of the road and dove on the ground. I could not believe the vehicle had gotten so close without us hearing it. We were now lying on our stomachs in the leaf litter watching. The vehicle came to stop just before it reached our location, and I felt certain the driver had spotted us and was about to exit the truck and call us out.

Being caught trying to catch someone else hunting bait was the worst. It rendered what was often a significant amount of time as wasted. Of course, you had stopped the violation from occurring, but that was little consolation for all the time and effort expended.

The driver stopped the truck and cut the engine. We were trying to hold our breath and hoping we had not been seen as we could hear the man moving around in the truck. I held my finger to my lips as though the intern needed to be told to keep quiet. It was an anxious time not being able to see who I felt certain was the violator.

After what seemed like an eternity but was probably about three minutes, the fellow came walking past us with his rifle in his arms. One thing I had learned rather quickly was you didn't want to startle a man with a gun. I allowed the man to pass our hiding spot, and I employed a tried-and-true technique: I whistled. This would usually stop the person in their tracks, and this time was no exception. I think it took people walking in the woods and not expecting anyone else to be there a second or two to recognize what they had heard as a human whistle. While thinking about it, they stood still, which was the desired result rather than to have them spin around toward me with their weapon in hand.

I remained on the ground and announced to the man I was the state game warden and I wanted him to place his rifle on the ground. The man gingerly put the gun down, and Jeff and I got up and moved over to him.

"Man, am I glad to see you," the man said in the way of a greeting.

I was thinking, "Probably not." Before I offered any response, the fellow began to explain how a poacher had been hunting the property, and he sure did want him caught, seeing how he was the only person who possessed a permit to hunt there.

I was thinking this guy would soon be sorry he told me that. I asked, "You're the only person with a permit on this property?"

"Yes sir," was his quick reply.

"So, I guess the bait out here is yours?"

This question didn't get such a quick response. The fellow stammered a little and in a very unconvincing tone said, "I don't know what you're talking about."

I had retrieved and unloaded the man's rifle and suggested we walk out to the field in front of us. We made our way into the opening, and I pointed out the mineral blocks and alfalfa cubes and asked if he had placed them there. He denied any knowledge of the bait. As we walked back to the truck, I was considering whether or not we had enough on this guy to arrest him. We had not let him get to the field, although he was within sight and shooting range of it when we stopped him. He claimed no knowledge of the bait but had told me he was the only person with a permit to hunt the property. However, he had also claimed a local outlaw was regularly poaching on the property, and I felt sure it would soon dawn on him to claim the poacher had baited the field.

As we neared the truck, I planned to read him his rights and hopefully get him to come clean about the bait. We arrived at the vehicle and I laid the unloaded firearm on the hood and glanced into the front seat. There is no substitute for being observant. I took the card from my wallet and read the subject the Miranda warning. He stated he understood his rights, and I began questioning him.

I started by asking what time he had left home coming to hunt. This kind of question would often confuse a subject since they did not anticipate it. He said he had left home around 2:30 p.m. I asked how long it took him to reach this location from his home. The answer to this question was totally irrelevant; however, having to think about an answer to my questions did not give him time to work on his defense. I asked if the loaded rifle he was carrying in fact belonged to him, and replied it did. I asked if he was the only person with a permit to hunt this property. He replied, "Yes." Jeff was looking at me with a curious look, and I was sure he was wondering why I was asking these benign questions and was not asking about the bait. However, I was about to get the attention of both the hunter and the intern.

"Can you tell me what would be the chance of the mineral blocks on the front seat of your truck matching those in the field?"

A smile broke across Jeff's face and the hunter lowered his head and did not reply. I told the man he was under arrest for hunting by the aid of bait. On several occasions, a quick peek in a violator's vehicle provided the evidence needed to solidify a baiting case.

As I prepared to write the man a citation, I asked if he had any hunter orange.

He looked at me with a sour "I'm guilty" look but then rebounded and said, "Well nobody hunts here but me," as if that negated the need for the safety equipment.

I replied, "I thought you had a poacher hunting all over you." He once again lowered his head. I wrote the man a ticket for hunting by the aid of bait and hunting without wearing hunter orange. I explained the area could not be hunted for ten days after the bait was removed. We made our way out to the edge of the road and waited on Hershel to come and pick us up.

Looking back, I hoped our intern was paying attention since there were several lessons that could be learned from this encounter. Do your best to watch your back. Don't startle a man with a loaded firearm. Be a good listener, and always be observant. That was a full day of class rolled up in about thirty minutes.

Although he did not end up as a CEO, Jeff did become a police officer. He has remained a friend of conservation and has assisted me several times in his positions of business owner and firearms dealer.

The violator in this story worked hard at claiming his innocence. Unfortunately, each of his explanations fell apart. Although he denied any knowledge of the bait, his story crumbled when I found the bait in his truck. He thought being the only person possessing a permit for the property would exonerate him; it in effect convicted him. He tried blaming it on someone else; however, he was the only one there. He was just like most of us. He tried to blame someone or something else for his transgressions. Again, just like with us, that will not work. The book of Samuel says, "Do not boast so proudly, or let arrogant words come out of your mouth, for the Lord is a God of knowledge, and actions are weighed by him." He knows it all. He can't be fooled. And yet, He still offers forgiveness and salvation. Wow, what a Savior!

WOMEN!

THE MAN WAS FACED with a decision that had him between a rock and a hard place. It was a difficult call. Do you face the wrath of lady justice or the lady you live with? He had to make a quick decision, and either way there were consequences.

As I have documented several times, it was not at all unusual for people to lie to the game warden. It often seemed folks would rather climb a tree and tell a lie than stand on the ground and tell the truth. This tendency permeated every activity, whether it was the person who had just shot from the road or the guy who had just crossed a barbed wire fence onto the property with a posted sign on every other tree. It also occurred with fisherman. I kid you not, many fishermen have an aversion to telling the truth.

Now everybody knows a fisherman will tell a lie about the size of a fish they caught or even more likely about the one that got away; however, in my experience it was more likely for them to tell a lie about whether they were even fishing or not. Although I didn't work a lot of fishing, during many years, the most frequent game and fish violation statewide was fishing without a license.

Let me attempt to explain a phenomenon you may not be familiar with. For many years, fishing rod manufacturers have utilized a mysterious material in the construction of their products. I do not know what it is exactly; however, I do know what it does and the catalyst needed to activate it.

There have been many advancements in rods over the years. The use of fiberglass, graphite, and other materials have greatly influenced their effectiveness. However, it is interesting that no matter whether someone is utilizing a rod containing a space-age polymer or a cane pole, they all appear to contain a compound that causes an immediate and significant increase in the temperature of the rod handle. The catalyst to activate the burning sensation is the sight of anyone who even resembles a game warden! It was not at all unusual to round a bend in the creek, come walking along the bank, drive alongside a stream or pull up at a boat launch, and see folks whose rods suddenly got so hot they had to throw them to the ground or even into the water.

Our normal protocol was to approach these folks and ask for their fishing license. Their normal quick response was, "I wasn't fishing."

When we would ask, "What were you doing?" there would usually be a lot of stammering and stuttering.

It is interesting how many people simply want to be associated with fishing. They like to be near water. They enjoy having a rod and reel and bait nearby, but they aren't fishing. It's uncanny!

Our officer in Chilton County shared with me the story of how he was sitting in his boat watching with binoculars as a fellow fished from a pier across the lake. After watching the man make several casts, the officer headed toward the pier. You guessed it; the phenomenon once again occurred. The rod immediately became hot, and the man promptly dropped it on the pier. The officer eased his boat up to the pier, greeted the man and woman, and asked to see the man's fishing license. The man gave the normal response that he wasn't fishing. The officer advised the fellow he had been watching him fish for several minutes. He

WOMEN!

again asked if the man had a license, and he admitted he did not. He asked for his driver's license and began writing the man a ticket for fishing without a license. The officer climbed up on the pier with the man and explained the ticket to him and showed him where to sign it.

As the man reached for the ink pen the officer offered, the man's wife said, "You better not sign that!" As you can guess, this left the man in a quandary. He looked at the officer and his wife. He again reached for the pen, and his wife repeated more forcefully, "You better not sign that."

The man looked at the officer and said, "I guess I'm not going to sign it."

The officer responded by telling him to turn around and put his hands behind his back. He handcuffed the man and helped him down into the boat. The officer turned and looked at the woman and told her she could come and pick him up at the Chilton County jail. With that, the woman turned and ran toward her lake house screaming all the way.

There is another interesting phenomenon that often takes place. When you put the metal bracelets on, the wearer begins to see the events that just transpired much more clearly. Such was the case with this man.

As the men rode through the choppy water toward the boat launch, the man turned and looked at the officer and said, "I screwed up, didn't I?" The officer responded that he would agree with that. The man hung his head and with a big sigh said, "Women!"

I'M CRAZY

During an active night hunting season when you were receiving multiple complaints, it was often a difficult decision as to where to work. It never seems to fail that the complaints would be strung out across the county. Although we sometimes picked the perfect spot, it was much more common for us to be a few to several miles from where the shots-fired reports would come from. This would require another decision of whether we would stay put or try to run down the shots. The old school officers would always say you were better off sitting tight and hoping the violators would come your way. The younger officers were always ready to try to go and find the shooters. While the stay-put method was probably the wisest, sometimes that wasn't an option.

Thursday night found Conservation Enforcement Officer Hershel Patterson and me sitting in the dark about eight miles west of the town of Rockford, the county seat of Coosa County. We had been receiving multiple complaints of people hunting deer at night during what was proving to be an extremely long deer season. The deer season had been underway for 104 days, and I felt like we had worked every one of them. Of course, the truth of the matter was there had been a few days we did not work, but they were very few. It was January 28, and with just three days left in the Alabama deer season, if experience was any kind of a teacher, the roads would be busy and the complaints numerous.

We were monitoring an area where we had recently had some success. It was not at all uncommon to apprehend numerous night hunters in the same area. We had been there for about an hour when the radio came to life and the county dispatcher said, "Base to 910" (910 was Hershel's radio call sign). Hershel answered the call, and the dispatcher stated someone had just shot in front of Randy Spivey's house, and they were in the field looking for the deer. I told Hershel, "Let's go."

Although they lived one mile away, Randy and Annette Spivey were my next-door neighbors, and I had previously caught night hunters in front of their house. We immediately sped toward their location, which unfortunately was about ten miles away. I radioed the Rockford police department officer and asked that he go out to the location and hold the suspects until we could get there. I hoped they would do it; however, they had not been inclined to take the lead on any game and fish calls in the past. I understood they were not comfortable trying to enforce our laws and regulations, but I hoped they would at least go to the scene and identify our suspects.

Hershel was getting all he could out of the Dodge Ramcharger as we entered Rockford. As we approached the four-way stop in the center of town, my heart fell when I saw the Rockford police car sitting at the four way. This was not the first time I had asked a police officer to respond to an armed violator and they had waited until I arrived to proceed to the scene.

We were still two miles from the scene, and I knew the chances of the violators still being there were slim to none. However, two minutes later, we were pulling up behind the suspects' vehicle and spotted the two men coming out of the field.

As I illuminated one of the men with my flashlight, I immediately recognized him as someone I had arrested five years earlier hunting "squirrels" with a shotgun loaded with slugs. When I said, "Good evening Mr. White," the man's head jerked back as if I had slapped him in the face.

"How do you know my name?" he asked, and I replied, "I know a lot of things, but what I want to know is what y'all are doing in this field." He gave me the age-old night hunter answer, "We were just using the bathroom."

It was amazing how many people would stop on the side of the highway to use the bathroom at night during deer season in areas where shots had just been reported. I mean it was uncanny. It happened so frequently I thought about making my first question, "Are you just using the bathroom?"

As I reached into the vehicle and retrieved a semiautomatic shotgun, the man immediately said, "I don't have any shells for that."

I replied, "You don't need any," and carried the gun and placed it in our truck. I asked the fellow what he was doing in Coosa County late at night, and he said they had just been riding around looking at deer. I asked where they had been, and he told me the route they had taken. During his answer, he named three of the county roads that traversed the areas of the county with the highest deer concentrations, telling me it wasn't his first time riding the county at night.

I asked him if he always brought his gun when he was looking for deer. He again told me he didn't have any shells for the gun, and I countered with, "Then why do you have it?"

He lowered his voice and said, "Well, sir, I don't like some people."

I did not know whether or not I was in that group, but I wouldn't be surprised! I asked him if he knew what you called a gun without shells. The blank look on his face told me he did not know, so I told him, "A stick."

I decided I would try another technique, so I told him to sit tight, and I went to talk with the passenger whom Hershel had been talking with. I asked Hershel what he had found out, and he replied, "This guy is crazy. He blew his ear off trying to shoot himself."

I must say that was a new one on me, and judging by his demeanor, it was a new one on Hershel too. I escorted the fellow to the back of our vehicle so we could not be heard, and asked him what was going on. Although Hershel had just told me this guy was crazy, I must admit I had not anticipated what he would say.

He immediately said, "I'm crazy, I'm crazy, you can ask my psychiatrist." He pointed to his right ear and said, "Look here, this is where I blew my ear off trying to kill myself. I'm crazy."

It was obvious I wasn't going to get far with this guy, so I returned to Mr. White and informed him I had talked with his accomplice and had received a totally different story from the one he had provided. I reached into the front passenger's floorboard and retrieved a hatchet I had seen earlier. I held it up and looked at Hershel and said, "Just like he said it was."

Although this had nothing to do with anything, I could tell it made Mr. White uneasy. I told the suspect I needed his driver's license. As he fished out the license, he was protesting and saying he had just stopped to use the bathroom. I countered that most people didn't stop on the side of an Alabama highway in front of someone's house and walk around in their field for fifteen minutes to use the bathroom! The man hung his head. Although what we had was shaky at best, we began writing tickets. While these would not be the strongest cases we had ever made, I felt very confident when the landowner told the judge the story, we would be okay.

The landowner had heard a shot and looked out and saw a vehicle sitting on the edge of the road in front of their house, where deer were known to frequent. They had watched as two men got out of the car and searched in the field until we arrived. We would add we had found a shotgun in their possession, and they had told us they were here, twenty-five miles from their home, looking for deer. I felt this story, coupled with the fact our judge was more than fed up with all of the night hunting that was occurring in the county, would work well in district court. I did not anticipate any problems.

The next month the defendants appeared in the district court before the honorable Judge Bobby Teel. I had prepared a detailed narrative of the events of the evening, being sure to include the strong points I hoped would work in our favor. The judge glared at the defendants and stated they were charged with hunting at night, hunting from a public road, and hunting without a permit and asked how did they plead. There was a brief pause before the pair dejectedly mumbled, "Guilty."

I had to fight the urge to look at the pair and say, "I thought y'all were just using the bathroom!" Truthfully, I was thankful for their plea and the ability to conclude the case without answering any questions.

These guys pled guilty because they were guilty. We are all guilty. The Bible says all have sinned and come short of the glory of God, but the gift of God is eternal life through Jesus Christ our Lord. It is free for the asking. Choose it today, while there's still time.

IF THAT GUN COULD TALK

LAW ENFORCEMENT IN A RURAL COUNTY is often a joint effort. Many times, I have responded to calls having nothing to do with game or fish. In Alabama, a conservation enforcement officer (CEO) has full police powers and can enforce any state law or regulation. The leadership of our department frowned on our involvement in anything other than wildlife law enforcement; however, they also weren't working in the field. I did my best to curtail enforcement activities outside our purview; however, there were times when I was the only officer available, and during those times I felt it was my responsibility to respond. Many times, it wasn't that we were asked to answer a call but rather to provide a backup to another officer. I was always more than happy to do this since there was always the possibility I would be the one needing the backup the next time. Most officers in the field were always good to assist one another.

CEO Hershel Patterson and I were working night hunting in the south part of the county when we heard our local trooper requesting assistance. He had been pursuing a vehicle on Highway 259, also known as Fish Pond Road, but had lost sight of it. He felt certain the suspect had either taken a side road or ducked into a driveway. We were close by and offered our assistance. He requested we set up on the Tower Road, a dirt road connecting Alabama Highway 259 and Alabama Highway 9. He gave a brief description of the vehicle and asked that we check anything coming through.

We soon arrived at our designated spot and began our vigil. Within a couple of minutes, a vehicle approached our set up. Not wanting them to turn and run, we waited until they were pretty close and activated our blue light and stopped the car. I immediately noticed the vehicle was occupied by two black guys and one white guy. This was years ago when that was not a common occurrence in our rural county. My experience had taught me when you observed this in a vehicle there were often drugs involved. (That statement has nothing to do with profiling; it has to do with experience.) This immediately put us on high alert.

The car description we had received had been somewhat vague, so we weren't sure if this was the suspect vehicle or not. I moved to the passenger side of the vehicle while Hershel spoke with the driver. The passenger lowered his window and I asked to see his identification. While he retrieved his wallet, I scanned the interior of the vehicle with my flashlight. This scan revealed a rifle between the passenger and the door. This wasn't the first time I had seen a rifle carried in this manner, and it was always indicative of night hunters. I told all of the passengers to raise their hands over their heads. This of course alerted Hershel to the fact something was amiss. I opened the door and removed the rifle. A more thorough look through the vehicle did not turn up any other weapons, and I took the rifle and placed it in our car.

We removed the three men from the car and separated them. I recognized the driver as a local guy from Rockford. Talking with him revealed the other guy was his brother and the rifle-toting guy was his brother's military buddy from Texas. I asked where they were coming from, and the driver stated they had been to their sister's house on Highway 259 for supper and were now on their way home to Rockford. When I asked why they had the rifle, he replied he wasn't sure. I moved to the gun owner and asked him where they had been. He stated they ate supper at a home on Highway 259 and were en route back to Rockford. I asked why he had the gun, and he explained he had come out from Texas to do some deer hunting. I asked where he had been hunting, and he replied on the family's property in Rockford. I asked if he had a hunting license, and he hesitated and then admitted he did not. Obviously, he did not need a hunting license to ride in a car with a rifle; however, pointing out that he had been in violation when he was hunting served to sort of place him behind the eight ball, so to speak.

When I questioned whether or not he thought there was going to be some trouble while they were eating, he initially appeared confused; he then chuckled and said no. I came back with, "Then why did you bring the rifle with you tonight?" After hemming and hawing for a few seconds, he stated he had brought it in case he saw a deer to shoot. I said that sounded a lot like night hunting to me. He simply nodded his head up and down. Further questioning of the other two revealed they all knew why the rifle had been brought along.

Hershel and I discussed the situation, and the decision was made to take a statement from the three and bring charges against them for hunting at night. We knew it was risky to make a case based on what they had said without any other corroborating evidence. However, we felt their collective confessions would likely carry enough weight to convict them. We decided to try it.

As I was completing the paperwork on the guy from Texas, I inquired about the make and caliber of his firearm. I had noticed it wasn't your basic night hunting rifle. It was a lever action, which was common enough; however, I had noticed it had an octagon barrel. The fellow told me the rifle was a Winchester 32-20 caliber. He added it had been in his family for many years and stated, "If that gun could talk, it could sure tell some stories."

I responded with, "Now it can tell about the night you lost it in Coosa County, Alabama."

"What do you mean lost it?" he nearly screamed. The alarm was very evident in his voice.

I explained any items used night hunting were subject to being confiscated, and he probably wouldn't get it back. Things had quickly gone from fairly lighthearted to very serious.

"I can't lose that gun," the man almost pleaded. "I'll do anything to keep that gun."

I informed him it would be left up to the judge. Visibly shaken, the man got in the car, and they went on their way.

The dread over the possibility of losing a gun used while night hunting was not at all uncommon. During this time, it was very common for the judge to condemn the gun. More than once I have had a violator literally beg me to let them replace the old "family" gun I was holding with a new, much more expensive one. Of course, this wasn't allowed.

The court date rolled around, and the trio appeared very anxious. The local guy approached us and asked if there was anything they could do to get the gun back. Hershel and I discussed it briefly. To say the case was weak was no doubt a gross understatement. It basically hinged on their confession, and we knew if they changed their mind and now said they had no intention of shooting a deer, we would be hard pressed to convict them, although that was what they had been doing. We told them if they wanted to plead guilty, we would recommend the minimum fine and cost and *request* the gun not be confiscated. However, we made it abundantly clear the decision on the gun was totally up to the judge, and we had no control over it. Our district court judge was a wild card in every case. We spoke with the assistant district attorney and explained the trio wanted to plead guilty if they could get the gun back. Fortunately, the judge was in a compassionate mood and honored the plea agreement.

This wasn't the last time assisting another officer would translate into a case for us. You know, if that gun could talk, it would be interesting to hear it tell the story about the night in Coosa County when you couldn't have driven a pin up its owner's rear end with a sledgehammer!

KEEP YOUR HAND OUT OF YOUR POCKET

IT WAS OBVIOUS when the man placed his hand back in his pocket after my third warning: there was something important in there. I had already made him empty his pockets but had not patted him down as I should have. I ordered the man to walk with his arms held straight out from his sides. We finally reached our vehicles, and I had him place his hands on the tailgate of his pickup. I then learned what was lurking in his pocket. Looking back, I realize I made many mistakes. Of course, this guy was a veteran outlaw, and I was a wet-behind-the-ears game warden.

    I had been working as an area biologist on the Coosa Wildlife Management Area (WMA) less than thirteen months when I made some of the most memorable cases of my law enforcement career. Conservation Enforcement Officer (CEO) Earl Brown and I were patrolling the WMA in my new Chevrolet four-wheel-drive pickup. The WMA was thirty-eight thousand acres in size and contained two hundred miles of roads open to the public. It was difficult to cover the entire area, so when we located a set of fresh tracks in the rain-moistened road, we were on the hunt. As we approached a stream crossing, Earl made the comment that with the recent rains, the stream would probably be deeper than normal. I asked if he thought we could make it through, and he replied, "Yes, if you'll get on through it."

This is a good point to make a comment concerning clear communication. During a thirty-two-year career, I learned almost every endeavor hinges on a clear exchange of information. Communication that is unclear leads to people drawing their own conclusions, which may be correct or incorrect. My interpretation of Earl's comment to "get on through it" was to hit the stream faster than normal, so I accelerated and hit the water pretty hard. Hard enough the truck almost immediately sputtered and died. Fortunately, I had approached with enough speed to get to the other side; however, that was as far as we would get. Fortunately, Earl had been a master mechanic before becoming a game warden; however, there was nothing he could do with the truck, which was hopelessly drowned out.

We soon realized we would have to call my assistant on the WMA, Lois Culver, for assistance. Lois was an interesting character. First, he was the first and only man I've ever known named Lois. When I began working on the WMA, I was twenty-four and Lois was sixty-three. Lois had held a variety of jobs during his life. He explained to me that when he worked for the county as a road hand, he would climb on any idle piece of equipment and learn how to operate it. This initiative had served him well when he got to the WMA seeing how there was always plenty of equipment work to do on the 200 miles of road around the area.

The former area manager, Mr. James Nix, had once told me that Lois had a split personality. He said Lois was a great worker on the area, but when he got around other people he just couldn't help but cut up and carry on. I found that to be a pretty accurate description. Lois taught me a lot, and I appreciated all of his hard work.

I called Lois on the radio and gave him our location and asked him to bring a chain. There is evidently a rule that says that although you are in an area that normally has traffic moving through on a regular basis, if you break down and need assistance, no one will come along. That rule was obviously in force.

My helper soon arrived and towed us back to the shop. I'm sure Lois thought this was nothing new. In my one year on the area, he had helped me out of many situations. After arriving at the WMA shop, Earl somehow developed a bad headache and decided to go home. I decided I would take Lois's truck and go back to the fresh set of tracks we were following prior to taking my truck for a swim. I shared my plan with Lois, and he said he would accompany me.

As I had mentioned earlier, Lois Culver was sixty-three years old. He had no law enforcement experience or authority. However, he was definitely a one-of-a-kind individual. Lois was about five feet four inches tall and weighed maybe 130 pounds. Although small, Lois was a scrapper, and I gladly accepted when he said he would accompany me on my patrol.

Although I was accustomed to working the area alone, it never hurt to have someone with you. One of the aspects that makes a conservation officer's job so dangerous is the fact you are often alone in the middle of nowhere and often, in our case, without any radio communication and/or backup. These are probably the factors that led one of my police academy instructors to tell me I was just asking to be killed by working with game and fish!

Lois and I returned to the northwest part of the area and picked up the set of tracks. Following the easily seen impressions, I soon spotted a pickup truck parked in the road ahead. The first thing that caught my attention was the truck was parked literally in the road. Blocking a road on the WMA was a regulation violation. I pulled up behind the vehicle and exited the truck.

Almost immediately, I heard what sounded like a shotgun blast. The shot sounded as if it came from down in a hollow off to my left.

The only hunting season currently open on the WMA was for rabbit. The pine plantation I was standing in was about twenty-five years old with a closed canopy and little understory. Knowing this was very unlikely rabbit habitat, I decided things might not be kosher and I should investigate the shot. I was thinking deer season had ended five days earlier, and this might be someone who had decided to extend it a little bit. I told Lois to stay at the truck while I went to check things out.

I began working my way down through the woods toward where the shot had come from. After going maybe one hundred yards, I observed an individual working his way toward me. I moved behind a pine tree and observed. As he moved closer, I could see it was a lone white male, probably forty-five or fifty years old, which seemed old at the time. He was carrying a shotgun in an unconventional manner. He held the shotgun by the barrel with the stock over his shoulder. I also noticed he did not appear to have any game with him. As I watched intently, the hunter's head suddenly snapped up as he spotted the green game warden truck parked behind his own. I almost laughed out loud when he immediately did an about face and started back down into the hollow. I stepped from behind my hiding spot and started toward the subject. My shout of *"Stop*, state game warden!" had little effect on the man, who hurriedly walked farther into the woods. I soon realized this fellow wasn't stopping, and I had better get moving. I was soon running downhill toward the subject. I did not want to run down and grab an armed subject, nor did I want to be out in the open with no cover if he decided to spin around and shoot at me. Therefore, I was trying to keep some trees between us.

When I got within about fifteen yards of him, I again yelled, "Stop!" Seeing he was not going to get away, he stopped. He did not turn around and face me; he stood still facing away. This was unusual and a little unsettling. In my most authoritative tone, I ordered him to put the gun on the ground, and thankfully, he did. I told him to turn around toward me. I did not recognize the man. I asked to see his license and permit. He retrieved his wallet from the rear pocket of his camouflage coveralls and fished out his licenses and permit.

At this point, I still wasn't sure what I had. My suspicion was he was probably illegally hunting deer. I knew a look at his ammunition would tell the tale; however, I was trying to play it cool. While examining his permit, I asked him, "What are you hunting?"

"Uh, uh, uh, rabbits," he replied.

"Rabbits!" I shot back. "Down in this pine thicket?"

While waiting for his answer, I picked his shotgun up off the ground and opened the chamber only to find it was empty. "Let me check your ammunition?" I said.

He replied, "I don't have any."

"Why not?" I inquired.

"I shot it all," was his answer.

Let me pause here and ask you a question. Have you ever gone hunting for anything and shot up all your ammunition? I know that can happen on a really good dove shoot, but for the most part, that doesn't happen.

Where are your rabbits? I asked.

"I missed them," was his reply. I noticed he had nervously placed his hand in his right front pocket, and I told him to remove his hand from his pocket and not to put it back in there.

I asked him how many rabbits he had shot at, and he responded he had shot at one cane cutter. A cane cutter was a slang name for a swamp rabbit that often inhabited areas of canes along drainages and wet areas.

It immediately seemed pretty odd to me that someone would go hunting rabbits and carry only one shell with them. I asked him if he had only brought one shell, and he replied, "Yes." I knew something was up, I just wasn't sure what it was.

The fellow again put his hand into his pocket, and I again told him to remove it. I wasn't sure whether the fellow was trying to get rid of a slug or maybe a buckshot he had brought to try and kill an out-of-season deer or whether he might be trying to reach a pocket knife or pistol, but I knew I didn't want him to put his hand in his pocket again.

I ordered him to empty the contents of his pockets on the ground. He removed his hand from his pocket, dropping a stick of lip balm and a pocketknife onto the pine needles covering the ground. I asked if that was all he had, and he replied it was. I picked up the items and instructed him to head toward the truck.

As he walked in front of me, we hadn't gone very far when he once again put his hand into his right front pocket. I guess it was a lack of a good place to stand him up and pat him down that kept me from doing so. Instead I told him to take his hand out of his pocket and to extend his arms straight out to his sides and walk to the truck without putting them down. So, he walked the rest of the way to the truck with his arms out to his sides.

Once we reached his vehicle, I told the man to place his hands on the tailgate of his truck. I handed the shotgun to Lois and asked him to place it in our truck. I began to pat the subject down and although I really was just interested in the right front pocket, I started up at the chest and did a thorough pat down of the man. I had only been out of the academy for a few months and remembered the instruction not to develop tunnel vision but to look at everything. Satisfied he did not have any other weapons on his person, it was time to search his pockets. Now this was before law enforcement officers were afraid of being stuck with a needle or something and I had no qualms about going into his pockets. As I slid my hand in the right front pocket, it took a couple of seconds for me to realize what it was that I felt. Once I realized what it was, the whole ordeal quickly came into much clearer focus. I grasped and pulled from his pocket the feet and beard of a wild turkey gobbler!

At the same time, I was both excited and repulsed. Excited I had just found irrefutable evidence the man had taken a turkey in closed season and repulsed that someone would kill a magnificent bird and simply cut off its feet and beard and leave the rest of it for the buzzards and other scavengers. Experiencing all of these emotions, my heart was about to beat out of my chest. I told the man he was under arrest and not to move off of the tailgate. I turned and showed the beard and feet to Lois and laid them on the hood of my truck.

Never having made a case like this before, I went to the truck and began calling the local game wardens on the radio. Although he was off duty, CEO Hershel Patterson was monitoring his scanner and, hearing the excitement in my voice, went to his vehicle and answered me. I quickly explained the situation to him. He asked for the man's name, and I gave it to him. Being familiar with the man, he informed me the man had probably killed the turkey over bait. Although it should have, this was something that had not occurred to me. However, thinking back on the situation, the fact he was in a pine plantation with nothing on the ground except pine needles should have tipped me off to this. Of course, I was a green-as-a-gourd rookie, but I did know enough to call the veteran officer and glean from his many years of experience, which I did many times in my career. Even after he had retired, I regularly conferred with him on various cases and situations. (As matter of fact, we still talk every week!) Hershel told me to simply ask the man if he was hunting over bait, and if he would not admit it, I would have to go and find it.

I returned to the subject and informed him he could make this easy or he could make it hard. I asked if he had killed the turkey over bait, and he calmly replied, "Yes." I told him we would be going and getting a sample of the bait and retrieving the turkey. To that he replied, "I don't think you'll be able to do that."

I immediately assumed he was inferring that I, a kid half his age, would not be able to make him go back to where he had killed the turkey. I felt certain he was questioning my authority, and I shot back, "Why not?"

"Because I threw it in the creek and it's really rolling," he said.

This statement really ticked me off. Not only did he disrespect the turkey by killing it over bait, in my mind it was even worse that he threw the thing away. I know I wasn't doing a very good job of hiding my disgust when I angrily asked, "Why did you do that?"

"To keep from getting caught with it," was his matter-of-fact reply.

Having been studying the regulation book, I knew that statement would be helpful during his prosecution.

We headed back into the woods. I followed the violator as he led me straight to where he had shot the bird. I retrieved a sample of the scratch feed, which he had used to bait the turkey. I asked where he had been when he shot the gobbler, and he pointed to a small depression in the ground where he had been laying. I spied the spent shotgun hull and retrieved it. I had him show me where he had thrown the turkey into Weogufka Creek and realized he was correct when he said we would never find it. We headed back.

Once back at the truck, I again placed the man on the tailgate of his truck and informed him I was going to search his vehicle. One of the advantages of being on the WMA was Alabama law gave a law enforcement officer the right to search any automobile, game bag, coat, and so forth within the boundaries of the WMA. This right to search was challenged many times in the field by people who weren't familiar with the rules and regulations on the area and who argued we could not search their vehicle without a search warrant. Unfortunately for them, the Alabama legislature had decided the fact someone was on the WMA was sufficient probable cause for the search. This was also often argued in court; however, we always prevailed. We didn't always win the case, but the searches were always upheld. This search authority resulted in many arrests and was soon to result in another one.

I searched through the subject's truck, looking for anything illegal or incriminating. When I slid my hand under the driver's seat, I felt a plastic zip lock type bag. When I pulled the bag from its hiding place, my blood pressure once again shot through the roof. In the bag was the breast of a small turkey. The size of the breast led me to theorize it was probably from a turkey hen. I held up the bag and asked the man if this was a hen, and he nodded his head that it was. With my pulse racing, I thoroughly searched the remainder of the truck but found no more contraband. I carried the bag containing the breast to my truck and retrieved my ticket book. It was now time for the ink to flow.

CEOs in Alabama enforce both laws and regulations. Laws were enacted by the legislature, while the conservation commissioner could promulgate regulations. Wildlife management areas have many rules and regulations that area users must know and abide by. This individual was soon to become familiar with many of the laws and regulations! The first ticket was actually for the state law prohibiting hunting by the aid of bait. Next was a ticket for taking a protected species, a wild turkey hen. The fellow's eyes seemed to get larger every time I finished a ticket and turned the page and started another one. The ink kept flowing as I stroked him a citation for hunting during the closed season.

Many people, including some judges and some supervisors, frowned on officers who stacked charges. I understood this and did my best to avoid that practice in many cases, but not in the case of what I considered to be premeditated and/or heinous violations. Unfortunately for this defendant, I felt this incident fell into each of those categories, and therefore, with three written, I started on number four. Distributing grain was illegal on the WMA and spreading the scratch feed was sufficient, so I wrote him up for that. The fact he had admitted he threw the turkey in the creek to keep from getting caught with it and the fact he had skinned out the hen put him in violation of regulation 220-2-.15 Destroying Sex of Deer or Wild Turkey Prohibited. This regulation states,

> It is hereby made <u>unlawful</u> for any person who kills, captures, or possesses a deer or wild turkey, in order to evade or attempt to evade any law or regulation, to destroy or attempt to destroy the evidence of sex, or to mutilate the carcass of such deer or wild turkey so as to make the determination of the legal status of the deer or turkey uncertain. Nothing in this regulation is intended to prevent any person from dressing for consumption any deer or wild turkey which has been killed legally. This regulation is designed to prohibit the killing or capturing of illegal deer and wild turkey hens.

I felt this incident was a perfect fit for this regulation. Having the hen in the plastic bag under his seat violated another regulation, which states game must be transported openly, and prompted ticket number six. Did I mention I was more than a little ticked off? Last, the fact he had thrown the turkey gobbler's carcass in the creek earned him ticket number seven for wanton waste of a game animal. Although I could have written two tickets for destroying the sex of an animal and a ticket for blocking the road, I decided seven tickets were probably enough. Hey, I have a heart!

It took quite some time to write the seven citations. After checking over each one, I explained the bonds to the outlaw and had him sign them. I gave him his copies and told him I would see him in court. I placed the evidence in my truck, and Lois and I left the area. As we drove away, I asked Lois if he was familiar with the man, and he stated he was and the fellow hunted there often. I couldn't help but wonder how many times he had gotten away with this type of behavior.

We returned to the shop, and I hoped my truck had dried out enough to crank. Thankfully, the truck started, and I drove straight to the courthouse and began signing warrants in the clerk's office. Although I had not written anyone for some of the offenses previously, I had no problem finding all the needed information until I reached the wanton waste case. I knew I had read the law concerning wasting animals, yet after a thorough search of the law and regulation books, I could not come up with it. Therefore, I phoned Hershel and told him I could not find the wanton waste law. He told me that didn't surprise him since that law or regulation did not exist. He went on to explain we did have a law against wasting fish but not game animals. He agreed with me that we should have such a charge but reminded me we didn't create the laws, we only enforced them. I asked Hershel what would be the proper procedure to follow when you had written someone a ticket for a charge that did not exist. He advised probably the easiest thing to do would be to contact the defendant and advise him I had decided to drop the charge and leave it at that. I agreed that was probably a good way to handle it; however, I remembered I had not written the man for blocking the road, and maybe I could just change it to that. Hershel told me he felt I probably already had more than enough charges, and letting the one go wouldn't hurt anything. I took his advice.

Within a few days, I received a call from the assistant district attorney (ADA) who inquired about why I had written the individual so many charges. I explained to him the defendant had committed a heinous wildlife offense and he should have the book thrown at him. Unfortunately, I was about to learn who had the power in the court system. I had not known that the district attorney or his assistant have the power to decide whether or not to prosecute the cases brought by officers. Even if they don't refuse to prosecute the case, they can fail to earnestly pursue the case. After learning this lesson, the ADA and I agreed to compromise where the defendant would plead guilty to four of the charges and pay fines and costs in the total of $1,065.

I assure you that was a huge fine-and-costs total for management area violations; however, I later learned this defendant received a much harsher penalty. It seems the word of the arrest somehow made its way to his work place, a large paper mill. The paper company actually owned the majority of the property in the WMA, and several of the mill employees hunted on the WMA regularly. I was told that for weeks after the incident, his locker remained filled with corncobs. He was greeted by turkey calls anywhere he ventured in the mill, and for several days a line of corn kernels led from his locker all the way to his truck in the parking lot. I also learned his reputation as a big-time turkey hunter would never be the same.

One of the things I still don't understand after all of these years is the person who portrays himself or herself as the great white hunter, when in fact, they are just an outlaw. I was told this individual had hundreds of turkey beards and feet displayed at his home. I was thankful the truth of how those "trophies" were obtained came to light!

Believe it or not, we will all soon be in the same situation faced by this outlaw. Everything will come to light. We are good at hiding our sin and even better at convincing ourselves we are good folks. The Bible says our righteousness is like filthy rags. It also regularly warns us: be not deceived. That's good advice. The man in this story had deceived himself into thinking he was a great hunter. The truth was he was simply an outlaw. Be not deceived, your sin will find you out!

YOU KNOW THE KIND

I KNOW YOUR KIND. That was an expression I used a lot. Most of the time I would use the phrase in jest with a friend or fellow officer, and sometimes I would use it to indicate I did in fact know the kind of person I was dealing with. I sometimes would have someone ask what the phrase meant, and sometimes folks would act a little offended. But I never received such a surprised look as I saw on the judge's face when the defendant said to him, "You know the kind."

During a thirty-two-year career as a conservation officer in a small rural county, I had thousands of encounters with violators. Multiply that by every officer in the county, and you come up with the number of violators our district judges had to deal with. Granted, many of our cases were settled prior to court; however, the judge has seen and heard it all. Of course, some heard more than others.

It was my good fortune to have had some good judges to work with. Believe me, working with a bad judge, one who doesn't take violations of wildlife law seriously, was an extremely frustrating undertaking. One local district court judge wasn't always a staunch friend of conservation. However, one day the judge had an experience that would forever change his view of conservation law violators. An epiphany if you will. Upon arriving at the driveway to his home in rural Clay County, he found the drive was partially blocked by a jeep and two men with guns. I will not refer to them as hunters, although that was what they would call themselves. The fellows were obviously intoxicated and were apparently upset with their vehicle. This was evident, seeing how they were shooting it! You can't make this up!

After this episode, the judge summoned my fellow wildlife biologist, Gene Carver, to his office, where the judge apologized for not having taken seriously what we were up against. However, he vowed he would never again take lightly wildlife law violators. The judge held true to his word, and from that day forward, many violators took it on the chin when they found themselves standing before him. It was my pleasure to be able to support his nomination for Judicial Conservationist of the Year and to see him receive the prestigious honor from the Alabama Wildlife Federation.

I had many memorable cases before the judge; however, one of the most memorable was one I had nothing to do with. It seemed a state trooper had reason to charge a woman with indecent exposure. The woman pled not guilty, and the case was set for trial.

This judge's court was run much differently than the one in my home county. Witnesses were required to take the witness stand, and everything was pretty much by the book. The trooper took the stand and testified that while on routine patrol, he was flagged down by a motorist who reported seeing a half-naked woman on the side of Highway 148. The man making the report informed the trooper the woman was looking over her shoulder and waving at passing vehicles. The trooper testified when he arrived on the scene, he observed a woman who was indeed naked from the waist down and waving at him while looking over her shoulder. He exited his vehicle and instructed the woman to pull up her pants. He testified the odor of alcoholic beverage was overwhelming. The woman failed a couple of quick field sobriety tests and was promptly placed under arrest for indecent exposure and public intoxication.

Following the trooper's testimony, the defendant took the stand. The woman looked to be about fifty years old but was probably closer to thirty-five. It appeared to have been some sho' nuff hard years. I thought if the lines in her face had been a road map, she had been halfway around the world. However, when she opened her mouth, her twang told me she had never ventured far from where she was sitting.

Bear in mind this wasn't some *People's Court* TV show; the judge conducted court in a straitlaced, professional manner. There was no funny business, no talking, and interruptions were not tolerated. This made what happened next so much more entertaining.

The witness stand was only six feet from the judge's position. The woman was sworn in and seated in the witness chair. The judge asked her to tell the court what had happened. The woman turned to face the judge and began her testimony. "Well judge, first, I was not "nay-ked." She continued, saying, "I had on a pair of them G-string panties." As if this wasn't enough of an explanation as to why she wasn't "nay-ked," the woman went on to describe the garment she was wearing, saying, "You know the kind, with the string going up your butt!" What I would have given for a snapshot of the judge's face.

The sure contempt of court citation and accompanying jail time were the two things that kept me from saying, "Yeah, judge, you know that kind."

The judge's face had turned bright red. As I fought to keep from laughing and the judge attempted to regain his composure, the defendant didn't miss a beat. She went on to explain she was simply using the bathroom, and her boyfriend was holding his foot on the brake to keep the lights on "'cause she didn't want to squat down on no snake!"

The judge regained his composure and asked, "Why were you waving when the trooper pulled up?"

She replied the trooper must have been mistaken because she wasn't waving, she was just using the bathroom.

The judge asked the defendant if she had any questions for the trooper, and she replied, "Naw, I don't reckon I do."

He told her she could step down and announced he found the woman guilty.

It's stories like this that you just can't make up! You know the kind!

KOTEX SHOOTER

WHILE I WAS THE AREA BIOLOGIST on the Coosa Wildlife Management Area (WMA), the decision was made to build a shooting range on the WMA. I was instructed to find a location on the WMA where there were no houses for at least two miles. Seeing how the area was thirty-eight thousand acres in size, I did not think this would be a problem. However, they also wanted a location close to a paved road and where the ground was fairly level. Those requirements were a little more difficult to locate. After a considerable amount of searching, we did find a suitable area, and the range was developed.

I must admit I was somewhat skeptical as to whether or not developing the range would turn out to be worth the effort, seeing how most people in our rural county had ample opportunity to sight in firearms on their own property or hunting club. However, I was amazed at the amount of use the shooting range received. While locals did utilize the range, the majority of users came from surrounding towns and cities, some as far as fifty miles or more. While the range was busiest prior to hunting season, people regularly used the range year-round. One Saturday prior to daylight and just before deer season, I went to the range and picked up all of the high-powered rifle brass. I returned that evening and picked up 375 high-powered rifle shell casings that had been fired that day. This number obviously did not include the rounds fired by folks who picked up their brass nor those people shooting rimfire cartridges and shotguns. The amount of use on the range was phenomenal.

The range had several regulations that applied, one of which stated shooters were only allowed to shoot paper targets. This rule was frequently violated and created a major problem of having to continuously clean up the trash shooters left behind. We had people who shot everything from rocks to washing machines and most things in between.

There were several folks who used the range on a regular basis, and for the most part, these people did a good job of cleaning up after themselves and policing others. One regular was a fellow who was around eighty years old. I encountered the old man on several occasions. I assumed the man was a navy veteran based on the tattoos—or what used to be tattoos—on his forearms. I went to church with a couple of navy veterans who both had the same green blobs on their arms, so I felt it stood to reason that he was a member of that cohort.

Early one morning, I stopped by the range and found the old fellow there shooting his pistol. As I was looking at the spent brass to see what all had been shot (over the years I found a little bit of everything), I noticed the man had a target on the ground approximately fifteen yards downrange. The "target" was unlike any that I had ever seen anyone shoot previously. He had a small piece of wood driven in the ground, and resting against it was what appeared to be a sanitary napkin. This obviously got my attention and brought some questions to mind. However, I wasn't really sure just what or how to ask. The guy was standing there with a loaded gun and was doing his best to poke holes in a feminine hygiene product. What do you say to that? I tried to be nonchalant when I commented about the unusual target the fellow was shooting at.

The man didn't skip a beat when he replied, "It's a Kotex."

Once again, I was at a loss for what to say next. I looked at the fellow with what I thought was a good "I need more info" look, but he simply went back to loading his pistol. There was a lot going through my mind. Could the man not find any other "paper" to shoot or did he have something against women or what?

I regained my composure and asked, "Do you find that makes a good target?"

He replied, "Yeah. It has powder on it, and that way I can tell whether or not I hit it."

Whew! Was I ever relieved! I had hoped there would be a reasonable explanation. I would not have thought of that myself, and evidently very few others have thought of it either since this was the only "Kotex shooter" I ever encountered.

You've heard it said that necessity is the mother of invention. This guy found an interesting way of being able to know whether or not he was hitting his target. If you don't have a target or goal, it is often difficult to know whether or not you are making progress. This fellow was of the generation who, when they came up against a problem, found a way to solve it. Unfortunately, I fear that skill is falling by the wayside daily.

LIKE MARSH MADILLON

CONSERVATION LAW ENFORCEMENT is not for wimps. FBI statistics show conservation enforcement officers (CEOs) are nine times more likely to be assaulted with a dangerous weapon than are traditional law enforcement officers. While many of the duties of a CEO are dangerous, one I considered extremely dangerous and one of my least favorites was approaching a baited stand. Do not misunderstand me. I thoroughly enjoyed apprehending those who would place an attractant out for wildlife and illegally attempt to ambush the wildlife that responded to the bait. Although the laws concerning baiting have been loosened across the country, I continue to believe the practice of baiting is unethical and detrimental to wildlife. There is no doubt that congregating wildlife by supplying them with what is often harmful feed should not be allowed. Anyone who has the well-being of the resource at heart would not allow such to occur. I digress.

Approaching someone who is armed, who knows they are in willful violation of the law, and who understands they will surely receive a ticket that will cost them several hundred dollars is not an enviable position. Most CEOs are in this position multiple times each year. Whenever possible I would attempt to lessen the danger by approaching the stand overlooking the baited area from behind.

Unfortunately, this wasn't always possible. Furthermore, you never really knew if anyone would be hunting the bait, and if they were, there was no guarantee they would be in the stand you had located. On numerous occasions, I have stealthily approached a shooting house overlooking bait only to find the hunter either in a climbing tree stand or sitting on the ground. There is no way of knowing how many times I simply did not find the hunter who was somewhere other than where I thought they would be.

Another technique I would often use to minimize the danger and lessen the chance of a hunter spotting me approaching them was to enter the area long before daylight and wait on the violator to come to me. This was the tactic I employed on opening day of the gun deer season on a parcel adjacent to the Kaul Timber Company property in northwest Coosa County.

Coosa County is 92 percent forested and therefore used to be home to many timber companies. One of the largest was and still is today the Kaul Timber Company. Kaul, as we referred to it, was comprised of nearly thirty thousand acres of primarily longleaf pine forests. Longleaf is the native pine in this area of the state. The longleaf pine ecosystem dominated the southern landscape covering ninety-two million acres historically. Beginning around 150 years ago, over-exploitation began to accelerate exponentially across the landscape, taking a toll on the resource. Eventually, mechanized harvest methods allowed the resource to be impacted unlike ever before. Previously, the ecosystem was managed naturally by low-intensity frequent fire. Over time, fire was minimized, and the resource suffered. Unbelievably, the longleaf pine ecosystem dwindled to only three million acres. Fortunately, in the past few years, through the efforts of groups such as the Longleaf Alliance, the Natural Resource Conservation Service, and the US Forest Service, there has been a major push to reestablish longleaf in its historic range. This ecosystem is a major benefit to wildlife when the stands are managed with prescribed fire. I digress. I do that a lot.

Due to receiving some good information during the archery deer season, I had located a ladder stand in a pine plantation overlooking a tripod feeder filled with corn. I assumed it was a bow-hunting setup since the stand was only about fifteen yards from the bait and was located in fairly thick woods, which did not allow a long shot in any direction. Bow hunters would normally get as close to the bait as possible to hopefully insure they could make a killing shot on any deer that came in close proximity to the bait. I had checked the area several times during the bow season but had yet to find anyone in the stand. As was always the case with every trip into the area, you increased the risk of someone spotting you and telling the illegal hunter of your presence in the area. The odds of me being at the corn at the same time the hunter was were slim enough as it was, and I didn't need anyone tipping them off. People just didn't seem to understand these outlaws were stealing from them by taking deer illegally.

After hiding my Tahoe on the Kaul property, I was thinking surely the culprit would hunt the corn this morning. I made my way along the now familiar path in the dark without using a light. I followed a firebreak, an eight-foot-wide dirt lane along the property line used to control prescribed fire and protect from wildfire, for a couple of hundred yards until I reached the small pine tree lying across the path. I stepped over the tree and turned into the woods toward the feeder, which was about twenty-five yards off the fire lane. I couldn't help but think I had created a better path into the area than the violator had!

As I slowly closed in on the feeder in the predawn darkness, suddenly directly in front of me appeared a small red light. "Laser sight" was my first startled thought. Although I am no Marshal Dillon, I think Matt would have been proud of how fast my hand instinctively dropped to my Glock model 35 handgun and removed it from the holster. At the same time, I was moving to my left behind the cover of a pine tree, as if the six-inch-in-diameter pine would afford my near three-hundred-pound frame much concealment. Simultaneously, I was also finding my flashlight with my left hand. Looking back, it was amazing how all the training kicked in just like the instructors always said it would.

Although I'm sure it took only a few seconds for all of this to occur, a lot was going through my mind. Since I failed to hear a loud boom, I reasoned the red light was not a laser sight. At least, if it was, luckily no one had fired a shot. The beam of my flashlight revealed the red light was emitting from a camera. That revelation gave me a measure of relief; however, it took a minute or two to regain my composure. As I was allowing my heart rate to return to a somewhat normal range, I came to the realization that in all likelihood there would be a picture of me with my pistol pointed directly into a camera plastered all over Facebook by the end of the day! The huge influx of cameras over the past few years had made it somewhat common to see the photo of a game warden who had been "caught" by one of the cameras on social media. I figured if the camera had captured me with my handgun pointed directly into the lens, it would likely go viral!

I made my way to my hiding spot and waited on the violator. I knew if he didn't show up today the chance of catching him would probably go out the window. He never showed, and if the photo ever showed up on social media, I never heard about it. Yes, working bait was a dangerous endeavor!

A note of clarification. One of my all-time favorite television shows is *Gunsmoke*. As a matter of fact, at the time of this writing, I watch *Gunsmoke* reruns almost every weekday! When my youngest son was very small, he shortened Marshall Matt

Dillon's name to Marsh MaDillon. Hence the name of this story. Today that "little boy" is six feet six inches tall (one inch shy of James Arness—Marshall Dillon) and is a senior at Mississippi State University, where he is completing a degree in criminology with a goal of becoming a United States marshal. This one's for you, son.

LITTERING!

SOME VIOLATORS ARE just a little harder to reach than others. One such violator was Donnie Philbert. My first encounter with Mr. Philbert was while working the deer decoy along with Conservation Enforcement Officer (CEO) Hershel Patterson on the Kaul Timber Company property in north Coosa County. The Kaul property was a favorite for violators. The property had been managed as a quail plantation for many years. It was thousands of acres of mature longleaf pine trees. With the exception of some areas of rampant bicolor lespedeza, the thinned pines offered good visibility. The area had a good deer population and a good road network, which constituted a substantial temptation for "window shoppers," our pet name for those who enjoyed hunting illegally from the comfort of their truck seat. These "road warriors" were our target early one frosty December morning.

Hershel and I had set the deer about one hundred yards off the paved county road in the big pines. Soon after setting up, a small pickup eased to a stop in the road, and the passenger let loose a blast from a 7mm magnum rifle, sending a bullet through the decoy's neck. We pulled into the road behind the truck and moved toward the two violators. While approaching the cab of the vehicle, a quick glance in the bed of the truck revealed what appeared to be a freshly killed doe fawn. The subjects, local constables no less, were arrested, and the deer was seized. The culprits were charged with hunting from the public road and hunting by the aid of a vehicle. Normally a fistful of tickets and the embarrassment of getting caught will slow down criminal activity; however, some violators are a little slow on the uptake. Such was the case with Mr. Philbert.

In response to complaints, wildlife biologist Gene Carver and I were working a decoy detail in a remote area of the county on Holly Springs Road; once again on Kaul Timber Company property. We had already had a good day catching three road hunters right off the bat. Believe me when I tell you the "road warriors" were out in force. We were back in position waiting on the next prospect when a pickup eased along the road. "Get ready," Gene whispered into the radio. Within seconds, *py-yow*, a shot rang out, and I was spinning and sliding down the muddy road toward the violator.

As I came around the curve in the road, I observed the passenger walking back to the open door of the truck and placing his rifle inside. I noted the driver was sitting behind the steering wheel. I pulled up and exited my vehicle and immediately recognized the passenger as Mr. Philbert and the driver as his son. Mr. Philbert immediately pointed at his son and exclaimed, "He did it! I told him not to, but he shot it!" I told him I had an officer who would tell me what happened.

Violators often did not realize we were normally watching them when they shot the decoy. Therefore, they were prone to deny what we were accusing them of. It was imperative that we had an officer situated so they could see the manikin and hopefully to keep someone from stealing it. Yes, we had that happen!

LITTERING!

Gene soon arrived and told me the passenger had exited the truck with his rifle and ran around behind the truck, and the driver had shot from inside the vehicle. I read the duo the Miranda warning, and they stated they understood. I asked dad, the local constable who Hershel and I had apprehended earlier in the year, what was going on.

He stated they had seen the deer, and he had gotten out of the truck and started into the woods to hunt the deer when his son shot from the truck.

I asked, "So you were going into the woods to hunt the deer?"

He emphatically replied, "Yes!"

I asked if he had a permit for the property, and he replied he did and produced one from his wallet. I again asked if he was going into the woods to hunt the deer, and he again replied, "Yes."

I could tell he was feeling pretty good about things until I asked where his hunter orange was. He stammered around and finally stated he didn't have any. He then qualified that statement, saying he did have some orange, but he had forgotten to bring it with him. I could tell it was very important for him to tell the truth!

I asked for the driver's license from both subjects and began writing the tickets. I wrote the driver for hunting from a public road and hunting by aid of a vehicle. I explained the tickets to the driver and allowed him to sign his bonds. He had very little to say. Gene had prepared the tickets for Mr. Philbert. He explained he was being charged with hunting from a public road, hunting without wearing hunter orange, and littering. Mr. Philbert took the first two charges in stride, but when he heard the littering charge, he hit top limb!

"Littering!" he yelled. "What do you mean, 'littering'?"

To which Gene replied, "I mean when you pulled up and threw that beer can out. That's littering, and you're under arrest for it!"

Although he could have easily bitten a nail in half, the violator signed the tickets and was on his way.

At district court, seeing how he had been in court the previous month for the same offenses, the judge had not forgotten Mr. Philbert and was not happy to see him again. Our judge used to have a saying he liked to use that went something like, "This isn't Sears and Roebuck, and we don't want your repeat business!"

I was somewhat surprised that the judge did not erupt on the man as he was prone to do. Mr. Philbert did receive the maximum fine and costs on each charge, including a $500 fine for littering. In addition, the judge levied an additional $1,000 worth of restitution for damage caused to the decoy. I quietly informed the judge that although the son had shot the decoy, Mr. Philbert had not.

The judge replied, "That's okay, we'll have a deer on every corner."

I don't know if this trip to court broke the fellow of his road hunting habit; however, I do know our complaints on him sure slowed down!

Although I wrote many littering tickets during my career, I never received a $500 fine for any of them. I worked with Gene Carver for many years, and we made many cases together, but that littering case was one of the best he ever wrote. Thanks Gene.

We all do things every day that we feel are insignificant. Throwing a beer can out the window was probably something this violator did several times a day without a second thought.

What about you? Do you have anything you do on a regular basis without even thinking about it? Is it a habit or maybe a phrase you utilize regularly? If you listen to folks speak, you will find many who will say "You know what I mean" or "By Golly," or if you are of today's generation, you may say "like" before and after every word. Unfortunately, it may be something much worse. The Bible says we will give an account for every idle word. Every thoughtless action. The key fellow in this story is no longer with us. I do not know where he is spending eternity, but I know where I will spend it. You can know too.

NO HEADLIGHTS IN TEXAS

Responding to a not-in-progress domestic violence call in a trailer park, Coosa County Deputy Mike Rudd and I turned onto Trailer Park Road. Calls in the trailer park were commonplace, and we had made the trip many times. As we reached the crest of a hill, we met a car driving down the middle of the road with no lights on. We immediately pulled to the right and activated our blue lights. The driver stopped about forty yards down the road. There was a young man and a small boy in the car.

As we approached the car, Mike said to the driver, "Don't you know you are supposed to have your headlights on at night?" While I knew this was a rhetorical question, the driver evidently didn't.

The man replied, "I didn't know—I'm from Texas." I must admit that response surprised me a little bit. I don't know for a fact, but I would assume every state has a law that says when driving a vehicle at night you should have your headlights on.

I asked the man if he had a driver's license, and he replied he did not. I was waiting to see if he would say he didn't know he needed one since he was from Texas. He didn't try that. When I asked why he didn't have a license, he responded he could not pass the eye test. I found that interesting, seeing how he was wearing a set of eyeglasses.

Seeing me looking at his glasses, he removed the glasses from his face and said, "These aren't any good. They are the ones I got in prison."

I thought to myself, "This just keeps getting better."

The fellow explained the prescription was not right, but he had been to an eye doctor and would have some new ones soon.

Deputy Rudd asked why the young child with the man was not in a child restraint, and the fellow replied the child was six years old. The child then replied, "We ain't got no car seat."

It was obvious there wasn't going to be anything right about this stop. We instructed the man to turn around and return to his home and not to get back on the road until he had a proper child restraint, some glasses he could see with, and a driver's license.

You can't make this stuff up!

I have had many violators use the defense that they didn't know. That doesn't work. Not now or later.

I'M A NATIONAL GUARD COLONEL!

WHEN YOU ARE IN LAW ENFORCEMENT, you quickly learn there is no shortage of folks who think the law doesn't apply to them. Every officer has encountered the individual who, for whatever reason, has the mindset they are above the law. Officers are normally pretty good at helping these folks understand anyone can receive a citation or a trip to jail. If a problem arises, it is normally on up the line. The bane of the officer is to be called into the supervisor's office and asked to, or worse yet instructed to, drop a ticket or help someone out. I doubt there is an officer working who hasn't experienced something like that.

My partner, Conservation Enforcement Officer (CEO) Hershel Patterson, related to me an incident where he and CEO Charles Reames encountered a boater who the laws and regulations obviously did not apply to, at least according to him. Lake Martin is one of the largest manmade lakes—if not *the* largest manmade lake—in the country, and it just so happens to cover parts of Coosa, Elmore, and Tallapoosa Counties in east-central Alabama. Obviously, when you have a forty-four-thousand-acre lake with 750 miles of shoreline, it is a tremendous draw for recreational users. The lake is covered up in the summer with swimmers, boaters, fishermen, skiers, and campers. Anytime you put that many user groups together, there will be some conflicts and some danger.

Hershel and Charles were working the lake, checking fisherman just after dark, when they observed a boat moving along the lake with no running lights. While this wasn't necessarily a game and fish violation, the game wardens regularly enforced the water safety rules and regulations as well, especially when it was a significant safety violation. The pair headed toward the darkened craft and stopped it. They informed the boater he was in violation by running along the lake with no navigational lights displayed. He countered that it wasn't dark enough to need lights.

Although it may not seem like it, whether or not it is dark is often a point of contention between game wardens and the public. On many occasions, I have encountered hunters coming out of the woods as much as an hour after sunset. When asked why they stayed in so late, they would often claim they could still see through their scope, so they had stayed in their tree or shooting house. I would normally counter with on a moonlit night and with a good scope you could see at midnight, but that didn't mean it was legal to be hunting then. The lake was really no different in that many folks would claim they could still see, even though to even the most casual observer it was dark. I'm sure you have probably witnessed this on the road with drivers who refuse to turn on their headlights because they can see without them. This is definitely one of my pet peeves.

As the officers wrote the citation, the man continued to plead his case to no avail. They explained the bond and showed the man where to sign. At that point, the man played his hole card. He informed the officers he would have them to know he was a colonel in the Alabama National Guard, and he should definitely not be subjected to such treatment. Although they appreciated his service, it did not amount to a get-out-of-jail-free card, and they instructed him to sign the bond or go to jail. He reluctantly signed the bond and was on his way.

Based on the man's vehement opposition to having received a ticket, the officers debated whether any repercussions would stem from the encounter. While that was difficult to know, there was an interesting phenomenon that often occurred. It seemed it was often the case that the more trouble the violator gave you at the scene the less you would hear from them. Even harder to understand was the fact that the encounters that normally came back to bite you in the last part over the fence were the ones where you didn't arrest anyone. Go figure!

Unfortunately, this guy was a little too important to take this citation lying down. The next week he called the Montgomery office to lodge his complaint of how he was wronged by the two officers who obviously could not tell daylight from dark. Seeing how important the man was, he would not waste his time with any low-level supervisors. No, he went straight to the top. Soon he was on the phone with longtime Game and Fish Division Director Charles Kelley. Serving as the director for an unprecedented thirty-nine years, I'm sure Mr. Kelley had handled his share of disgruntled sportsmen.

Evidently the man was using the same argument he had pressed with the officers and wasn't getting very far. Therefore, he again went with the ace up his sleeve. He informed Mr. Kelley he would have him to know he was a colonel in the Alabama National Guard and demanded to be treated with respect. At that point, Director Kelley, a brigadier general in the Alabama National Guard, began to put his many years of military supervisory vocabulary into action. It is my understanding those in the adjacent office were afraid the phone was going to melt. The tongue-lashing culminated with the general informing the man he had better not ever hear of him attempting to use his position in the guard to get him out of anything or he likely would not have a position in the guard. The fine was paid the next day. Imagine that.

What about you? Can you relate to the guy in this story? Are you just a little too important to have to play by the rules? Do they not apply to you? It is amazing how things change when we come face to face with real authority. We will all one day meet the real authority. We will stand before Him and give an account of our life. Are you ready? For by grace are ye saved through faith; and that not of yourselves: it is the gift of God. Not of works, lest any man should boast.

LOOK DADDY

KIDS SAY THE DARNEDEST THINGS. That is especially true when they are young outlaws in training. It was a bad way to get taken down; however, it could have been worse.

I have heard several statistics through the years concerning how much more likely it is for a conservation officer to be assaulted than for other police officers. I remember well my feeling when my first partner told me that when he began his career, 10 percent of all officers working had been shot. He went on to explain how an earlier partner of his had been shot and killed by night hunters. Suffice it to say all law enforcement jobs are dangerous. However, if you really want to talk about something dangerous, we should talk about those conservation officers who work covertly. Unlike other covert officers who had hidden cameras, audio equipment, and officers listening nearby ready to rush in, the covert conservation officer was often totally on his own with only his wits to guide him and allow him to survive. The stories these guys tell can leave a tough man curled in the fetal position, sucking his thumb!

Years ago, our department had no covert "unit." We had one officer, who worked in uniform in a county, who handled basically all of our undercover investigations. He was worked to death, but he was great at his job. So good, in fact, he was requested by numerous state and federal agencies to assist them with covert operations all over the country.

Obviously, there was much more work than one man could handle; therefore, from time to time, he would enlist the assistance of other officers. I listened with interest as one officer relayed the details of his short-lived covert career. He was asked to assist the undercover in infiltrating a rogue bunch of dog deer hunters who were running roughshod over landowners and wearing out the resource in the north part of Alabama. Our covert officer had already made an initial contact with the group and hoped to "hunt" with them and catalog their violations. The plan was to "inadvertently" bump into the group on Saturday morning and hopefully have plenty of evidence by the end of the day.

The two officers easily located the hunters as they were assembling on a county road and preparing to release their dogs. Making cases for illegally hunting with dogs was often difficult in that the officer really needed to see the people releasing their dogs in an area where they did not have permission to hunt. The fact these folks were getting ready to do just that was encouraging. Our undercover had engaged one of the group leaders in what appeared to be some light banter, but in truth he was gathering pertinent information that would likely come into play shortly. In addition, he was solidifying his role as an outlaw. Things were looking good.

Research has repeatedly shown that most violators participate in their first violation at an early age. The term *like father, like son* was one we often used. In our wildlife vernacular, we would often say the acorn didn't fall far from the tree. This group of hunters was your typical group in that it contained grandpas, daddies, and juniors.

I would venture a guess that the juniors probably were the last thing on the officers' minds. It is difficult to keep your head on a swivel, watching everything that is going on without looking like you are watching everything that is going on. Working undercover demands that you make a lot of mental notes that you will record later to be used in court down the road. While details vary, you may go to court the next month, or it could be several months. Therefore, documenting everything is essential.

Oddly enough, it was one of the kids who quickly ended this covert operation. A young boy, maybe eleven or twelve years old, walked over to the newly covert officer, pointed at his feet, and exclaimed to his nearby father, "Look Daddy, he's wearing game warden boots." As the expression goes, you couldn't have driven a pin up the officer's rear end with a sledge hammer! For many years leading up to this time, all officers were issued green Browning boots. Wearing the boots every day, it did not cross his mind that he should wear something else.

The youth's proclamation, coupled with the fact that the officer's entire head was now beet red, prompted the experienced officer to come up with a good reason for them to leave. Fortunately, they survived what could have been a life-changing mistake. Unfortunately, the covert recruit saw his covert career come to a screeching halt. Dang kids.

What about you, have you ever made a mistake? We all have sinned and come short of the glory of God. Rarely do we have someone step up and point out our sin. That's all the more reason we need to understand what sin is, do our best to eliminate it from our life, and most importantly understand forgiveness and salvation are available through Jesus Christ.

Ironically, as I am preparing to send this to the editor, it is Father's Day. My dad went to be with the Lord almost three years ago. My father-in-law did the same this year. I praise the Lord for having those fine men in my life and for what I learned from them. I pray I have passed on some Godly wisdom to my sons. What are you passing on to those who are learning from you?

NO FIRST CLASS FOR YOU

I KNEW SOMETHING WAS WRONG when the plane backed away from the gate and then pulled right back in. Soon the captain came over the intercom and informed us they had discovered a problem with the hydraulic system of the plane and were going to need to have it looked at. Shortly thereafter, I spotted a guy wearing coveralls and carrying a roll of duct tape coming toward our plane and then disappearing under the wing. After a forty-seven-minute delay, the captain again came on the public-address system and told us things had been patched up, and we were good to go. I didn't have a good feeling when we backed away from the gate. While that was a fairly long delay, on my next trip I would learn, as folks around here say, that wuttin nuthin!

A highlight of my career was working with the 4-H Wildlife Habitat Evaluation Program (WHEP). This is a tremendous program designed to teach kids from nine to nineteen years of age how to evaluate habitat for wildlife. Students must learn about a wide array of species in their area. They learn to identify the species, what the species requires as food and cover, and how to manipulate habitat to provide benefits for selected species. In addition, the participants are required to evaluate habitat from aerial photographs and give oral reasons as to which property was the best habitat for the target species. They are also required to develop a written management plan, complete with a habitat evaluation and recommendations for habitat improvement. It was a comprehensive undertaking.

Much more than just learning about wildlife, the students developed critical life skills and how to work as a team. I literally saw participation in this program change the lives of kids in our county. I began as a coach for our county team and ended up serving on the national committee for fourteen years. I had the opportunity to work with many great wildlife professionals and to train a lot of great kids, many of whom went on to become my coworkers. I was afforded the opportunity to travel all over the United States, and it was often a wild ride.

These adventures were interesting, to say the least. For many years, I traveled with Dr. Jim Armstrong, who chaired the national committee for several years and who had extended me the invitation to be part of the group. Jim was the wildlife specialist at Auburn University, which was only sixty miles from my home, so we often rode and flew together to 4-H events. Although many of these trips are memorable, one really stands out.

Jim, wildlife biologist Ashley (Rossi) Lovell, and I had flown from Atlanta to Dallas and then to Kansas City. The contest moved to a different state each year. It was generally hosted by the state extension wildlife specialist. By moving state to state, the participants and their coaches were often exposed to vastly different habitats than they were accustomed to. I remember when we took a team to Utah, and our team members asked, "Are there not any trees out here?" I also remember when the contest was held in the Chihuahuan Desert. I guarantee you that didn't look much like Alabama!

This contest was hosted by my good friend, Charlie Lee. We often called Charlie "Mr. Excitement," since nothing seemed to excite him. Whatever came along, he took it in stride and never seemed to get worked up over anything. That says something when you are hosting one hundred teenagers, their coaches, and many parents. Charlie had it all together.

Things went fairly well with the contest. The committee usually had to be on-site for five or six days, and by the end of that time, we were more than ready to return home. The flight back to Dallas was uneventful; however, that was where the uneventful part ended. I had flown enough to know anything could happen when it came to planes and airports. That knowledge was about to be reinforced. It began when our flight was delayed due to the lack of a flight crew. It seems our crew had logged too much flight time and had to get some mandatory rest. That sure sounded like poor planning to me. We were assured another crew was on the way. That assurance wore thin after the first hour. After several hours, we were told we had a crew, but the airplane would now have to be cooled down before anyone could board, and it would take a while. Even in a large airport like Dallas, there is only so much you can do to entertain yourself in an airport in the middle of the night.

After waiting yet another hour, I went to the desk and inquired as to how much longer it would be. The lady was very apologetic. She assured me we would be in the air soon and again apologized. She told me due to our long ordeal she was going to upgrade me to first class. I thanked her and returned to my seat. Jim had gone to the restroom, so I told Ashley to go to the desk and ask the lady to upgrade her. She did. When Jim returned, we told him they were giving us an upgrade to first class, and he needed to go and see the lady. Jim went over and soon returned, and he was not happy!

Now I have worked with Jim for many years, and I can count on one hand the number of times I've seen him get upset. This was the first time I had ever seen him mad. We asked what happened, and he stated, in an angry, belligerent tone, "First class is full!"

Soon the call came to board the plane. If you've ever flown, you know that they board the first-class passengers first. It was a little awkward when Ashley and I left Jim behind to go and find our seats. We quickly got settled in on opposite sides of the first-class cabin. It was then I remembered one of Jim's biggest pet peeves about flying. On numerous occasions, he had commented about how much it irritated him that people in first class would not make eye contact with the coach passengers passing through. I looked over at Ashley and I told her, "When Jim comes through—*no* eye contact."

As we waited for Jim to board, I obtained a newspaper and was holding it ready to put it in front of my face as soon as I knew Jim had seen me. After a brief wait, it was time for the common folk to load the plane. Soon Jim rounded the corner. As soon as we made eye contact, I immediately pulled the newspaper up. I guess I had underestimated just how upset he was. This was the second time I had seen Jim *mad*.

"Oh, that's real funny," he sputtered as he made his way to the back of the plane.

When I say the back of the plane, I mean the very back of the plane. He was seated right beside the toilet. Furthermore, nearly the entire coach section of the plane was occupied by a family who was returning from a family reunion in Jamaica. While they were all in a celebratory mood, each time I was able to sneak a peek into the coach section, Jim looked like someone who had to sit next to the toilet while his friends sat in first class!

Fortunately, we all survived the trip. As I relayed the events of our ordeal to my seat mate in first class, he told me I probably should not expect my bags to be in Atlanta when we arrived. He was prophetic. I got them two days later.

I want to take this opportunity to thank Jim for allowing me to serve on the national WHEP committee. As I said earlier, it was one of the highlights of my career. I thank Roger Vines, our county extension agent, for allowing me to assist in coaching the teams. It did not cross my mind when I began training our students that one day I would be working right alongside some of them. I am very proud of their accomplishments and cherish the memories of seeing them develop.

RIGHT PLACE, RIGHT TIME

ONE OF THE MOST FRUSTRATING THINGS for me as a conservation enforcement officer was the complainant who called me after the fact. Don't misunderstand me; it was always good to get information. However, hearing about someone shooting at night a week after it had occurred wasn't nearly as helpful as getting the call immediately. Many people would say they hated to wake or bother me late at night, or they were sure the people would be gone before I could get there. However, many times I would have to tell them if they had called when the incident occurred, I was only a mile from their location. Fortunately, every once in a while, when the shooting became too regular, some landowners would begin calling as soon as they heard the shot. Such was the case late one night.

The hunting of deer at night was widespread across Coosa County. The deer standing along the road proved to be too much of a temptation for folks. It seemed many folks were of the opinion there was no need to spend all day outside in the cold when you could see more deer and get an easy shot at a deer right on the side of the road at night. Furthermore, they reasoned the chances of getting caught were between slim and none since the game wardens were spread thin.

In response to complaints, wildlife biologist Gene Carver and I had been working a night hunting detail in the far north part of the county and decided to head for home around midnight. As I was south of Weogufka, I received a call from the sheriff's office stating they had just received a night hunting complaint from the Mt. Moriah area. My heart skipped a beat as I realized I was within a quarter mile of Mt. Moriah Church and had to be right on top of the night hunters. Believe me when I tell you when you were trying to cover an entire county of 652 square miles, that didn't happen very often.

The dispatcher went on to say the caller had said they had heard a shot on the Foshee place. The Foshee property was somewhat of an anomaly in Coosa County in that it contained actual farm land. This was rare in our county, which was 92 percent forested. We didn't grow many vegetables, but we grew millions of pine trees! I knew the Foshee place pretty well and turned in front of the church and headed in that direction. I radioed Gene and told him about the call, and he said he would come in from the north, and hopefully we could box them in between us. It was indeed rare to have two units in the area with one on each side of the violators. We hoped that was the case.

I quickly made my way to a high point overlooking the Foshee bottoms and turned off my lights. I had not seen any vehicles on my way in, and I now stood in the dark silence, listening for anything. The night was overcast, which hampered my ability to hear; however, I soon heard a vehicle approaching quickly from the north, and figured it was Gene. After the vehicle came pulling up on me with no lights on, I sure hoped it was Gene. Running without any lights on was a standard technique we employed until our department developed a policy forbidding it. It was often an effective technique. Not necessarily the safest thing to do, but effective.

Gene exited his truck and stated he had not met any vehicles on the road. This meant they either got out ahead of us or were still in the bottoms. You never really knew how long the caller had waited before calling in the complaint nor how long it took the dispatcher to get the report to us. We hoped it had been quick enough that the culprits were still in the area.

The Foshee property contained several large fields encircled by a paved county road; however, the fields could not be seen from the road. As Gene and I stood listening, we both looked at each other and simultaneously said, "Four-wheeler."

As we searched the darkness, we saw what we thought was a light in the fields below. We began racking our brains, trying to decide where the off-road vehicle would emerge from the fields. Obviously, being an ATV, it could make a way out in any direction. Our hope was they would take the path of least resistance and use the paved road we were sitting in.

The main entrance to the farm was north of us about one-half mile up the county road, and Gene decided he should move to that area in case they exited there and went in the other direction. I advised I would stay put and stop anything that came my way. Without turning on any lights, Gene started toward the farm entrance. He had gone maybe a couple hundred yards when I saw his headlights come on. Illuminated in the road in front of his vehicle was a four-wheeler. I immediately started my truck and took off toward his location. As I was nearing his truck, I observed that one four-wheeler was stopped in front of him, but another was headed straight at me. I pulled on my headlights and activated my blue lights, while sliding sideways in front of the fast-moving vehicle. The ATV slid to a stop, and I quickly recognized the riders as Johnny and his wife Janey. I jumped out of the truck and ordered Johnny to cut the machine off. He did so and quickly said, "We ain't doing nothing but looking, Mr. Glover."

The fact they had been looking was evident by the million-candle spotlight in the front rack of the ATV. While Johnny was telling me they didn't have a weapon, I was scanning them with my flashlight. Not seeing a weapon, I shot a glance toward Gene and saw him taking a rifle from the driver of the other ATV. At this point I used a technique that often worked in this type situation. I did not ask what was going on, I simply stated matter-of-factly they knew this kind of thing was wrong. Johnny started to protest but then just lowered his head and said, "I know it."

With Johnny and Janey secured, I moved to Gene to see what he had. When I got to where I could see the individuals on the second four-wheeler, I realized it was Johnny's brother, Bobby, and his wife, Betty. When Bobby saw me, he started shaking his head. I asked him if they had killed a deer, and he said they had not. I asked where all they had been hunting, and he said just in the fields on the Foshee place.

We gathered all four together and, seeing how it had started to rain, we told them we would follow them to their home, which was only about a mile away, and would handle all the paperwork there. I thought this was a good idea; however, Janey immediately spoke up with an emphatic, "No!" This took me by surprise. I asked her why not, and she replied, "Because my father-in-law is over there, and I don't want to embarrass him."

Therefore, the four sat in the rain while Gene and I wrote them tickets for hunting at night and hunting by aid of a vehicle. I explained to Johnny and Bobby their four-wheelers were subject to being confiscated in the event they were convicted of hunting at night. Johnny replied that if that was the case, he was going to stop making the payments on his machine. I assured him that would be between him and his finance company. The two couples headed for home.

Gene and I marveled at how quickly things could go from

nothing to something. We were fortunate to have been in the right place at the right time, proving the old adage even a blind hog finds an acorn every once in a while.

The four defendants appeared in court the following month. In a plea agreement, they pled guilty to the charges and paid fines and court costs totaling over $3,000. They were allowed to retain their rifle and four-wheelers. You may be wondering why we would make an agreement in a case like this one. If you were paying close attention, you may have noticed I did not mention advising them of their rights prior to asking some questions. While that wasn't unusual in some cases and wasn't insurmountable, we didn't want it to become a factor.

You may have also noticed we didn't technically see the group "hunting." They did not deny they were hunting; they fulfilled the elements of the crime and indicated that was what they were doing. They were obviously guilty. However, you need to understand guilty folks walk out of court every day on technicalities. Therefore, we decided to be more than pleased with convictions on all counts and $3,000. We were glad to be in the right place at the right time!

NOT WHAT THEY WANTED
(SORRY ABOUT YOUR GUN)

AFTER HEARING A SHOT and receiving a call from his partner, the "chase" vehicle headed to the location of the decoy deer. As he neared the location, he saw his partner with his gun drawn and pointing at an individual on the side of the road. He raced to the scene and slid to a stop. He noticed the violator staring a whole through him with a sick look on his face.

So many times in my career, someone put an action in motion that ended up resulting in the opposite result than what they wanted. This often had to do with our receiving a complaint and then apprehending the "wrong" person. Speaking with other officers, I have learned this wasn't unique to me. Talladega County Conservation Enforcement Officer (CEO) Jerry Fincher shared with me the story of how he received complaints from two brothers. While one complained of people shooting deer at night, the other brother complained about people hunting from the public road.

Jerry and his partner, Greg Gilliland, decided to utilize the deer decoy to see if they could help squelch the complaints and protect the resource. The decoy was "the" mechanism to put the quarry, the outlaw, and the officer in the same place at the same time. It was and is a tremendous tool. The fake deer was placed along a field edge, and CEO Gilliland positioned himself in the ditch directly across from the manikin. Fincher waited in his truck a couple of hundred yards down the road. We called this the "chase" vehicle, which was a misnomer, seeing how we had it there to avoid having to chase someone. I was in several chases during my career, more with the sheriff's office than with game and fish. Chases were dangerous and often ended in torn-up vehicles and injuries. They were best avoided.

It wasn't long until a van traveling along the road came to a stop, and the driver exited the vehicle with his rifle in hand. While most people shot while seated in the vehicle, it wasn't unusual for someone to get out of the vehicle and shoot. As Greg watched, the man knelt in the center of the road and fired at the decoy deer. Greg called for Jerry, and then stepped out of his hiding spot. He ordered the man to put his gun down. Instead, the man urgently started toward the officer pleading his case. I have had this happen, and it is a very difficult and dangerous situation for everyone involved. While the shooter likely didn't mean to threaten the officer, his coming toward him with a loaded gun in hand is a serious interaction. Greg again gave a loud verbal command for the man to stop and put his rifle down. He put an exclamation point on this command by drawing his pistol and coming to ready gun. The man complied by placing the gun down in the road; however, he still kept advancing on the officer, wanting to plead his case.

Greg again ordered the man to stop. During this time, Jerry was quickly coming down the road toward the two. When he realized Greg had the man at gunpoint, he pressed the accelerator a little harder. As he slid to a stop and quickly exited his truck, he noticed the defendant was looking at him with a very sick look on his face. While this isn't uncommon of violators who have just been caught red handed, this look was a little different. As Jerry approached the now speechless man he asked where his firearm was, and the man dejectedly pointed to Jerry's truck, where his tire was resting on the man's Belgium-made Browning rifle and Zeiss scope.

With the situation under control, the violator was allowed to plead his case, which sounded so familiar. He started by saying he was the man who had called about the night hunting in the area. Unfortunately for him, he did not know his brother had called about the road hunting!

The man appeared in court and was found guilty and was fined a smashed scope and scraped-up gun by the judge, who felt he had suffered enough damage. You can't make this stuff up!

There is a lot in life that will not turn out the way we wanted. Much of it we have no control over, and much of it we cause. Therefore, we should do our best to properly handle what we do control. It is your choice where you will spend eternity. The truth is you have already made that choice. You have either accepted the salvation Jesus offers or you haven't. If you haven't, it isn't too late. Choose wisely.

YOU CAN CAMP OUT WITH THE SHERIFF!

THE COOSA WILDLIFE MANAGEMENT AREA (WMA), where I was the area biologist for almost eighteen years, was a nonstop source of work. Since the area had two hundred miles of roads open to the public, it drew all types of folks. Along each road was a multitude of bright yellow signs, which informed folks they were on the WMA and special rules and regulations applied. I don't have an exact number, but to say I had posted a thousand of the signs would not be an exaggeration. The regulations not only covered hunting on the area but also the many recreational opportunities the area afforded users. Enforcing the WMA regulations was one of my many duties.

One of the "attractions" on the WMA was an area known as the underwater bridge. I think most people in Coosa and all surrounding counties were familiar with the underwater bridge. The "bridge" was actually a concrete ford across Weogufka Creek. When I went to work on the area, the ford was in pretty bad shape, with many large holes in it. Since we crossed it on an almost daily basis, I thought it would be a good idea to repair it. Unfortunately, neither my BS degree in environmental biology nor my MS in wildlife ecology had provided me with much information in the area of bridge construction. In addition, I had no clue about making concrete repairs in running water. Therefore, I contacted the paper company, which owned the land, for assistance.

The paper company wasn't normally very free with money; however, they did have a full staff of skilled workers who were always helpful. To my good fortune, I found they too wanted the bridge repaired. Therefore, we started on the project. I contacted our office in Montgomery about purchasing the concrete, and surprisingly, the chief agreed.

I contacted the workers and told them we were ready to proceed, but I didn't have a clue as to how. They told me we would build a coffee dam. This was something I had never heard of but soon learned a coffee dam was basically an earthen berm that would temporarily divert the water to the other side of the creek while we poured the concrete. It worked really well. The next day we repeated the scenario on the opposite side of the creek. Things went relatively smoothly except for the fact I had told the chief it would take about nineteen yards of concrete. It took thirty-eight! The chief came up with the money, and the final product was a good bridge that is still in good shape today, some thirty-two years later.

Unfortunately, the new and improved underwater bridge proved to be a major attraction. It evidently was a great place to have a party and leave all your trash, especially used baby diapers! I can tell you many littering tickets were written at the ford. The area was a popular place for parties, bonfires, four-wheelers, and even camping. Of course, many of these activities were in violation of the management area regulations, yet that did little to dissuade people.

Summer was a high-traffic time on the WMA with its two hundred miles of backwoods roads open to traffic. This necessitated that I try to patrol the area fairly regularly. One night, County Forester Blake Kelley and I were riding through the area checking things out when we came around the curve to the underwater bridge. We observed a pickup parked on the south side of the road and a tent pitched on the north side. As I was coming to a stop behind the truck, my headlights illuminated an individual who ran and dove into some small trees and lay still on the ground. Not exactly sure what we might have, we cautiously exited the truck, and I ordered the man lying on the ground to raise his hands, which he did. I told him to get up on his knees. He complied, and I moved in and handcuffed the man. At the same time, Blake was scanning the area with his flashlight and located another man hiding in the bushes. He moved in and handcuffed him. Further scanning of the area didn't reveal anyone else. I asked the men what they were doing, and they stated they were cutting firewood. Keep in mind this was taking place around eleven o'clock at night. A chainsaw was on the ground next to the first subject. When I asked why they were hiding, they replied they did not know who we were and thought they should hide. They stated they did know they were on the WMA; however, they did not know it was against the law to cut trees on the WMA. I asked if they cut trees on the property of other people they did not know. Although it wasn't a rhetorical question, I took their silence as a no.

I had assumed since there was only one vehicle present and two guys cutting firewood near it, the tent and truck belonged to these guys. Well, you've probably heard that saying about assuming. When I informed them I was going to search their truck, they replied, "That's not our truck." A little confused, I asked, "Well how did you get here?" They answered they had arrived in the truck, but it wasn't theirs; it belonged to the guy who was in the tent with his wife. This was interesting information. I did not ask, but I wondered where these two guys had planned to sleep.

I decided to search the truck prior to searching the tent. One luxury we had on all state management areas was a state law giving us the right to search any vehicle within the boundaries of the area without a search warrant. This type of leeway very often led to arrests for a little bit of everything.

A search of the truck revealed a loaded shotgun and rifle. No weapons were allowed on the WMA except during the hunting season, and no loaded firearms were allowed in vehicles at any time. I told Blake we needed to talk to the owner of the truck. I asked the subjects we had in custody for the name of the truck owner and went to the tent.

Unzipping a tent and sticking my head in wasn't something I wanted to do near midnight nor any other time for that matter. After yelling the man's name several times, the subject's wife unzipped the tent and stepped out. I identified myself and told her I needed to talk to her and her husband.

She replied, "He's asleep," and I replied, "Wake him up!"

I asked if there were any weapons in the tent, and she said there was not. She finally got him roused up, and it was painfully obvious when he came out of the tent he wasn't a morning person! He came out grumbling and growling and wanting to know "what the hell" I wanted. From the fragrant smell of alcoholic beverage I could detect from several feet away, he had obviously drunk himself to sleep. And it evidently wasn't beauty sleep.

As he was staggering his way down the incline toward the truck, something told me we were going to have some trouble. I moved to my truck and radioed the sheriff's office and asked if they could send a deputy to the underwater bridge. That was one positive aspect of the spot's popularity. Although it was several miles from a paved road and literally in the middle of nowhere, everyone knew where it was. The dispatcher advised she would have someone en route.

I moved to the front of my truck and began trying to talk to the individual. I inquired as to whether or not the pickup belonged to him, and he belligerently replied, "Hell yeah, what's it to you?"

I informed him I was the area manager and he was in violation of several management area regulations. I advised he was under arrest and needed to place his hands on the hood of my truck.

"F*** you," was his curt response.

At this point, for some reason, I got the distinct feeling this guy wasn't going to cooperate. I had dealt with belligerent people in the past, but this guy was trying to take the cake. I took a deep breath and informed him he was about to make the decision as to whether he would receive a ticket or would spend the night in the Coosa County jail. Although I used my most authoritative tone, I got the distinct impression he wasn't impressed in the least. Fortunately, his wife was sober enough to realize I meant business, and she began pleading with him not to cause any trouble and to do what I had asked.

After a couple of minutes of staring at each other, he reluctantly put his hands on the hood of the truck. As I moved in to handcuff the man, I felt sure the fight would be on when the cuff hit his wrist. I had already decided where I was going to throw him if he resisted when I put the cuff on. I instructed him to put his left hand behind his back. He did not move. His jaw was clenched, and I was thinking he was going to spin around and start swinging at any second. His wife once again starting begging him to comply. Since she had already had much better luck than me, I decided to let her handle it. Another minute passed. I had not said anything while she continued to plead with him. Finally, he reluctantly put his hand behind his back. I put the cuff on it and asked for the other hand. He had to think about it for a few seconds, but he gave me the other hand. I looked at Blake and saw the look of relief on his face and was sure it resembled the look on my face.

Now it was time to sort out what all the violations were. Although I could have written more, I wrote the truck owner a ticket for illegal camping and possession of a firearm without a permit. I also wrote the fellow with the chainsaw a ticket for damaging trees on the WMA. A deputy soon came roaring up, and, although things were under control, I was glad to see him. We uncuffed everyone and allowed them to sign their bonds and we were on our way. On the way out, I once again thanked Blake for agreeing to accompany me. More often than not, a conservation officer worked alone. This was one of those situations where, had I been alone, it may have gotten ugly.

The next night, Blake and I once again decided to patrol the area. With thirty-eight thousand acres to cover, it normally took a few nights to get over the majority of the area. I decided we would work the opposite side of the property, and we started by checking the area known as the public launch. Public launch areas had been built across the state by our fisheries section to provide the public with areas where they could launch their boat. These areas carried several rules and regulations in addition to the long list that applied to the WMA. We pulled into the launch parking area and immediately spotted a pickup, a tent, and a fire. Camping and fires were both violations of launch regulations, so I pulled over to have a talk with the folks sitting near the blazing inferno.

Before exiting the truck, I was keeping an eye on the people and noticed they looked awfully familiar. About the time I was saying, "I don't believe this," Blake said, "That's the people from last night." We exited the truck and slowly walked over to the foursome. I must admit they were a lot more hospitable than they had been the previous night. Of course, I didn't know how long the hospitality would last once I informed the people they were once again in violation of multiple regulations. This time they were so contrite and cooperative I decided a written warning would suffice. I did the paperwork and told the man to show the ticket to anyone else who might check them.

The court date came around the next month and when the cases were called, the defendant and I approached the judge's bench. The judge attempted to read the charges; however, the code for the camping offense was abbreviated in such a way he could not make it out. He asked me what the charge was, and I replied it was an illegal camping charge.

The judge looked at the man and asked, "What's your plea?" The defendant offered a "not guilty" in a somewhat belligerent tone.

This response sort of ticked me off, seeing how I had written him two tickets when it could have been eight; however, I knew his tone would not sit well with the court. The judge told us to raise our hands and be sworn and asked me for the facts of the case. I gave him the short version of how the subject was camping in an illegal area and possessed two loaded weapons in his vehicle. The judge looked at the subject and asked why he had pled not guilty, and he replied he didn't know he couldn't camp there.

Without any fanfare the judge said, "The court finds you guilty. That will be one hundred and fifty dollars fine and costs and thirty days in jail in each case." The judge asked his patented question, "Are you going to pay it or sit it out?" This meant you could either pay the fine and court costs and have the jail time suspended or start serving your sixty days.

The defendant stated he didn't have three hundred dollars, once again using a gruff tone. If the defendant had known the judge like I did, he would have known he wasn't helping himself by acting tough. I wasn't sure how the judge might respond, but I knew it would likely be memorable.

I was not disappointed when the judge looked at the man and said, "Well a man with no money can just go and camp out with the sheriff!" A deputy took the defendant by the arm and sat him in the holding area and began preparing to take him to jail.

In a few minutes, I was approached by the wife of the defendant, who gave me the sad tale of how they were in bankruptcy, and she could only pay $150. I told her if she didn't pay the $300 plus the $180 in court costs, her husband would serve the sixty days in jail. She left near tears.

A few minutes later, I noticed the wife speaking with a local bail bondsman. She returned to me and said she was going to get an appeal bond to keep her husband out of jail. I told her that would be fine; however, the judge would have to set the bond amount. She asked if I would ask the judge to set the bond, and I stated I would.

During the next lull between cases, I approached the bench and informed the judge "the camper" had requested an appeal bond be set in his cases. The judge stated he would gladly do that and asked his secretary for the files. The judge, through his clenched teeth, mumbled something about being tired of frivolous appeals and promptly set the bonds in the amount of $5,000 each. I thanked him and returned to the defendant's wife and told her that today just wasn't her day. She asked what I meant, and I told her the judge had set the bond at $10,000!

"Ten thousand dollars!" she almost screamed. "He can't do that."

I told her unless she wanted to be in jail with her husband, she didn't need to tell the judge what he could and could not do!

At this time, a bail bondsman would typically charge 10 percent to post a bond for someone. The cost on a $10,000 bond would compute to $1,000 dollars, more than double what it would cost to pay the fines and court costs. I again informed her it would be best if she came up with $300 plus costs, and miraculously, before court was over, she did!

It was amazing how often the defendant who appeared before the judge and claimed not to have a cent to their name would end up coming up with enough money to pay their fine to avoid going to jail. While jail is much better than it has ever been, it is still no picnic. Spending time incarcerated served as a deterrent to most folks. Unfortunately, today judges are persuaded by politicians to severely limit the number of folks they send to the pokey to try to control costs. I understand jail is expensive, but so is turning criminals back out on the street so they can go back and do it again. There are a lot of folks walking the street when they need to be camping out with the sheriff.

A DOG NAMED CEDRICK

WHILE DRIVING DOWN a rural Talladega County road, Conservation Enforcement Officer Jerry Fincher noticed a small beagle dog tied in the front yard of a mobile home. The dog closely resembled his dog, which had come up missing a week earlier. He decided it couldn't hurt to stop and inquire about the pup.

The setting was not unlike many low-income areas of rural Alabama. A weather-beaten mobile home or trailer, as they are commonly called, with a red wood porch. That is not a porch made out of redwood; it is a porch made out of wood that has been painted red. This was a common site many years ago.

Feeling the sponginess of the steps, Jerry knew he had to tread lightly lest he might drop through into the pile of beer cans and other trash below the porch. His rap on the door was answered by a young girl maybe eighteen or nineteen years old. Her hair was tied in a heap on top of her head and a cigarette dangled from her lips. Her red tank top and cutoff blue jeans resembled her bare feet in that they all could have used some soap and water.

Although his uniform and corresponding green state truck sitting in the yard would have normally been enough to identify himself, Jerry introduced himself as a state conservation officer.

He told the young lady he was interested in the dog secured by a chain tightly wound around the stake in the front yard. He explained he had previously had a dog much like that one and asked where she had acquired it. She replied her boyfriend had given it to her. He asked how long she had had the dog, and she replied about a week. He told her his dog had been missing for about a week, and he was wondering if this could possibly be his dog. There was a pregnant pause as she contemplated her response.

Suddenly it was as if a light had come on, and she asked the officer, "What was your dog's name?"

Jerry had for some reason not anticipated this question, maybe because it was totally irrelevant, but he answered, "Buddy."

With a look somewhere between relief and smirk, the girl replied, "Oh, that can't be your dog. That dog's name is Cedrick!"

Somewhat baffled by the "logic," Jerry stood there grappling with his response. As she stood giving him an "I'm pretty proud of myself" look, the officer decided there was no need to respond. With a curt "thank you," he turned and negotiated the spongy steps. He entered his truck and drenched himself in hand sanitizer. He wondered if he rubbed some on his ears if he might could forget what he had just heard. You can't make this stuff up!

ON THREE WHEELS

I FEEL CERTAIN every county has its own set of characters. I have read many officers' stories in which I could easily exchange some of my violators for theirs. Obviously, people are the same all over. I love a quote I heard that says, "Remember, you're unique—just like everyone else." Believe me when I tell you our backwoods county had its share of characters.

One character we dealt with on a fairly regular basis would have probably met anyone's definition of a redneck. There were numerous cars up on blocks in the front yard. One end of the deer-skinning rack was attached to the end of the house trailer. There were at least four dogs that lived under the red wood porch. That was wood that was painted red, not actually redwood; seriously, this was popular in the south many years ago. I trust you have the picture.

The fellow worked for the county road department, which allowed him to have a county radio. At that time, the county shop and the sheriff's office shared a radio frequency. This was a real problem. More than once, I've heard an officer reporting a serious situation be talked over by a road crew member requesting someone grab his lunch out of the truck or bring him a shovel. It was a bad situation that thankfully was straightened out eventually.

Conservation Enforcement Officer Hershel Patterson and I were set up working the night hunting of deer that was rampant in the south end of the county when I heard the county worker's familiar voice come over the radio, calling "Base." The dispatcher told him to go ahead, and he informed everyone listening he had just seen a small white car going past his house, and he didn't think the occupants had any business being there. Now while I am all for people feeling secure in their home and their right to defend that, the problem was this fellow's house was fifty feet from the paved public county road. This road was open to traffic, and anyone with a driver's license and a properly licensed vehicle was allowed to drive down the road. This was probably the reason the dispatcher answered him with a simple 10-4, and nothing else was said. We sat in the darkness and speculated there had to be more to the story than what we had heard. Not hearing any more radio traffic, we didn't give it much more thought.

Approximately fifteen minutes later the fellow again came on the radio with a totally different demeanor. His voice was now high pitched as he screeched, "Base!" The dispatcher answered, and the man told him the car had just come back by his house, and he had blown the rear wheel off with a 30-06, and they are going down Highway 231 on three wheels. Although we were having some trouble believing what we heard, I immediately started my truck and headed toward Highway 231. Coosa County Deputy Brett Oakes called the dispatcher and stated he was en route. We contacted him, informing him we were near the area and would see if we could locate the vehicle and make sure no one had been injured.

As we neared Coosa County Road 10, we spotted a small white car on the right side of the road. Realizing the car was parked in front of what was known as Killingworth's old store, we feared the situation may have gone from bad to worse. Although the store had been closed for several years, the cantankerous old owner still lived in the old building. I had been warned by the two game wardens in the county not to stop in front of the store since the old man had been known to come out and shoot the tires of vehicles. A couple of years earlier, a local state trooper told me he had stopped a car in front of the house one night, and the old man had come out and attempted to run him off. I was thinking this is all these folks needed.

There were three people standing outside the small car, and they were indeed changing a rear tire. Without letting on that we knew anything about what had transpired, we asked everyone's name and gave them every opportunity to tell us what had happened. Not one of them mentioned what had caused their flat tire. Fortunately, no one came out of the old store, and the trio soon had the spare in place and took off down the road.

We made our way back to our night hunting surveillance location and sat there in the dark wondering why three guys, who had just had someone, apparently unknown to them, shoot the tire off their car as they drove down the public road, would not take the opportunity to report that to law enforcement. We got to thinking the shooter may have been on to something when he said they were up to no good.

While it was totally unrelated, and we will never know what was going on that night, I found it interesting that one of the three in the car was convicted of a home invasion murder a few years later!

SEVERE HANDICAP

"I'M 10-100." Those words would always get the attention of any officer monitoring the radio since 10-100 was the radio code for a pursuit. Pursuits were fairly common early in my career. However, in the latter years, due to increased liabilities and resulting stricter pursuit policies, these chases became fairly rare.

Conservation Enforcement Officer Hershel Patterson and I were working one night when we heard our local state trooper call the Coosa County sheriff's office and state he was 10-100 southbound on Highway 231 north of Rockford. Seeing how we were in Rockford directly in front of him, we decided to head toward him and lend any assistance we could. We were hurriedly moving his way when he again came on the radio and reported he was still in pursuit, but the offender had slowed to about ten miles per hour but was refusing to stop. That was good news, seeing how it was raining lightly and the road was pretty slick.

When the trooper's blue lights first came into our view, the fleeing driver decided to pull over. As we pulled to a stop, the trooper was removing the driver from the car and placing him in his patrol vehicle. He briefly spoke with us, telling us the subject was obviously drunk. I noticed the trooper made a pretty quick decision without the benefit of any field sobriety tests; however, I knew he had been doing this for a while, and I figured he knew what he was doing.

We followed the trooper to the jail in Rockford. The officer removed the man from the back seat of his patrol car and pointed him toward the door of the jail. The jail was across the street from the "old" jail. Don't let that fool you into thinking the current jail was anywhere close to new. It was not. It was in fact quite intimidating. It was a two-story brick structure, surrounded by a rusted chain link fence with rusty concertina wire across the top. I'm not sure, but it would not surprise me to learn that escape attempts had been thwarted by the fear of a cut from the rusty razor wire! The old jail would be torn down and replaced with a new one a few years later.

The arrested subject was a fairly small guy, maybe five feet seven inches tall and about 135 pounds. His clothes were disheveled, like many intoxicated folks, and he had a full head of unruly black hair. He was very unsteady on his feet and had problems negotiating the four-foot-wide gate that led to the front door of the jail. We followed them into the jail and straight to the Intoxilyzer room.

At that time, the rules stated you had to observe the subject to make sure they did not take anything by mouth for twenty minutes prior to administering the breath test. During this time, the trooper took down the pertinent information and filled out the many forms necessary to use the breath test as evidence in court for a driving-under-the-influence (DUI) charge.

When the time had elapsed, he began the test. The first step was to inform the subject they were now being advised to take a test to determine the alcoholic content of their blood. There was a rather long diatribe that had to be read to the subject. It included the penalties for not taking the test and several other facts. I always thought it was sort of odd you had to explain all of this to someone who you obviously felt was too drunk to know what was going on. However, that was the rule. Near the end of the instructions was the part where you told the individual when they began blowing into the tube, they would hear a tone. Once the tone started, they needed to continue to blow until they were told to stop. With the instructions completed, a fresh mouthpiece would be inserted into the tube, and the test would begin.

During my many years working, I had the opportunity to observe many subjects who were given the breath test. The reactions to the instructions segment of the test varied widely. While some were argumentative, others were inquisitive, and yet others were basically out of it. I think my all-time favorite response was by a guy that our local game warden and I had arrested for DUI. When the local police chief, a young man in his late twenties, began reading the subject the instructions, the drunken driver interrupted him by saying, "Boy, I was blowing these things up before you was born!" That was a good one; however, I was about to witness another "classic" response.

As the trooper was finishing the instructions, the subject stood up and began to remove his shirt. The trooper quickly told the man there was no need to remove his shirt; however, he continued to disrobe. With his shirt now off, the fellow pointed to his chest and said, "Look here."

We both looked at the man's chest and noticed a series of scars. The trooper commented, "You've got some scars there, don't you?"

The man looked him straight in the eye and stated, "I ain't got no lungs!"

I must admit this revelation took both of us by surprise. "Ain't got no lungs?" the officer replied. He then said, "Man, you gotta have one lung, or you wouldn't be here, and a man with one lung can blow this machine up."

SEVERE HANDICAP

The man again stated he didn't have any lungs. He was told he was breathing pretty good for a man with no lungs, and he needed to blow in the tube. The man tried to blow into the machine, but it proved to be just too much for a man with such a severe handicap.

When someone could not blow enough to give a sample, it was listed as a refusal of the test. The necessary paperwork was completed, and the man was booked into the jail on the DUI charge. Shockingly, the judge didn't believe the "no lungs" defense, and the fellow was convicted. Afterward, I told the trooper I would have thought he would have had some compassion for a person in that kind of shape!

Many times in my career, I thought I had heard it all; however, I learned early on people would say and do anything. That continued to be the case for as long as I worked, and I'm sure it is still the same today! You can't make this stuff up!

SITTING ON THE CORN

WHEN I BEGAN MY CAREER, I was fortunate to have the opportunity to work with several veteran conservation enforcement officers (CEOs) or game wardens, as they called themselves. One of those was a crusty old fellow named Lee. Although I am now nearly the age Lee was when I went to work, I feel I can refer to him as old considering the fact he began his career the year prior to me being born! I found Lee to be a good game warden. He had a definite idea about how things should be done, and that was the way they were done. He wasn't fond of newfangled things such as the deer decoy, and he didn't like messing with anything that wasn't a pure game-and-fish case. He was all business and was well respected by the hunters he policed and other officers.

I worked with Lee several times on the Hollins Wildlife Management Area (WMA). The majority of the WMA was in Clay County, where Lee was assigned. One day, while checking hunters on the area, we engaged in a conversation about how it seemed some people would rather climb a tree and tell a lie than stand on the ground and tell the truth. One of the most difficult aspects for me to become accustomed to early in my career was the fact it seemed the vast majority of people I encountered while working enforcement would lie to me. Even when the question was not anything significant, a truthful answer was difficult to come by. It wasn't like I had not been lied to in the past, but it definitely had not been an everyday occurrence. It didn't seem to matter how "red-handed" the people were caught, they would deny whatever they had done.

Lee, having been working for twenty-six years when I started, understood very well what I was talking about. He related to me an incident he had been involved in with someone who had to be the quintessential liar.

Early in Lee's career, there were very few deer in the state. Therefore, he did a tremendous amount of enforcement on small-game and turkey hunters. One season, he had located an area baited with corn to attract turkeys. In the center of the baited area was a blind fashioned out of limbs and small trees. The blind was just large enough to conceal a man and offered an easy shot at any turkey utilizing the cracked corn that had been strewn in the area. On a cool March morning, Lee decided to go and check the blind. As he slowly approached, he spotted a man sitting in the small blind. The officer gingerly approached as close as he could before making his presence known.

Approaching a baited area was always one of the most dangerous moments in the life of a CEO. Although I loved catching people hunting by the aid of bait, and especially turkey bait, it was a dangerous undertaking. Walking into an area where you suppose an armed predator is hiding in camouflage just waiting to shoot something isn't the best situation to be in. Turkey bait was even worse, due to the fact the sound of a man walking in the woods is difficult to distinguish from the sound a turkey makes walking in the woods. Add to this the violator knows he is in violation and will be facing a hefty fine and possibly jail time if caught. The sum of these circumstances doesn't bode well for the man in green with the badge on his chest. Baited sites that had a known observation point or blind seemed to be a little less dangerous since you knew where the violator was "supposed" to be. However, every officer who has worked much bait has been surprised to find a hunter somewhere other than where he was anticipated.

After creeping in as tight as possible without being seen, and not wanting to startle a man holding a loaded shotgun, Lee quietly called to the hunter. Once the hunter turned his head and acknowledged the officer, Lee cautiously approached the man and asked to see his shotgun. Rule number one in almost every situation was to get control of the firearm. While Lee checked the shotgun, the fellow was telling him he was glad to see him working in the area and all the usual banter a violator would spout. Not being one for chitchat, Lee got straight to the point and told the man the area was baited with corn.

Immediately, the man became defensive and began denying any knowledge of the bait. The man was quickly getting irate and said he knew some people hunted that way, but he did not hold with that type of activity. Lee interrupted the man's tirade and told him to step out of the blind, and he would show him the corn in the leaves. The fellow acted as if he didn't hear a word Lee said and went back to vehemently pleading his case. He stated in no uncertain terms he did not believe in baiting and would not hunt over bait. It didn't take Lee long to get his fill of the denials, and this time he more forcefully ordered the man out of the blind to view the bait. Knowing what was coming, the man lowered his head, stood up, and stepped out of the blind. The about-face in the man's demeanor did not escape Lee's attention. He watched the man closely as he exited the blind. Viewing the area where the man had been sitting, Lee quickly realized why the chatty fellow had now gone silent. It would be difficult to continue to convincingly argue you weren't aware of the bait when you were sitting on a bag of yellow corn! Liars, give me a break!

I always thought it was so funny that Lee had been working as a game warden a year before I was born. However, a couple of years prior to my retirement, Captain Darrell Askew contacted me and explained an officer from his district was transferring to my county and asked if I would assist him in learning the county and give him the benefit of my many years of experience. Darrell had been a lieutenant in our district years earlier. He explained the officer was young but was a good, aggressive officer. I told him I would be happy to work with him.

CEO Drake Hayes moved into the county, and I stopped by to introduce myself. When he answered the door, it was all I could do to keep from asking if his daddy was home. I swear he looked to be all of sixteen years old. Talking with him, I learned he had actually been working as an officer for a couple of years. I also figured out I had been working for five years before he was born! Somehow that wasn't so funny! Go figure.

SOMETHING NO OTHER GAME WARDEN HAD EVER DONE!

PEOPLE ILLEGALLY HUNTING DEER at night definitely kept us busy all winter long. The overpopulation of deer in our rural county was a magnet for those who wanted to ride the roads after dark, attempting to kill a deer or two. Unfortunately, this illicit practice was simply a game to many of the participants. Many times, I have had people not familiar with illegal hunting ask me if the culprits were merely poor people trying to obtain food. I can say without reservation I never apprehended anyone who I felt was actually hunting deer at night due to the need for food. Yes, many of the folks who killed deer illegally would eat those deer; however, just as many would not even bother to retrieve the slain animals. Many of them were actually engaged in a sick game of seeing who could kill the most. Others were selling the deer they killed or trading them for drugs or other items. However, I truly believe the motivation for many violators was simply to hunt deer at night without being caught by the game warden. While not being caught was a source of pride, oddly enough, many of those caught wore their apprehension as a badge of honor. The guy in this story ended a family tradition and provided me with my first felony arrest of a night hunter.

SOMETHING NO OTHER GAME WARDEN HAD EVER DONE!

Even after being lied to by violators for over thirty years, it still baffles me how people will lie, even when you catch them red-handed. Believe it or not, it isn't unusual for people to deny ownership of items found in their pockets, purse, or hand. Although this really bothered me when I first began working, eventually it became what I expected. While I was rarely disappointed, like with everything, there were exceptions.

The deer decoy gave us a real advantage when it came to catching people hunting deer both during the day and night. Many nights were spent sitting in remote areas, watching a county road or little-used highway, when we would hear the *py-yow* of a rifle shot in the distance. Even with our learned skill of placing where a shot came from, it was still difficult to try to move to that location and locate a violator. Placing shots was rarely totally accurate. It was influenced by weather conditions, and multiple roads in an area made it difficult to pinpoint. Furthermore, if you did find a vehicle, the sound of a shot was sometimes weak probable cause for a stop, and by moving through the area, you increased the risk of being spotted. This was problematic since word traveled fast among night hunters. The deer decoy put the officer, the violator, and his objective, a deer, or what they thought was a deer, all in the same place at the same time. It sure saved a lot of time running around. Of course, there were drawbacks. Read on.

Conservation Enforcement Officer (CEO) Shannon Calfee and I had positioned our deer decoy in a pasture alongside Alabama Highway 22, west of Rockford, in an area where we had received recent night hunting complaints and had just settled in for our vigil. No sooner had I turned off my truck's engine than I received a call from the Coosa County sheriff's office (SO), stating someone was spotlighting in the bullpen area of Coosa County on County Road 15. Dang! The bullpen area was at least twenty miles from our current location. While I hated to leave our current setup, where we had received complaints of nighttime shooting, we did not have a lot of options.

This was one of the problems with using the decoy. With the deer deployed, you were pretty much tied to the location. You did not need to try to work the deer with only one vehicle, and you obviously could not leave it set up. Trying to decide whether or not to retrieve the decoy, I reasoned that pulling into the field now would increase the likelihood of being spotted by the very folks we were attempting to apprehend. After weighing the options, we made the decision to just sit tight. We reasoned it would take us at least thirty minutes to retrieve the decoy and travel to the location of the complaint, and the culprit would no doubt be long gone by then. The report had not stated that a shot had been heard, and for all we knew, they might come our way eventually. Have you ever noticed how we are pretty good at justifying what we want to do in the first place?

Our decision seemed good until the radio once again came to life. The dispatcher stated they had received another call from the same area. The dispatcher stated a landowner had gotten the tag number of the vehicle and gave us a vehicle description. That was it. I told Shannon we were going to have to pull the deer and head to the complaint. To expedite things, we decided to drive out into the pasture and quickly pick up the decoy.

As I felt my pickup sinking into the soft earth, I realized driving into the field was not the best idea. Although I did not want to destroy the pasture, I knew my only option was to keep moving. With tires spinning, I made a loop around the deer and headed back toward the road, fortunately avoiding getting stuck. We jumped out of the truck and ran into the pasture, yanked up the deer, loaded it, and headed to the complaint in separate vehicles.

I had worked the area of the complaint several times in the past and had a couple of hiding holes in mind as we neared the location. I radioed Shannon and suggested he should set up on the hill on Coosa County Road 55, an area where he had a good vantage point and where we had caught people before. I informed him I would go to a spot I knew on Coosa County Road 56. This would have us about a mile apart as the crow flies and about three road miles apart.

At approximately 11:00 p.m., I arrived at my hiding spot, only to find some four-wheel-drive enthusiast had been climbing the road bank and had rendered it impassable for my Dodge four-wheel-drive pickup. I knew of another road near a close-by hunting camp but remembered it had a cable across it. Although I did not want to run the risk of sitting on the side of the road while trying to find my key to unlock the cable, there weren't many choices. While I always encouraged landowners to limit the access to their properties to decrease entry by trespassers, it made it a pain for when we needed to get on the land. It usually would take some time for me to find which one of the three-hundred-plus keys on my key ring would fit the lock. You know those darn things all look alike.

As the woods road came into view, I was excited to see the cable was down. I debated whether to pull into the road or to turn around and back in. Wanting to get out of sight as quickly as possible, I decided I would pull into the road and find somewhere to turn around. As I started into the road, I realized this might be a problem, seeing how there was a vehicle coming out. Don't get ahead of me, but yes, it perfectly matched the description I had been given.

I allowed the vehicle, an older-model multicolored Chevrolet pickup with a Talladega County tag, to pull into the paved road before I activated my blue lights. The driver immediately pulled over. I radioed Shannon and told him I had the truck stopped and to come to my location. As I approached, I observed a scoped rifle on the seat beside the driver, who appeared to be maybe twenty-five years old. I gave the loud verbal command for the man to raise his hands and exit the vehicle. I had him step to the rear of his pickup, and I patted him down for weapons.

While waiting on Shannon to arrive, I asked the fellow if he was a member of the club he was coming off of, and he replied he was not. I asked what type of rifle he had on the seat, and he replied, "It's a 17," indicating it was a .17 caliber. I saw headlights approaching and did not ask any more questions until Shannon arrived. Shannon walked up, and I asked him to retrieve the rifle from the truck while I asked for the subject's driver's license. I read the man the Miranda warning from my card, and he stated he understood his rights. Although I had the Miranda warning memorized, I always read it from the card in my wallet. That way, if questioned in court as to whether or not I had sufficiently advised them of their rights, I could positively state that I had.

I realized I had not observed the subject do anything except come off of a property he did not have permission to be on. However, not having seen him out of the vehicle on the property, I really didn't have anything. Nor had I observed him doing anything that would constitute hunting at night. It was not illegal to ride around with a loaded rifle in the seat beside you. All I had was a vehicle matching the description called in by two complainants. With that being the case, I knew his answers to my questions would be critical.

I decided to go with the straightforward approach and told him we were investigating a night hunting complaint, and giving him my best "I know you did it" look, I said I felt he was the one doing it. What happened next took me totally by surprise. He simply replied, "Yeah." I could not believe it. Had this guy just confessed to night hunting? After I got over the momentary shock, I realized a simple "yeah" wasn't going to hold up in court, so I began to shoot the questions rapid fire. I asked if he had been shining a light from his truck into fields along the road, and he replied, "When I saw a deer, I tried to shine it with my flashlight." When I asked him if he understood that shining a light from a vehicle trying to see a deer when you have a loaded rifle at night constituted night hunting, he replied, "Yes, I understand that." He said he had not planned to shoot a deer, and if he had intended to do that, he would have brought a .22-caliber rifle because the rifle he had was too loud. I was once again surprised when the man stated he had killed many deer at night and had no problem with doing that if he needed meat. I could not believe this was happening. While it was totally unusual for any night hunter to spill the beans in this fashion, it was unbelievable that it was coming from this guy, seeing how he was a member of a well-known outlaw family. I again asked if he understood shining his light at night with his loaded gun in the truck was night hunting. "Yes," was his instant reply. I inquired what he was doing up the road he had just driven out of, and he said he was just riding around. I pushed forward and asked if he had shined the fields up the road, and he said he had. When I asked if he had a permit for the property, he replied he did not and added, "It sounds like I'm going to get several tickets."

I must admit I was still having a difficult time believing this was really happening. I was trying to process everything the guy was saying and what I needed to do. Even with his "confession," I knew I would have to get with the witness who had actually seen him shining from the truck and get statements. I asked the fellow if at any time during the evening had he had anyone else riding with him, and he said he had not.

When I had initially approached the suspect, I had noticed several items in the bed of his truck that seemed somewhat out of place. In plain view was a wood-burning heater, an air compressor, an orange extension cord, a pistol safe, a yellow bench grinder, and a camouflage bag containing clothing and bedding. I probed as to where the items had come from, and he said the heater had come from his friend, and the other things were items he used at work as a mechanic. I noticed some blood on the tailgate of the truck and, thinking it might be deer blood, I asked where it had come from. He replied it was his blood from a cut on his finger. As I scanned the items in the truck, I noticed blood on the wood-burning heater as well. I left Shannon with the subject and went to my truck and called the SO and asked if they had had any burglaries reported that evening. They stated they had not.

I returned to the subject and advised him I would be obtaining warrants for his arrest and would be in touch with him soon. We made sure we had a good address and contact information, and the subject was allowed to leave, sans his two-cell flashlight and .17-caliber rifle.

As the fellow drove away, I looked at Shannon and told him something was definitely not right with this situation. First, I could not believe the fellow would admit he was night hunting, and second, the stuff in the back of his truck came out of somebody's house. I said to Shannon I felt we ought to check the hunting cabin up the road and make sure it was secure.

As we pulled up to the cabin, a light was on inside, but there were no vehicles in the yard. A quick check revealed the side door of the cabin standing open, and a window in a bedroom was broken out. I called one of the owners and told him the cabin had been broken into, and they would need to come down and see what was missing. I went to the SO and reported the cabin had been burglarized, and I suspected our night hunter was responsible.

The next day, I followed up with the cabin owner, who stated he would be down around 1:00 p.m. to see if anything was missing. In the meanwhile, I contacted the complainant from the night before and asked what he had seen. He said the individual in the truck had come by his house, shining at least three times. He said his grandson had followed the vehicle and observed him shining a light from the truck and had gotten his tag number. I contacted the grandson and he stated he had observed the truck go past his house, shining the fields with a light. I asked him for the tag number and vehicle description, and they matched the vehicle I had stopped.

At 1:00 p.m., I met with the cabin owner. He stated they were missing a large camo bag, some hunting clothes, and some bedding. He described the bedding as having a Southwestern motif. I told him the bag had been in the back of the truck I had stopped the night before. I called the Coosa County SO investigator and advised him of the situation. He asked that the cabin owner come to the jail and make a report.

I traveled to the courthouse, where I met CEO Calfee. Armed with our statements and the statements from the complainant, we obtained warrants on the suspect for hunting at night, hunting from a public road, hunting by aid of a vehicle, and hunting without a permit. The permit case was a request from the cabin owner, who also owned the property where the fellow had admitted to shining the fields.

We met the county investigator late in the afternoon, and we prepared to go and serve the warrants on the subject. Before we left, we were met by a deputy, who had just taken a report of a stolen wood heater, air compressor, and grinder. He also stated some glass had been broken, and there was blood at the scene. The investigator, deputy, CEO Calfee, and I all headed to a residence in the nearby town of Sylacauga in Talladega County to confront our suspect.

Upon our arrival, no one was at home. However, we heard music coming from a storage building in the backyard. We went to the building and knocked on the door. Receiving no answer, we looked through the window and observed the wood heater I had seen in the truck. We immediately went to the Talladega County sheriff's office to prepare a search warrant. At the SO, we were met by the Sylacauga police chief. He stated he had heard the traffic on the radio and had contacted the mother of the subject we were looking for, as she was a clerk for the police department. She came to the SO and gave us consent to search her home and storage building.

We returned to the residence and immediately went to the storage building. Opening the door, we were surprised to see the wood heater had been removed. We did, however, find the grinder that had been in the back of the truck. We searched the house without finding any of the missing items. It was extremely aggravating to me to know that while we were talking to the homeowner at the police department; her son was removing the evidence from the building. When we asked the whereabouts of her son, she stated she had no idea, nor did she know when he would return. We advised her we would wait.

A few weeks prior to this incident, I had received some training on how to question a suspect using the Reid interrogation technique. I felt this would be a great opportunity to utilize these new skills. The technique involves asking baseline questions that will be answered honestly to begin with and judging the suspect's demeanor and body language. Then, as you get into further questioning, you watch for cues as to whether or not the suspect is telling the truth. I had developed my questions and had them printed and ready.

It wasn't very long until the subject arrived home. I had shared with the SO investigator I had prepared some questions for the subject. He asked if I wanted to question him first, and I advised he could start, and I would follow up with my questions.

My thinking was I would observe the man's reactions to the investigator's questions, and that would strengthen my analysis. I thought it was a pretty good plan.

The investigator read the subject the Miranda warning and then paused for several seconds while formulating his first question. I was all ears. I could tell he hadn't spent nearly as much time preparing his questions as I had when he asked the man, "Did you break into those houses?" I could not believe he had totally omitted any baseline questioning and went straight to an in-your-face question. Just as I was thinking, "This will never work," the man answered, "Yes." My jaw hit the ground. So much for my fancy questioning. He asked the man where the stolen items were, and he told him. I was dumbfounded. The investigator turned to me and asked if I had some questions for the man, and I simply replied, "No." I informed the fellow I had written a statement containing what he had told me the night before and asked him to read it and, if it was correct, to sign it. He read it and signed it.

We retrieved the stolen items and transported the violator to the Coosa County jail. While en route to the jail, Shannon and I talked freely with the young man, who informed us we had done something no other game warden had ever done, "caught a member of his family night hunting." Once at the jail, we handled all the paperwork on our charges, and he was placed in jail on two counts of burglary and two felony counts of theft of property.

The defendant's attorney offered they would state to the facts of the case and plead guilty to the hunting offenses and asked that they be appealed to circuit court. I had never had that happen and don't know exactly what it means other than you leapfrog over the district court level and move straight to the circuit level. *Leapfrog* may not be a real legal term! The case ended up going to the grand jury. They returned an indictment, and the man was later found guilty.

When you have grown accustomed to being lied to, it is a little disconcerting to have someone admit to everything you confront them with. I could not get it out of my head that something was wrong with this case. Although I felt this guy was obviously trying to cover up his burglary and thefts by admitting to the hunting charges, I was convinced the subject had been accompanied by someone else, whom he had let out of the truck prior to my stopping him. The witnesses each reported he was shining with a spotlight, yet the only light in his vehicle was a small two-AA-cell flashlight (believe me, I searched the truck thoroughly). The witness who followed him down the road assured me there were two people in the truck at that time. However, I asked he man numerous times if he had been accompanied by anyone that night, and he denied it every time. An accomplice was never identified.

While the defendant paid hefty fines and court costs in the hunting cases and ended up with a substantial criminal record, not to mention paying the sizable fee of his high-powered attorney, you might say he got by with one, and, in a sense, he did. However, you must remember, there are a lot of violators who are never brought to justice in this life. I'm certain these folks erroneously believe they won the game. And while they may have snuck one by me, I feel certain God has had or will have something to say about the way they treated his creation. The Bible says nothing will remain hidden and vengeance is mine, I will repay, saith the Lord. That applies to everything in this life, and we would all do well to remember that.

THEY TOOK OFF!

IT SHOULD BE BLATANTLY OBVIOUS to even the most casual observer that conservation officers can't be everywhere. I often commented that with both of our conservation enforcement officers (CEOs) and myself working in Coosa County, we still needed to be covering over two hundred square miles apiece. That's only 128,000 acres. No problem. Yeah, right. With these kinds of odds, it was no wonder some folks would decide to take matters into their own hands when game and fish violations occurred. Some handled it better than others.

My telephone got a work out during the hunting season. Calls with complaints and questions were normally a daily occurrence. Of course, mine wasn't the only one. Gene Carver was a fellow wildlife biologist on the Hollins Wildlife Management Area in neighboring Clay County about twenty miles from my house. Gene and I spent many days and nights working together. He had begun his career about a year and a half before I was hired and, therefore, being a seasoned veteran, served as one of my mentors. He related the details of a call he received one night that was another one for the "you can't make this stuff up" category.

Gene answered the phone and heard the familiar voice of a local landowner. He said it was blatantly obvious the landowner was more than a little excited. The man had a pressing question he had to ask. "If someone shoots at a deer beside your house can you shoot at them?"

Gene, sensing something was up, replied, "No, you should not shoot at someone for that."

To which the caller responded, "Well, you don't need to come over here then!"

Of course, this indicated to Gene he had better get over there as quickly as possible. Arriving moments later, Gene noticed the road was full of automotive glass. He exited his truck and spoke with the landowner, who relayed to him the recent events. It seems he had observed some deer standing beside his house, which was a common occurrence. Not long after he had checked on the deer, he noticed a vehicle had stopped in the road in front of his house. As he made his way to the door for a better look, he saw a gun barrel come out of the driver's side window. *Py-yow!* A blaze of fire billowed out as a shot shook the house. Although initially startled, the homeowner grabbed his shotgun from behind the door and stepped onto the front porch. He said that as the car began to pull away, he "blew the back glass out of it and they really took off!"

Believe it or not, this type of incident was not that uncommon. I have had numerous officers share stories of this type. Fortunately, many of the folks did not shoot directly at the vehicle. It was interesting that while this shot obviously hit its mark, to the best of our knowledge, no one ever came forward concerning the damage. Imagine that!

THE DEFENDANT WILL SPEAK WITH YOU NOW
(THANKS, GRANDPA)

Police officers are bound by a multitude of policies and procedures and basic civil rights of individuals. While these things are absolutely necessary, they often tend to bind the hands of law enforcement. Despite what the media would have you believe, officers learn early in the police academy that people's rights must be upheld. We must not unlawfully infringe on these rights; However, non-law enforcement folks aren't necessarily encumbered by such things, and that turned out to be a major turning point in this story.

Night hunting for deer was rampant during the mid-nineties in central and south Alabama. This preponderance of illegal activity mandated that we work both day and night. Night hunters come in varying ilks. While some are content to kill whatever deer they see, others fashion themselves as trophy hunters, meaning they only shoot large bucks. Of course, the definition of *large* varied greatly among outlaws. For those who were of the "trophy" variety of night hunter, it stood to reason they would be more successful if they lurked in areas known to have better deer. In Alabama, the area known as the Black Belt holds that type of deer, and most hunters know it. Macon County is located in the upper edge of the Black Belt. Like Coosa, it is sparsely populated with people but heavily populated with deer. That combination made it an ideal area for illegal hunting activities of all sorts.

With the area's fertile Black Belt soil and high deer numbers, hunting leases and commercial hunting opportunities were both very expensive. More than once, I heard an outlaw make the comment that the low risk of being caught and paying a fine was a lot cheaper than paying to hunt! With that being the prevailing attitude, the officers in Macon County stayed super busy during the deer season, both day and night.

My good friend and mentor, retired Conservation Enforcement Officer (CEO) Byron Smith, began his CEO career in Macon County after serving as a crime scene specialist and police officer in Birmingham for twelve years. Byron was the decoy guru and put the fake deer to good use. As you can guess, Byron had a boatload of good stories.

Night hunting was wide open, and the complaints just kept coming. To give you an idea of how active it was, while on his way to set up on yet another area where shots had been reported, he had to make a quick stop. Seeing a piece of guardrail that had been mangled alongside the highway, Byron stopped and salvaged a broken reflector from the debris. This was necessary so he could create a new eye for his deer decoy, seeing how someone had shot the eye out of it the night before! Oh yeah, things were wide open.

With the repair material in hand, he continued toward the problem area where he would again deploy the decoy. This area was in sight of the largest employer in Macon County, the Victoryland dog track. As a matter of fact, it was some of the dog track folks he was after. The complaint he had received stated the folks who cared for the greyhounds that ran at the track were provided funds to purchase beef to feed the dogs. However, word was the people had decided to pocket the cash and feed the dogs deer meat instead. While that wasn't really any of our business, the fact they were acquiring the deer by shooting them at night was definitely in our purview.

Byron had located a large field near the dog training facility and decided to try his luck with the decoy. Finding an area with deer was no problem in Macon County. Finding the right spot where people would likely hunt was a little more difficult. Byron felt it stood to reason that the outlaws would try to kill some deer as close to the facility as they could. After quickly fashioning a new eye for the fake deer, he placed it in the field and moved to a hiding spot just in the edge of the woods that surrounded the field. From his vantage point, he could actually see the dog kennel. That would prove to be helpful.

Around midnight, the officer spotted the lights of a vehicle as it left the dog kennel and seemed to head straight for his location. Many people make the erroneous assumption that all night hunters will utilize a four-wheel-drive pickup truck. I have found that not to be the case. Game wardens have caught folks night hunting from motorcycles to tractor-trailer trucks and almost everything in between. In this instance the vehicle utilized was an older model Mercury Marquis car. I think Byron referred to it as a "land barge."

The driver piloted the large passenger car in such a manner that its headlights illuminated the field where Byron sat. Lo and behold, the headlights picked up the former guard rail reflector, now deer eye, and within seconds a shot rang out. As was often the case when a seasoned night hunter shot the decoy and it just stood there, it did not take them very long to realize they had been had. This was the case, and the vehicle took off at a high rate of speed. Fortunately, the route they took led right past Byron's hiding spot, allowing him to be right behind them in a matter of seconds. Byron got the tag number of the vehicle as they quickly made their way down the dirt road that bisected the field. It was obvious, as they ignored his lights and siren, they had no intention of stopping.

As the vehicle neared the paved road, they employed a technique often utilized by night hunters: they threw their gun out the window. I have had this happen a number of times. The best I can figure is the folks believe if they don't have a firearm when we get them stopped, we will not be able to make a case against them for hunting at night. As I said, I have seen this tried a few times; however, I have never seen it work. However, it sort of worked this time.

Instead of throwing the gun out the window and away from their vehicle, these brain surgeons threw the gun straight back at the pursuing green Bronco. While I feel that was a crazy thing to do and while I am certain they never intended for things to turn out as they did, it did work in their favor. Byron saw the gun come out of the car and didn't think much of it as he ran over it.

However, when the car reached the paved road and turned to the right, Byron's steering wheel would not turn at all. Yes, the gun had jammed his steering. He said all he could do was hang on as the Bronco bounded into the highway. However, when the front end slammed down in the paved road, the gun, or what was left of it, came flying out from under the truck and spinning down the road. Unfortunately, the momentary inability to steer the truck had allowed the shooters the opportunity to disappear down the road.

While they were able to escape, this wasn't Byron's first rodeo. During the pursuit, he had made a mental note of the vehicle's tag number. He called dispatch and learned the tag number of the vehicle came back to a fellow in the nearby town of Shorter, Alabama. Unfortunately, the address listed on the license was a post office box. This was before a physical address was required on all driver's licenses. Although it was now nearly two o'clock in the morning, Byron placed a call to the local postmaster. After several rings a groggy voice answered. The officer explained the situation and asked if she would have a physical address for the owner of the post office box listed on the license. She said she did, but it would be at the post office. He told her he could be there in fifteen minutes. To her credit, the woman said she would be there shortly.

The postmaster showed up looking like a lot of folks who have been woken from a deep sleep look at two thirty in the morning. Byron explained that time was of the essence if he was going to have a successful outcome for this incident. She located the address of the boxholder and gave it to him. He thanked her and left the post office.

With the address in hand, Byron went directly to the area. It was 3:00 a.m. when Byron rapped on the door of the dilapidated house with the well-kept yard and obvious garden patch containing some sort of greens off to the side. In a couple of minutes, an elderly man came to the door. Byron identified himself and asked if the man owned a Mercury Marquis car. The man said he did but his grandson had been using the car that night.

Byron explained to the man the car had been used in a night hunting incident and high-speed chase and asked if he knew where the car was now. The man did not hesitate to tell him the car was behind the trailer across the road from his house. He added it had arrived there about fifteen minutes earlier. Byron told the man he was going to need to talk with the grandson, and the man asked if he could go with him. Byron knew he really couldn't deny the request, and his read of the granddad was it might be beneficial to have him along.

The pair went to the trailer and the CEO knocked on the door. It took a couple of minutes for the grandson to open the door. The young man was rubbing his eyes and yawning and doing his best impression of someone who had been woke up from a deep sleep. However, the grandfather was having no part of it. He said, "You ain't been asleep!"

The young man attempted to protest, but the elder man was having none of it. Byron told the young man he needed to talk with him concerning the night hunting incident and chase that had occurred earlier. The man immediately told him he had no idea what he was talking about, seeing how he had been asleep for hours.

That blatant lie was more than the grandfather could stomach. He asked Byron if he could step inside and talk to the young man alone for a minute. Byron knew allowing the men to go into the house wasn't a wise tactical move; however, he followed his gut and allowed it.

As soon as the door closed, Byron heard a loud *whack* and then some loud "talking." In just a minute, the door opened and both men stepped out. The grandfather told the officer the young man had some information for him and was ready to speak with him. After Byron advised him of his rights, the young man gave a full confession, complete with the names of his accomplices.

While Byron would have likely been able to make this case without the assistance of the grandfather, the elder man obviously used some tactics of persuasion the officer couldn't employ. They no doubt made things a lot easier.

While we will never know what was actually "said" behind the closed door of the trailer, I do not doubt it had something to do with the fact the grandfather wasn't too keen on losing his vehicle due to a choice he did not make. On the other hand, he wanted the grandson to be accountable for the decisions he made.

Our culture today isn't very high on accountability or taking responsibility for our actions. What about you? We all make wrong choices. All have sinned and come short of the glory of God. Is it going to take your getting slapped up side of the head to get your attention? Maybe you need to have a talk with *the* Father. As the song says, just a little talk with Jesus makes it right.

DO YOU BELIEVE IN GOD?

As I DROVE ALONG Gold Mine Ridge Road on the south segment of the Coosa Wildlife Management Area (WMA), I noticed what appeared to be a machete lying in the roadway. I stopped and picked up the brush cutter and placed it in my pickup. I continued along the road and soon began to notice flagging tape hanging from trees, and it became evident a survey crew had been in the area. This was not unusual since this section of the wildlife management area was comprised of numerous private land holdings. I began to wonder if this meant we would soon be losing some property from the WMA, which often occurred when property changed hands. The Coosa WMA was thirty-eight thousand acres in size. The vast majority of the area was a contiguous block north of Hatchet Creek. The segment I was currently on was south of Hatchet Creek and east of the Coosa River. Since this was a small segment of the area that was probably twenty miles from the area headquarters, it did not receive as much attention as the larger contiguous section did.

During this time, the WMA system was comprised of thirty-five areas encompassing nearly eight hundred thousand acres of wildlife habitat available for public hunting of big game, small game, and waterfowl. Most folks erroneously believed that all of this property was state owned. The truth is we only owned a small amount of property. The remainder was held through some sort of lease. Many of the leases were simply an exchange of hunting rights for in-kind services, such as grading the road, maintaining culverts, and painting boundary lines. This worked well until the price being paid for deer and turkey leases began to grow exponentially. Once that occurred, we began to lose many tracts of land, and some entire areas were lost. I could not blame the landowners who opted for more money, but I hated it for the hunters who had grown up hunting the areas and many who didn't have the means to join a deer hunting club. Nonetheless, losing property became a common occurrence.

As I pondered whether or not we were losing this tract of property and the boundary line work and corresponding map changes that would be associated with it, I noticed a pickup parked in a side road. When I got closer, I could see a man was sitting in the truck. I rolled to a stop approximately twenty yards from the vehicle. I asked the fellow if he had lost a machete, and I held the one I had found out the window. He came over and took it and said he was sure a member of his crew had dropped it. I asked whose property they were surveying. As he began to explain, I observed two men walking along the woods road toward our location and noticed one of the men had a rifle slung over his shoulder. This got my attention since the man was on the WMA and the hunting season was closed. As the pair walked up behind their truck, the man with the rifle looked up, saw me, and immediately did an about face and started away at a fast pace. I hurriedly exited my truck and moved toward the man while ordering him to stop.

Although I could tell he thought about running, he fortunately decided against it. I approached him, identified myself as a state game warden, and asked for his rifle. As he handed over the old military rifle, he asked, "What's the problem?"

Although I was pretty sure he knew what the problem was, his belligerent tone let me know there might be more of a problem than I had anticipated. As I worked to unload the firearm, which was a chore since it was some crazy, sporterized military relic, I responded the problem was he was in possession of a loaded firearm on the WMA during closed season. I asked if he had a WMA permit, and he responded he did not. He added he wasn't hunting, he was surveying. I responded we usually considered people who were surveying with a gun over their shoulder to be hunting.

"I wasn't hunting. I have that gun for protection," he nearly shouted.

"Protection!" I shouted back.

"There are wild dogs in these woods," was his terse reply.

I asked who had told him that, and he replied everybody knew it.

I said I found that interesting seeing how I had been working in the area for fourteen years and I had never received a report of wild dogs.

I asked the man why he had turned and walked away upon seeing me, and he replied that he didn't. When I said, "Yes, you did," he shot back that he didn't. I carried the rifle and placed it inside my truck. I was not sure how this was going to go, but I knew if I ended up fighting this guy, I didn't want to be holding his rifle. I turned to the supervisor in the truck and asked if this was in fact his employee. It was obvious he wasn't happy having to acknowledge that it was. I inquired whether or not it was common practice for his employees to possess firearms while working. He said it was not common and, in fact, it was against their policy, and the man could lose his job for it. I asked the man who had accompanied the man with the rifle if he knew what the man's intention was, and he said he did not.

I returned to the gun owner and advised him he was in violation of several WMA regulations and he was under arrest for possession of a firearm without a valid permit. He went ballistic. He began ranting and raving, saying he could not believe he was getting a ticket. He wasn't bothering anybody and was only trying to protect himself. He added he had a Second Amendment right to possess a firearm. Surprisingly, he ended his barrage with the statement he knew there was going to be trouble when he saw me, and that is why he had started walking away.

My patience was wearing pretty thin, and things didn't get any better when I started writing his second ticket. Many people are evidently of the opinion that receiving a ticket gives them license to be as belligerent as possible. This guy was no exception. He decided he would really come undone on me. However, I stopped his rant long enough to point out I had plenty of tickets and plenty of ink, and I could write as long as he could rave. He was not a happy camper but did calm down a little. I explained the bonds to him and told him where to sign.

When he didn't immediately sign them, I explained his option was either sign the bonds or go to jail. While signing the tickets, he looked at me and asked, "Do you believe in God?"

I must admit I didn't see that one coming. I told him I did, and he said, "Well, you'll have to answer for this!"

I responded, "I've got that one covered." I handed him his copies of the tickets and told him I would see him in court.

The court date arrived, and I spotted the defendant as he entered the courtroom carrying a small child that appeared to be maybe three years old. This was a memorable day since it was the first court date for our new court clerk. I had known the clerk for several years when he had been a business owner and boat motor mechanic. Now he was starting a new chapter of his life as a public servant in the courthouse.

The judge entered the court room, took his seat on the bench, and began calling the docket. The defendant was soon called, and we both approached the bench. The judge read the charges and asked the man how he pleaded. I must admit I was again caught off guard when the man said, "Judge, the first thing I would like to do is apologize to this officer for the way I acted."

I said, "I appreciate that."

The man looked at the judge and said, "I plead guilty."

The judge said the court would accept the plea and sentenced the man to thirty days in jail suspended on the payment of fines and cost totaling $300 in each case. He asked the man if he was going to pay the fine or sit it out (meaning start serving his thirty days) and the defendant replied he would pay it. The judge handed me the case folders and said, "Take him to the clerk."

The man, carrying his daughter, followed me out of the courtroom and down the hallway to the clerk's office. I told the assistant clerk the man's name and he needed to pay $600. As I turned to go back to the courtroom, I noticed the fellow removing his checkbook from his pocket. I knew this would be a problem since the clerk did not accept checks. I told the defendant they would not accept a check. He asked if they would take a credit card, and I told him they only took cash. He said he would have to call his wife to bring the money. I asked where she was, and he replied she was in Montgomery, which was an hour away.

This was a problem, and I'm sure that was evident by the look on my face. I told him I would have to take him back to the courtroom, and I really didn't want to do that. He innocently asked, "Why not?" and I told him when we went back in the courtroom, the judge would in all likelihood put him in jail. He naively replied he didn't think the judge would do that. I was thinking he didn't know the judge like I did. I told him to go ahead and contact his wife, and we would take our chances with the judge.

I opened the door and entered the court room with the man and his daughter in tow. The judge immediately glared at me, stopped everything, and yelled, "He doesn't have the money, does he?" He followed that with, "I knew it! That's the only reason people bring their children to court."

While I wasn't convinced that was the reason this guy had brought his daughter with him, I knew the judge had seen this ploy several times. The judge then did something I had never seen before. He got up and came down from the bench and said, "It's not going to work." The judge told the man he was in the custody of the sheriff. He then informed him that his daughter would be taken to the Department of Human Resources (DHR). Although I knew the judge was aggravated, his demeanor had totally changed as he addressed the small child. He assured the little girl that everything would be okay. Evidently the child believed him, as she did not say a word and did not appear to be the least bit upset.

While the little girl wasn't upset, I can't say as much for the court clerk. He turned to me with a frantic look on his face and asked, "What are we going to do?"

I responded, "We aren't going to do anything." I reminded the clerk the judge was in charge, and he would do what he thought was best. Court soon resumed as if nothing had happened.

In about an hour, the man's wife arrived to pay the fines. I had the unenviable task of telling her she would have to retrieve her daughter from DHR and her husband from the county jail. I wasn't surprised when she didn't take it very well.

Seeing how I had never had anything like this happen before, I wasn't exactly sure how to proceed. I escorted the lady to DHR and told the workers she was the mother of the little girl the judge had "confiscated" in the courtroom. I could tell they were glad to see her, and that told me they would quickly be giving the child back. The little girl was still calm but was glad to see her mother.

I have thought back on this encounter and wished I would have answered the man differently when he said I would have to answer to God for my actions. My response that I had that covered was true. However, I wish I would have said we will all have to do that. The Bible says we will give an account for every word we've uttered. We really need to keep that in mind. Every knee will bow and every tongue will confess. Think about it.

VOLE CONTROL

My good friend, Dr. Jim Armstrong, was the extension wildlife specialist for Alabama for several years. I had the good fortune of serving with Jim on the National 4-H Wildlife Committee for about ten years. We had a lot of fun traveling together. Like me, Jim had some unbelievable stuff happen while working with the public.

Unlike many who hold doctorate degrees, extension professionals, at least in the south, rarely introduce themselves as "Doctor." I feel this comes from a fear that their audience might perceive them as "uppity," which might hinder their ability to connect with their clientele. To be effective in extension, you must be able to connect with folks at every level. Those who can't normally don't stay in it very long. Jim has been in it forever.

Jim is an authority on wildlife damage management and spoke with groups across the state concerning wildlife damage issues. There was no shortage of complaints about deer damage to crops, rabbit damage, even robins damaging the earthworm crop! (I am not making that up.) Suburban areas also had plenty of damage from species such as armadillos and voles. This being the case, Jim often spoke with homeowner groups and garden clubs across Alabama.

Jim shared with me a memorable garden club meeting. The audience was comprised of your typical Alabama garden club members. There was a lot of gray hair and numerous large straw hats and eyeglasses on chains. A couple of ladies had sweaters tied around their waist, and there was a plethora of rainbow-hued polyester pants above sensible shoes. The youngest member of the group, a forties-looking lady wearing a cap with a ponytail sticking out the back, sat on the front row with her pen in hand. It seemed she was attempting to capture every word. Fortunately, Jim's slow southern delivery made it pretty easy to keep up; however, the South Carolina accent was so strong it wasn't always easy to decipher the words.

Eventually the topic of voles in flower beds came up. Jim told the group that if voles were a problem in a flower bed, they could normally be controlled using a simple snap-type (mouse) trap. He told them a peanut butter and oatmeal mixture was good bait for the trap. He went on to say if you had problems with ants getting on the bait, you could add a little Sevin dust, and it would control the ants. This prompted a question from the ponytail wearer in the front row. She asked, "Won't the Sevin hurt the vole?"

Jim immediately replied, "Not for long it won't."

You can't make this stuff up!

YOU SPRAYED THE KIDS!

ONE OF THE GROUPS I was glad to be associated with during my career was the Coosa County Forestry Planning Committee (CCFPC). The planning committee was made up of representatives from all of the natural resource agencies operating in the county, as well as forestry and wildlife consultants and private landowners. I was asked to join the group by the chairman, Natural Resource Conservation Service District Conservationist Doug Watkins. I appreciated the opportunity. Unfortunately, Doug soon took a position in south Alabama. However, Alabama Forestry Commission County Forester Blake Kelley and I took the reins and moved forward.

The group normally had about ten or twelve members. I was the chairman of this committee for many years, and most of the time the group worked well together. I like to think we accomplished a lot for the county. We were fortunate to win several awards, including being named the Conservation Organization of the Year in 2008 and the Outstanding Planning Committee in the state three times.

The primary mission of the CCFPC was to educate citizens of the county, both young and old, concerning the proper management of our natural resources. The committee took on many different projects over the years. We developed a multiple-use manager's guide for landowners, we worked with a publisher to provide a plat book for the county showing every parcel of property in the county along with the landowners' names, and we promoted the TREASURE Forest program.

The TREASURE Forest program assisted landowners managing their property for multiple uses. The landowner chooses their objectives, and wildlife biologists and foresters assist them in achieving their goals. Once adequate accomplishments are made toward objectives, the property is certified and the landowners publicly recognized. Our committee embraced the program, and through the efforts of our county landowners, we had more properties certified as TREASURE Forests than any other county in the state.

The planning committee sponsored many programs for both adults and youth, one of which was the adopt-a-school program. Soon after we started this program, our county consolidated all of our community schools into one. Yes, there is one school in our entire county! The adopt-a-school program consisted of taking the entire fourth-grade class to a TREASURE Forest in the county where we had learning stations dealing with forestry, wildlife, soil, water, and soil erosion. We would rotate the groups of kids through the stations, and the day would culminate with lunch. As with almost any field trip, the kids were glad to be out of class and were sometimes a little wild. We, the instructors, normally enjoyed the day, with the exception being when there was a lack of chaperones to keep the kids reined in.

It was always evident this type of training was needed based on the answers we received to basic questions. When you ask a kid from the most rural county in the state with a tremendous volume of wildlife what noise a turkey makes and they answer "cock-a-doodle-doo," they need some outdoor education! Some of the answers we received from the kids were hilarious.

I normally used a couple of box turtle shells to demonstrate the importance of camouflage. I had one shell that was the normal brown color, and the other was faded to white. I would place the shells six to eight feet apart and sort of nestled in the leaves on the forest floor. I would talk about how it was vital for ground nesting birds to blend in with their surroundings in order to help them avoid being devoured by a predator while sitting on a nest. I would then tell them there was a turtle shell in the leaves, point to the area, and ask who could see it.

The kids would immediately spot the white shell and start pointing and hollering. I then would tell them there were two shells. They would normally spot the brown shell fairly quickly. To make my point, I would ask which one they spotted first, and they would answer the white one. When I asked them why they did not spot the brown one first, they would say because it was harder to see. In an effort to reinforce my point, I would again ask why it was more difficult to see the brown shell. Eventually someone would say, "Because it blends in." I would then talk about wildlife coloration and predation.

At the end of the segment, I would again ask, "Why did you not see the brown shell?"

Some of the kids would answer, "Because it blends in."

I then asked, "Why did you see the white one?"

I was so tickled when a young girl enthusiastically answered, "It blends out!"

My wildlife station was normally located between the water station and soil erosion station. My routine normally consisted of talking with the kids, showing them some animal parts, and trying, in twenty-five minutes, to teach them we needed to wisely manage our natural resources. We would rotate the kids from one station to the next, with my next group coming from the soil erosion station. For many years, the soil erosion station was manned by a Natural Resource Conservation Service technician named Darin Mosley. Darin was a real cut up and always had something up his sleeve. He eventually resigned from his job so he and his wife could become group home parents for kids. An admirable vocation.

One day as the new group of adopt-a-school kids arrived, I began my usual routine of introducing myself when I noticed the kids were acting a little peculiar. When I told the class we were going to talk about wildlife, they all began to sing "Happy Birthday." I must admit, this prank really did catch me off guard, especially since it wasn't my birthday. I let them finish and again started my talk. I asked the question, "Who can give me a definition of wildlife?" When I said *wildlife*, they again started singing. I glanced back toward Darin's station and, seeing him doubled over laughing, I figured out what the joke was and who was behind it. After that initial success, Darin would continue to give the kids a key word and tell them to either sing or bark like a dog or some silly something every year. It was often easy to tell when he had put them up to something by the snickering and grinning going on when they reached my station.

Unfortunately, the adopt-a-school normally took place in early May, in the heart of allergy season. Although I had never suffered with hay fever-type allergies until I reached the age of thirty, after that, spring was often a miserable time for me. It was not unusual for me to begin sneezing and sneeze over ten times in a row! In addition, my eyes were often red and sometimes nearly swollen shut. Anyone who hasn't experienced a bad allergic reaction cannot comprehend how tough it can be.

During one adopt-a-school, I was having a terrible allergy attack. My eyes were blood red and badly swollen. My nose was also bright red from repeated blowing. As I battled the allergy, my next group of students arrived snickering and giggling.

Noticing their demeanor, I knew my friend was back at work putting them up to something. Although preoccupied with their task, they could not help but notice something was definitely wrong with my face. One of the kids asked, "What's wrong with your eyes?" It was then I came up with a plan of my own.

When teaching the adopt-a-school, I would wear my law enforcement uniform, complete with gun belt. Many of the kids were not at all familiar with conservation enforcement officers and what their job was, and I found it a great opportunity to allow them to meet an enforcement officer in a friendly setting. Many people still do not understand a conservation enforcement officer is a state law enforcement officer with as much or more authority than most of the police officers people are familiar with. Numerous times I have been asked by adults as well as kids as to why I carried a gun. Obviously, they, like most adults, did not realize wildlife law enforcement is one of the most dangerous enforcement jobs in the nation.

The kids were all looking at my red eyes and wanting to know what the problem was. I responded by telling the kids when I had started talking to the prior group, they had, for some unknown reason, started singing or barking or something. This caused many nervous glances and snickers to be passed around the group. I went on to tell them I didn't appreciate being interrupted in that way, so I had taken the pepper mace from my belt and sprayed the kids, but unfortunately, the wind had blown some of the spray in my eyes.

The snickering abruptly stopped, and we all stood in silence. Finally, one of the kids exclaimed, "You sprayed the kids!"

I acted like it wasn't a big deal and said, "Okay, let's get started."

The kids were all astounded. As I began with my introduction, it was all I could do to keep a straight face when I said "wildlife" and noticed all of the nervous stares, and one child even put her finger to her lips in a warning to the others not to say or do anything. I knew I had found the magic word, so I used it several more times, and not one syllable was uttered by the crowd.

As I finished with the group and the next one approached, I once again read the faces and realized Darin hadn't given up on disrupting my class. Once the group was assembled in front of me, I called to a teacher who was walking past and asked if she had thought to bring back the handcuffs I had used on the kid the day before. As the kids looked on wide-eyed, the teacher did not skip a beat and replied, "No, I left them at school." I replied I had another pair, but I was sure we wouldn't need them with this group. I went on to say I didn't know what could have made that kid start barking like that in the first place. I turned back toward the kids and, reading the terror in their eyes, I knew I had once again deciphered the puzzle. In all my years, I never found a better use of an allergy attack!!!

TURKEY WHIPPING

I FEEL THIS IS A GOOD TIME to reiterate the stories in this book are true. I know many of them are hard to believe, and I would likely doubt some of them if I hadn't lived through the majority of them. Just wanted to remind you.

As a young game warden working in Wilcox County, Jerry Roach was on routine patrol when he located his first turkey trotline. Trotlining turkeys is a heinous wildlife law violation. It consists of attaching a hook to a line that is secured to a tree or limb and baiting the hook with corn. An unsuspecting turkey happens along and picks up the corn and is hooked. I found one turkey trotline during my career, and it made me sick. Unfortunately, this dreadful technique was employed by some outlaw slime, and in this case, the illegal ploy had worked, as there was a hen turkey attached to the line.

Although repulsed by the act, Jerry was excited over his discovery. He radioed his supervisor, Mr. Henry, and reported what he had found. When the officer told him where he had found the device, the captain became excited and told the officer not to move until he got there. He told Jerry he would be en route shortly and asked if he wanted him to bring him a coke. Although the question was a little puzzling, Jerry told him yes, he would like a cool drink.

The captain soon arrived. Much to Jerry's surprise, the supervisor showed up carrying a large cooler. He sat the cooler on the ground, opened it, and gave the officer a coke.

Just in case you are not from the south, you may not realize that in Alabama, a soft drink is referred to as a coke. It does not matter what the actual brand is; they are all cokes. You ask someone if they want a coke, and if they say yes, you ask what kind of coke they want. It's just the way it is. I remember having to explain this to my classmates in graduate school at Mississippi State University. Several of them were from above the Mason-Dixon Line, and for that reason, they referred to a coke as either *soda* or *pop*. Bless their hearts.

Jerry noticed the cooler contained more cokes, chips, and other food items. Mr. Henry informed the young officer he had been attempting to catch this guy for years, and they were going to stay as long as it took. Although Jerry was anxious to make an arrest, he hadn't planned to stay on the scene for days.

After keeping their vigil for a couple of hours, it was getting pretty close to dark when they heard a racket in the distance. It is interesting how far you can hear a vehicle driving along a gravel road. When you are in the vehicle, you don't realize it makes any noise, but when you are sitting outside and things are fairly still, you can hear it for a mile.

As the two officers observed, a raggedy, faded blue Chevrolet pickup eased down the road toward them. "That's him," the captain uttered. The truck rolled to a stop in the road. A tall, lanky fellow wearing a pair of blue denim overalls and a faded plaid shirt exited the truck and made his way to the trotline. The officer could not believe his good fortune. Although he had not worked for very long, he knew it wasn't every day that you caught a violator on the first day of your stakeout. The officers watched as the man reached down and removed the turkey from the line.

As the man stood up, a spectacle unlike anything Jerry had ever seen unfolded before his astonished eyes.

The captain, a somewhat small man, came out of the woods on a full run. He grabbed the much taller violator by the scruff of the neck with his left hand and grabbed the hen turkey in his right and began to whip the man with the turkey. While Jerry looked on with his mouth hanging open, the violator was yelling "No, Mr. Henry!" and running in a tight circle while the captain was flailing him with the turkey. Eventually the man fell to the ground, and the captain continued to wear him out with the dead bird, which was quickly being denuded of all its feathers.

When the man was sufficiently beat down, the captain advised him not to ever do anything like this again. The man scampered to his feet and ran to his vehicle. The supervisor turned to the rookie and stated, "I don't think he'll do that again!" No ticket, no judge, no fine. Just a lesson in what not to do.

Jerry went on to a full career; however, he said that was the only turkey whipping he ever witnessed! You can't make this stuff up.

VACCINATING THE RACCOONS

DURING MY CAREER, I found it interesting how so many people considered themselves to be experts when it came to game management. I had six years of college and thirty years of on-the-ground-experience, and I was still hesitant to call myself an expert. Of course, many of the folks I'm referring to definitely would not have called me an expert. Interestingly enough, the topics for which I received the most grief were normally ones that there should not have been much debate on.

One that comes to mind was when I got the call from a young reporter with the *Alexander City Outlook* newspaper, who wanted to question me concerning the black wolf that had been run over in Tallapoosa County. I explained that although I had not actually seen the animal, I had viewed the photos of the eighty-pound canine. I explained we had not had wolves in our area for probably ninety years, and those were red wolves that would not weigh eighty pounds. Therefore, I was confident it was not a wild wolf. I went on to state some people do possess wolf/dog hybrids that reach that size, and I could not rule that out. However, I felt comfortable stating we did not have a remnant wolf population.

Not to be deterred, the reporter asked about the possibility of us having a black coyote. I explained that would be very likely, and I had personally seen several black coyotes. However, I told them that a large coyote in Alabama might weigh forty pounds. Of course, the paper printed my opinion, and then came the tirade of those who knew so much more than me. The one I liked the best was the "expert" who stated he had caught several coyotes that weighed over sixty pounds, and maybe I needed to get out a little more. I thought about having the paper put out another article telling how I had assisted a friend of mine trapping on the wildlife management area and he had caught over a hundred coyotes in three years and the average weight was about thirty pounds. While that evidence could be considered anecdotal, I felt it was probably significantly more than the naysayer had!

That story reminded me of the time I received a call from a man who stated he had killed a red wolf. I explained that the wolves had been extirpated in Alabama and felt certain what he had killed was a coyote. He countered that there had been a picture of a red wolf published in the *Birmingham News* and looked exactly like the wolf he had killed. It was obvious the man would not be satisfied until I came and viewed the animal. Of course, I knew he probably wouldn't be satisfied then; however, I made an appointment to meet with him.

I traveled to the Marble Valley area and met with the man. As soon as he exited his home carrying a black plastic bag, I knew he did not have a wolf. The "wolf" weighed nineteen pounds and closely resembled a coyote. Go figure.

One species that many members of the public were very knowledgeable about was their favorite wildlife to have as a pet, the masked bandit raccoon. If I had a dollar for everybody who had told me they used to have a raccoon as a pet, I would have several dollars. Evidently, many years ago, having a pet raccoon was as common as having a little TV sitting on top of your big, nonworking console TV. (I'm telling you that was common.)

After numerous problems and many rabies shots, the decision was finally made to no longer allow anyone to possess wild raccoons. The decision did not go over well, and there were many holdouts. After the fight had finally died down, the USDA brought the raccoon back to the forefront. Based on numerous positive rabies tests, the USDA Wildlife Services group embarked on a major raccoon rabies project. A large component of the study was the distribution of rabies vaccine for raccoons along a corridor that traversed all of Alabama and several eastern states. The vaccine was placed in a bait packet that was made of fishmeal. These packets were distributed by hand on the ground in more densely populated areas and by air in the more rural areas.

The project was discovered by the media, which of course muddied the water concerning what was actually taking place and why. Once the story aired, I received several calls from dog owners wanting to know whether or not the vaccine would be harmful if ingested by their animals. I told the callers if their dogs ingested the bait pack, they would be vaccinated against rabies and would have a shiny coat. I understood the people's concern and felt it was justified.

A fellow wildlife biologist working for the group handling the project received many more calls than I did. Although most were the run-of-the-mill calls from people worried about their pet finding the bait, she also received a few from citizens who were irate to learn their tax money was being spent on such a project. These calls had done little to prepare her for yet another outraged caller.

The irate caller wasn't worried about his pet or the cost of the project; however, he was extremely upset with the haphazard method used to place the bait. She assured him the baits were being placed or dropped in areas where raccoons were likely to frequent and posed a minimal threat to any other species.

However, the guy continued to rant about the vaccines being scattered about.

The biologist said she had just about offered all the explanations she could come up with when the fellow finally revealed the basis for his concern. "What if some kid finds one of these vaccines and sticks themselves with the needle?"

Although taken back by the question, she dutifully explained these were oral vaccines, and no needles were involved. When she related this story to me, I couldn't help but visualize the raccoons in the forest finding the packet and injecting themselves! I asked her, "This guy didn't mention any really big coyotes, did he?"

You can't make this stuff up!

WELCOME TO COOSA COUNTY COURT

To the best of my recollection, the first time I was ever in a courtroom was as an arresting officer. Therefore, my courtroom knowledge was limited to having watched *Perry Mason*, *Matlock*, and later *Law & Order* on television. I had several court appearances prior to going to the police academy and receiving the little bit of courtroom training they gave. I found out quickly the Hollywood courtroom and the one in Rockford, Alabama (and every other one), were very different places.

While the courtroom itself was akin to most courtrooms I have ever seen, the makeup of the judiciary was another story. The Coosa County courthouse was by far the largest building in the tiny county seat of Rockford. Sitting at the intersection of US Highway 231 and Alabama Highway 22, the two-story building loomed over the town.

One of the first things I realized about the court was most of the cases were handled with the officer and the violator standing at the judge's bench. Even after thousands of cases, I can still count on one hand the number of times I had to sit in the witness chair to testify. Since most of our cases were misdemeanors, more often than not, the defendant was not represented by counsel.

Therefore, the elegant speeches by the learned defense attorney were basically nonexistent.

I was surprised to learn the assistant district attorney (ADA) didn't really investigate the cases and develop a strong prosecution like they did on the *Law & Order* television program. As a matter of fact, the ADA often didn't even approach the bench for our cases. In the rare event that we would have an actual trial, the ADA would walk over at the beginning of the trial and ask, "What happened?" So much for intense preparation. I knew early on I was on my own when it came to case preparation. Fortunately, that is one reason I can remember so many of the cases we made since I prepared a detailed narrative for them.

Let me take a moment and tell you about a trap many game wardens fall into. Since the majority of the cases we make are "on view," which means the offense was committed in our presence, many officers fail to prepare their case for court. I mean, how difficult is it to step up and tell the judge you saw the guy fishing and he didn't have a license? While that may work fine for a simple license case, all cases aren't that simple. Many officers have been made to look like idiots when they entered court unprepared and ran up against a seasoned defense attorney. I always encouraged young officers to, at the very least, make some good notes on even the simplest case. A detailed narrative was in order for cases that were more serious. This was extremely valuable when you were juggling numerous cases and when a case ended up continuing for several months. After a few years, I realized my ADA had done me a favor by making me prepare my own cases.

Although I learned a lot during my early days in the courtroom, probably one of the most interesting things I discovered in the Coosa County District Court was that the judge, the ADA, and the local defense attorney all shared the same last name! The defense attorney was the dad, and his sons were the district judge and the ADA. I kid you not. Believe it or not, a younger son later replaced his brother as judge. I didn't know much about court, but I knew this sure didn't sound like anything I had heard of previously.

Before you think I am complaining about my district court, let me assure you I am thankful I was fortunate to have good conservation-minded judges in my county. I worked counties where that wasn't the case, and it was totally frustrating. When you are attempting to apprehend an armed violator in the middle of nowhere at two o'clock in the morning with the nearest backup an hour away, it helps to know your judge doesn't like night hunters any more than you do. While we didn't always agree, my judges were a strong defender of Mother Nature and her sword bearers!

As a matter of fact, my first judge shared an interesting story with me. While relaxing in his recliner at about 9:30 p.m., he was jarred from his reverie by the *py-yow* of a high-powered rifle blast that split the night. He said having had some threats, he wasn't sure what might be happening. He grabbed his shotgun and moved to the front door. Looking toward the road, he spotted a stationary vehicle with its headlights shining off the side of the road. Not sure what the people were up to, the judge made a quick decision. He opened the door and shot up in the air. The folks hurriedly left the scene. Problem solved!

The next morning, as the judge pulled out of his driveway en route to the courthouse, he spotted a dead deer lying along the wood line. It was then he realized he had evidently interrupted someone night hunting for deer. Although I never tried it, I kept in the back of my mind the idea if I ever thought it was necessary, I could go by and fire a couple of shots in front of the judge's house the night before court. He would then surely enter the courtroom snarling, fired up, and ready to go. I never really did that. Seriously, I didn't.

Let me repeat, I appreciated the good judges. I felt sorry for the officers who worked in counties where the judge and/or prosecutor did not care about our natural resources. Unfortunately, there were many counties where that was the case. As my friend Terry Grosz was fond of saying, "Wildlife dies without making a sound." Conservation officers are their voice; however, they are only as effective as the judge they bring the violators before.

MISTER, YOUR DEER IS RUINT

EARLY IN MY CAREER, summers were a pretty slow time for conservation enforcement officers (CEOs). After the area lakes had been checked eight or ten times, the violations were normally few and far between. As an area biologist on a 38,000-acre wildlife management area, summers were not at all slow for me. I was responsible for maintaining two hundred miles of road, cleaning out culverts, planting wildlife openings, and a hundred other things, including performing enforcement duties on the area.

One hot summer day for some reason I can't recall, I wasn't on the management area but was at my office in Hanover. I was one of very few area biologists who actually had an office. This was possible only through the benevolence of my friend, Alabama Forestry Commission County Forester Blake Kelley, who allowed me to have an office in his building located along US Highway 231 in the Hanover community. CEO Hershel Patterson and I were at the office around lunchtime when one of the forest rangers, Buddy Adcox, came in and told me he had just seen a man on the side of the road, and he appeared to be dressing a deer. Seeing how deer season had been out for months, Hershel and I decided to go and check it out.

We soon arrived at the intersection of Highway 231 and the Newsite Road, and sure enough, there sat a faded blue van. When we looked into the edge of the woods, we spotted a fellow who was attempting to hoist a deer up in a tree. We noted the man appeared to be by himself. When we asked what he was doing, he said "they" told him he could have the deer, and he was going to take it home to his brother-in-law. He also added he didn't know anything about deer, but his brother-in-law in Florida did.

"Who is they?" I asked. A confused look came across his face. I again asked him, "Who is they?"

He stood staring at me with a look that said he had no clue what I was talking about. I realized I was going to have to clarify things, and I reminded him he had said "they" had told him he could have the deer, and I needed to know who he was referring to. Finally understanding my question, he replied the people who were picking the deer up had told him he could have it. We realized he was talking about the highway department crew that removed dead animals from the roadways.

A quick look at the deer revealed the highway crew definitely should have picked this deer up, probably about three days earlier! The deer was in bad shape. The eyes had been removed, I suppose by black vultures, and the hide on the stomach had already turned green. Noting this, I explained to the man that in the first place, the highway department did not have the authority to allow him to possess a deer in closed season, and it was illegal for him to do so. I went on to tell him this deer was not fit for human consumption. The man again stated he didn't know anything about deer, but his brother-in-law did, and he was taking it to him. I again told him he could not have the deer, and it wasn't fit to eat.

Once again, it was as if the guy did not understand what I was saying. I could not tell if the fellow was just totally dense or if maybe he was playing dumb to hopefully avoid a ticket, but for some reason the guy just couldn't seem to comprehend what I was telling him. Up until this point, I had done all of the talking. Sensing that the guy definitely wasn't the sharpest knife in the drawer, Hershel evidently decided to put things in layman's terms. He looked at the man and said "Mister, your deer is ruint! You can't have it! It's ruint!"

"Okay," was the man's quick reply.

Obviously, Hershel knew the proper vernacular to get through to the man.

The man began removing the rope from the deer, and we got back in our vehicle and headed back to the office. As we were discussing what had just occurred, we met Blake, the county forester, heading in the other direction. I radioed him and asked him to look when he got to the Newsite Road and let me know whether or not there was a van sitting there. About three minutes later, he called back and said there was a van there, and it appeared a guy was trying to load a deer onto the top of it. I wanted to throw up.

Minutes later, Hershel and I stood outside the forestry office, and sure enough, the van went by headed to Florida, at least two hundred miles away, with the deer strapped to the roof. I looked at Hershel and asked him if he wanted to run him down and write him a ticket. He replied, "No, if he hates his brother-in-law that bad, let him take it to him!"

What about you? Have you ever been told not to do something, but you went ahead and did it anyway? How did that turn out for you? We all go astray from time to time. The Bible says all have sinned and come short of the glory of God. However, it says if we will confess our sin and ask forgiveness, it can be obtained. God has a plan for you. Unlike the guy in this story, God's plan is to prosper you not harm you. He says take up your cross and follow Him. It won't be easy; however, the benefits are literally out of this world!

YOU ARE A LOT NICER THAN THE LAST GUY

While it was always good to receive information from the public, some folks understood the type of information we needed better than others. Learning that someone had shot sometime during the night around someone's house was good; however, being informed someone in a white car had shot in the hayfield beside the bridge at 1:30 a.m. was much better information! That was information I could do something with, and I did.

My friend Alabama Forestry Commission Forest Ranger Buddy Adcox was a source of good "detailed" information. If he told me something, I could count on it to be the case. Therefore, when he reported someone was shooting in his hay field around three thirty in the morning, I immediately made plans to work it. However, I was not totally elated. Complaints of shooting between two and four in the morning were the worst. I had learned I could handle working until 2:00 a.m., or I could come out at 4:00 a.m. and work the rest of the day, but for some reason coming out at two in the morning was rough. However, I knew if you wanted to catch 'em, you had to be there when they were doing it. Another thing that was always true was anybody you saw out at 3:00 a.m. was a dang good prospect!

I set my alarm for 2:05 a.m. Deep in the hunting season, the sixty- and seventy-hour weeks began to take their toll. It was somewhat of a mind game to set the clock for five or ten minutes later than what it needed to be to try and trick myself into believing I was getting a little more sleep. Of course, when I had a hot tip to work, I was normally awake prior to the alarm going off. Such was the case this morning, and I was in my truck and headed north at 2:15. Unfortunately, my system had not appreciated the early wakeup call and was letting me know with a very uneasy rumbling and pain in my "stomach." It was not a slight discomfort kind of pain; it was the type of pain that said you had better find a bathroom—*now*!

You must keep in mind where I was. In rural Coosa County, you were hard pressed to find a public bathroom in the daytime much less at two thirty in the morning. As a matter of fact, there was no public restroom anywhere in our county after ten o'clock at night through the week and eleven o'clock on the weekend! Fortunately, I was near the Forestry Commission Office, so I pulled into the parking lot and hurried toward the back door. It wasn't easy hurrying with my butt clenched together, but I did the best I could. As I tried to get my key in the door in the dark, it was evident a violent episode was taking place in my body. I got the door open and made it to the bathroom, but not before things really went south, if you know what I mean. As I was taking care of business in more ways than I care to write about, I was debating whether or not I should continue with my plan to work night hunting or head back home to the "comfort" of my familiar toilet. Either way, I would be going commando!

I decided to hope for the best, and, armed with a roll of toilet paper (a good game warden always had a roll of toilet paper in the truck), I entered my truck and made my way to my "hidey hole" overlooking Buddy's pasture. I got out and pulled back the webbed wire fence and backed up in between the large pine trees that lined the fence row. This was a good observation point. The area was high enough above the road that it allowed me to view the road and the pasture while staying hidden and at the same time provided quick access to the road. Sites with all these attributes were few and far between.

I turned the ignition switch into the "off" position and looked at my watch, which read 3:00 a.m. I found it interesting that even with my unexpected pitstop and clean up, I had arrived at my preplanned time. Literally as I was checking the time, I saw light in my peripheral vision. I couldn't believe it as a spotlight swept across the pasture. Seconds later, a small white SUV eased past me and the passenger kept the field lit up with the spotlight. I had not been in position for more than one minute!

I cranked the truck and picked up the radio microphone and called Conservation Enforcement Officer (CEO) Bud Philippi. Bud had said he would be out working; however, we had not talked about where, and I doubted he would be out this late. Therefore, I was a little surprised when he immediately answered the call. I told him I was on County Road 35 and was about to stop a white SUV that was night hunting. I was once again shocked when he replied he was also on County 35. I told him I was crossing the bridge and would be out of the truck. I activated my blue lights and the driver immediately pulled the vehicle to the side of the road. I exited my truck and ordered the four occupants to raise their hands. Bud and CEO Shannon Calfee arrived seconds later. I was glad to see them since multiple suspects always made the odds against the officer even worse than they were to start with.

As I eased up to the vehicle, I observed that each rear-seat passenger had a long gun. I once again gave the loud verbal command for everyone to keep their hands up. As I approached closer, I observed a shotgun between the front seat passenger and the console. I asked if there were any more weapons other than the three shotguns in the vehicle, and the front-seat passenger stated there was a rifle between him and the door. We gathered the four long guns and four spotlights and placed them in my truck. This was the only time I ever recall catching four night hunters and finding that each one had a long gun and a light. Two was common, three wasn't unheard of, but four was definitely unusual.

I began gathering identification from the violators and learned both rear seat passengers were juveniles. Any time juveniles were involved, it always complicated things. We decided to take everybody to jail and sort things out. Shannon placed one of the adults in the truck with him, and Bud drove the SUV to the jail.

On the way to the jail, I had the dispatcher run the driver's license numbers for the two adults and learned the driver's license was suspended and he had an outstanding warrant in Harpersville, a small town approximately forty miles north of Rockford. I asked them to advise Harpersville we had him in custody and were en route to the county jail if they wanted to pick him up there.

We arrived at the jail and began handling the paperwork for hunting from a public road, hunting by aid of a vehicle, hunting at night, and hunting without a permit. We learned the juvenile officer was out of town, and it took several attempts to reach her assistant who for some reason didn't immediately answer her phone at four thirty in the morning. She said to allow the juveniles to go with the adult present. Although that didn't seem like a good idea to me, seeing how he had just led them down a bad path, it wasn't my call.

The sky was just beginning to lighten when I told the younger adult and the juveniles they were free to go. The older fellow with the warrant extended his hand to shake mine and said, "I appreciate it," and added, "You were a lot nicer than the guy that caught me last year."

This revelation both tickled me and piqued my interest. I asked, "Who was that?"

He replied, "It was Fincher in Talladega County."

As we ended our handshake, Harpersville Police Department showed up and took the driver into custody.

I couldn't wait to call CEO Jerry Fincher. I had been Jerry's default training officer, as we did not have a formal field training officer program when he was hired. I had been working for fifteen years when he was hired, and I did my best to teach him what the veteran game wardens had taught me. He took to it like a duck to water and turned out to be a fine officer. I called him on the phone, and when he answered in his groggy voice, I told him number one he needed to keep his night hunting residents in his county, and number two I wanted him to be a little nicer to ones he apprehended! Of course, he knew that meant I had caught some folks from his county. I told him the whole story, save the violent stomach episode. While we were happy to catch anybody, it was always good to get a frequent flyer!

The defendants pled guilty in court and paid fines and costs and lost their firearms. It would not be our last encounter with all four of these defendants. Imagine that!

According to the violator, I was a lot nicer than the last guy that caught him. Fortunately, I heard that from time to time. Of course, I've heard the opposite of that as well. Early in my career I was known as someone who would write their own mother a ticket. Later on, I mellowed some, like most do. I wrote a lot of people tickets that they knew would cost them thousands of dollars, and yet, like the guy in this story, we shook hands when the paperwork was done. Many of them would tell me they appreciated it. They were not saying they appreciated getting a ticket, they were saying they appreciated the way they were treated. I strived for that response.

I've heard it said we should be more concerned with our character than our reputation since our character is who we are and our reputation is just what people think. I read a quote by the great preacher D. L. Moody that said, "If I take care of my character, my reputation will take care of itself." I did my best to live by that.

MURDER IN RICHVILLE

As I observed a man lying in a pool of blood, another individual approached me and said, "I did it." Although I had been told about things such as this in the police academy, this was my first spontaneous exclamation and my first murder case!

Being one of few law enforcement officers of any kind in a rural county, I had the opportunity to respond to many calls that were not related to the enforcement of wildlife laws and regulations. In Alabama, conservation enforcement officers (CEOs) are certified by the Alabama Peace Officers Standards and Training Commission and possess full arrest powers. I have responded to calls ranging from domestic disputes to elementary school discipline problems to drive-by shootings. One of my most memorable calls occurred one night while I was working a night hunting detail with my supervisor, Rick. We were in the southwest part of Coosa County, a favorite area for folks who would stoop to the level of shooting a deer at night. The night had been very uneventful, and we were dozing occasionally.

Having worked a lot of night hunting details, I had learned to sleep, carry on a conversation, and listen to traffic on the radio all at the same time. I know that sounds impossible; however, I have a list of partners who can verify it. Although the sound of the dispatcher calling my radio number would pull me out of sleep, I was not asleep on this night when I heard the sheriff's office dispatcher call the only deputy on duty and ask for his location. Deputy Bearden responded he was in the northeast part of the county. The dispatcher told him he needed to be 10-84 (en route) 10-17 (urgently) to a residence in the Richville area, where a 10-92 had occurred. Fortunately, I can count on one hand the number of times I heard the code 10-92 used on the radio. Although this was the first time I had ever heard it used, I knew it was the code for murder. I looked at Rick and told him we were only about two miles from the scene and the deputy was about thirty miles away, so we had better head over there. He wasn't happy about it but agreed. I called the dispatcher and told her we were close by and would be en route and secure the scene for the deputy.

In a couple of minutes, we were pulling up at the residence. There were several vehicles at the house, and a few people were standing in the back yard. As we pulled up to the rear of the house, I spotted the body of a black male lying about twelve feet from the rear door of the house. I exited the truck and started toward the body. The man was lying in a large pool of blood that appeared to have come from a wound on his head. I checked the man for a pulse and found none. As I stood up, I was approached by a young man who said, "I did it. He was going to shoot me, and I shot him."

I had never before been the recipient of what at the academy I was taught was a "spontaneous exclamation," especially not one concerning someone shooting somebody. I must admit I was somewhat taken aback. I told the man I needed to advise him of his rights. I read him the Miranda warning, and he stated he understood. I asked him where his gun was. He responded he would go and get it, and he took off around the end of the house. I shouted for him to stop and told him I would retrieve it, and he just needed to show me the location. He led me to the chimney at the end of the house and showed me he had placed it in the cleanout area of the chimney. I looked at the gun and noticed the slide was locked back. Later examination revealed the gun, a .25-caliber semiautomatic pocket pistol, had jammed after the one shot was fired.

I told the subject we would leave the gun there for now, and we returned to my truck, where I took a quick statement from him. He explained the now deceased man had gotten mad at him for some unknown reason and had come out of the house with a shotgun to shoot him. He said he had pulled his gun out and fired at the man, and the gun had broken. I left the man in my vehicle and went back to the area where the confrontation had occurred. The story seemed to coincide with the evidence in that there was a shotgun lying beside the dead man and he was struck once just above the eye. I began to take down the names of some of the people on the scene. After a few more minutes, Deputy Dan Bearden arrived and I briefed him on what I had, and he took over the investigation. He asked if I would take photos of everything, and I did. The funeral home personnel arrived and took the body. Rick and I left shortly thereafter.

I had the photographs developed and gave them to Dan. That was the extent of my involvement in the case, a fact I found interesting. The case later went to trial; the man was convicted and sentenced to prison. Although I took the initial confession from the man, Rick and I secured the crime scene, and I took the photographs and interviewed several witnesses, no one ever contacted me concerning the incident or subsequent trial. Although that was hard to figure out, it wasn't the most intriguing aspect of this case. What I did not mention earlier was this incident occurred at a party.

Now it isn't unusual for violence to erupt at a gathering, especially when alcohol is involved. The interesting part of this was the party never stopped! From the time we arrived until we left about an hour later, the music never stopped nor did the dancing and carrying on. It was unlike anything I had ever seen. People would exit the house and basically step around the body as if it were a mud puddle. I had never seen such disregard. While there were probably thirty-plus people at the residence, only one woman asked if we would cover the body with a sheet. The owner of the home, the girlfriend of the deceased, did not come out of the house until the deputy went inside and brought her out.

Looking back, I'm very thankful I responded to few murders during my tenure. I would have hated to have to deal with that type of situation on a regular basis. Dealing with the deer and turkey killers was bad enough!

BUMPER JACK

THE DEER DECOY is a great wildlife law enforcement tool and probably one of the best deterrents to hunting from the road. The decoys we used were made by my good friend and mentor Conservation Enforcement Officer (CEO), Ret., Byron Smith. They were simply mounted deer with some robotics thrown in. Various options were available. The typical model came complete with a head that would turn about 180 degrees and a tail that would wag up and down. This was necessary after the decoy had been in use for a while. I wish I would have kept up with how many times folks shot our stationary deer. I do remember our first stationary buck, with its dinky three-point rack, had forty-three holes in it when we retired it and went with the upgraded model.

I cannot tell you how many times I had someone tell me they had seen our decoy. They normally always reported they knew it was a decoy because it didn't move and it really didn't look real. Many of them would comment they didn't know why anyone would shoot it since it looked so fake. This was interesting since the areas of their reported sightings were seldom anywhere we had used the decoy. If they saw a deer there, it was a real one. There is no way to know, but I would guess the deer decoys saved the lives of thousands of deer in Alabama and across the country.

They looked good. Good enough to fool hundreds of road hunters during my career.

Using the decoy was usually productive, sometimes amusing, and occasionally aggravating. The aggravation came when someone would see the deer and decide they needed to scare it off so no one would shoot it, or they would sit and take numerous pictures of the stuffed wonder. Eventually we would have to come out of our hiding place and run these lookie-loos off. More than once, these innocent onlookers prevented our apprehension of a real outlaw.

One night, the Coosa County game wardens had deployed the decoy along the side of a rural county road and were hiding in the bushes on the opposite side of the road. About 8:00 p.m., a car rolled to a stop with its headlights illuminating the fake deer. CEO Earl Brown thought sure he was in business. The driver's-side door slowly opened. While most folks simply stuck the barrel of their rifle out the window and shot, some would get out of their vehicle to shoot at the deer. The driver emerged from the car and stealthily made his way to the trunk. He opened the trunk and removed what was thought to be a long gun and started toward the front of the car and the deer.

Having seen enough and thinking he could keep from having another hole or two added to the decoy, the warden left his hiding spot and pulled up behind the vehicle. As he exited his truck, he noticed the man turned toward his car and pitched the "gun" in the window. Earl gave the loud verbal command for the man to raise his hands and not to reach for the gun. The man replied he didn't have a gun. The officer had heard that many times before. He ordered the man to stand still, and he moved up to the car to retrieve the weapon. Shining his Maglite into the car, he was surprised when instead of a firearm, he was looking at a bumper jack!

The officer looked at the man and asked, "What were you going to do with that?"

The man didn't skip a beat when he turned and pointed at the deer and said, "I was gonna kill that deer. Look at it, there's something wrong with it."

A little baffled by the situation, and not wanting to explain what was wrong with the deer, the officer told the man it was illegal to try to kill a deer at night, and he needed to get back in his car and be on his way.

On another night, we had deployed the decoy across the ditch and on a hill approximately thirty-five yards off the roadway. As was more often than not the case, several vehicles came by while we were trying to get the deer set up. With things in place, we started back across the road. As fate would have it, about the time we stepped in the road, we saw headlights coming. Quickening my pace, I promptly fell in the middle of the road. I was not injured, but there was a problem. My eyeglasses had come off, and I was now feeling around in the road for them, all the while watching as a vehicle neared my location. After a few long seconds of searching, I located the glasses and scampered across the road. While I didn't find much humor in the situation, the two veteran officers found it quite comical. I was beginning to think they were going to need some oxygen, as they had laughed until they were losing their breath. I didn't find it to be that funny.

Once the laughter had died down, we began our night hunter vigil. The wait wasn't long. An older model Ford pickup eased along the road and came to a stop with its lights shining on the decoy. This always caused an increase of my heart rate. We waited in anticipation of a shot. However, instead of shooting the fake deer, the driver eased the truck through the ditch toward the deer. Several thoughts ran through our minds. We considered the possibility the driver was armed with a handgun and needed to get closer or possibly just wanted to see how close he could get to the deer. The suspense didn't last long. The driver eased up until he was within about thirty feet of the antlered manikin and floored the accelerator and ran over the $600 deer. I have not mentioned that our department did not furnish decoys for us. Although we occasionally had some benefactor who wanted to assist with the cost of a decoy, we normally ended up footing much of the bill.

With our decoy now up under the man's truck, our jaws all hit the ground. We quickly regained our composure and ran through the ditch and up the hill and pulled the driver out. His flimsy explanation was he had never killed a buck and just wanted to kill one. We informed him he still hadn't killed one. We examined the deer and found that it miraculously wasn't damaged. Despite my objections, the two senior officers declined to charge the individual. Man, someone tried to kill a deer with a bumper jack, I crawl around in the road in front of an oncoming car, and some Einstein runs over our decoy with his truck. I couldn't help but wonder what was going to happen next; a bunch of teenagers trying to kill deer with large rocks! Yep, that happened too.

Byron shared one of his more memorable decoy-related stories with me. He said he had just apprehended a fellow who had shot the fake deer. As he wrote the fellow a ticket, the man, who was staring at the decoy, asked, "How do you get that deer to just stand there like that?"

Stifling a laugh, the officer replied he had poured out a bag of corn, and the deer would stand there and eat it.

The shooter enthusiastically replied, "Really!"

Byron didn't skip a beat when he answered, saying, "Yeah, but we lose a lot of good deer that way."

The fellow just shook his head and got in his truck and pulled away.

BUMPER JACK

Believe me when I tell you, you can't make this stuff up. You never knew what would happen when the decoy and the public were involved.

IT'S NOT EASY WEARING GREEN

It's not easy wearing green

Being perceived as harsh and mean

Trying to police people's recreation

Striving to protect God's creation

Being known as one who holds to what's right

Getting calls all during the day and night

Harassing people who are just trying to have fun

Exploiting the resource with rod and gun

Chasing outlaws in the dead of night

Not knowing whether they will flee or fight

Watching what your family has to go through

Having people ask them if they know you

Having friends whose conversations end when you join the crowd

Being openly ridiculed and cussed right out loud

Because so many feel they are above the law

IT'S NOT EASY WEARING GREEN

It's only deer and turkey after all

Even in court they often get a slap on the wrist

By judges who fail to realize the danger and risk

It was hurtful when their actions said they didn't really care

That you were face-to-face with death in the middle of nowhere

Normally outnumbered and often ill-equipped

Just a badge on your chest and a pistol on your hip

And yet I made it through it

I faced the bad and mean

And there was good with the bad

That came with wearing green

The thousands of times the judge said "guilty"

Which more often than not was the case

The sense of accomplishment

Seeing outlaws put in their rightful place

Working with a landowner and having them understand

That it's the habitat on the ground not the feed spread around

Working with kids and after seeing the light come on

Understanding how a teacher feels

And why they would stay in a classroom with all of its ills

And though it wasn't easy and sometimes was downright mean

IT'S NOT EASY WEARING GREEN

I don't know what I'd have rather done
than have a career wearing green

And now those days are over, and I will fade away

Although some may recall, few will probably remember

Until maybe late one night in a dreary and cold December

When somebody shoots and someone rolls up on the scene

Gets out of their truck and they're wearing green

I pray God will richly bless you, as he has me

My blessings are many

My troubles are few

The Savior is waiting to hear from you

ANOTHER DIVINE APPOINTMENT

DURING MY CAREER, most folks in wildlife law enforcement preferred to fly under the radar, meaning we did not try to call attention to ourselves or our job. I think we erroneously thought maybe if folks didn't think much about us, they wouldn't be expecting us to be hiding and watching them or snooping around on their property. The reality was, the hunting public and especially the outlaw segment knew us very well. Many knew our work schedule, where we lived, and could recognize the tire tread on our vehicle. We weren't fooling many folks.

Unfortunately, what we were doing was preventing any recognition with the general public. The vast majority of the population have no idea who the game warden is or what they do. Several times I have had people wearing a surprised look on their face ask why a game warden would carry a gun. I have literally been asked if I carried a gun in case I was attacked by a deer. I kid you not. I am thankful for the conservation officer television shows that give the general public some insight into what goes on.

This anonymity being prevalent even in my rural county, many folks would regularly call the sheriff's office (SO) when they encountered a hunting problem. This was usually not a problem, except that it often delayed our response time when an immediate response would have made a difference. For the most part, the SO dispatchers were pretty good about routing the calls to us, but depending on the load of their own calls, there was often a delay.

One night about 7:30 p.m., I received a call from Coosa County Dispatch stating that Deputy Matt Cook was at a residence in the Stewartville area of the county and was requesting our assistance. As I got my truck headed in his direction, I called Matt and asked what he had. He explained a landowner was complaining that a neighbor had shot a deer, possibly on their property, and had definitely come onto their property to retrieve the deer. They had asked the fellow previously not to come onto their property and had placed Posted signs on the land. They reported the neighbor was currently cleaning the deer he had taken earlier at this time. I told Matt my ETA was approximately twenty minutes.

These type situations were often problematic. Although the landowner had advised the neighbor not to be on the property, when it came down to the neighbor being arrested, the landowner would often back up and decide they just wanted to have the person warned again. On many occasions, I have advised they could either prosecute the violator or write them a permit to hunt the property. While I definitely understand wanting to keep peace in the neighborhood, I also understand that when you tell someone to stay off of your property and they come on it again and you just let it go, then they often become a perpetual problem. As I thought about the address of this complaint, I realized I had been there the previous season to handle a complaint about their neighbor. Therefore, I didn't have a good feeling about this.

I shortly arrived on the scene, and sure enough, it was the same folks from last year. I approached the deputy and the landowners and asked what was going on. The landowner explained his wife had heard a shot right at dark and had then seen someone walking across their property. Minutes later, she saw the neighbor pull his truck to the edge of the property. He later emerged from the woods and loaded a deer onto his truck and drove off. I asked if she could identify who it was, and she said she could and provided me with his name. I asked what they wanted done about this. Since I had not witnessed anything, if a case was to be made, it would have to be the result of investigation, and she would need to be willing to testify. She and her husband briefly discussed the matter. The husband told me the man had been asked to stay off the property and they had posted the property with signs. I told them I would talk to the neighbor and, if need be, I would be back and get a written statement from them.

Deputy Cook and I went two doors down to the neighbor's house and there found a young man cleaning a doe deer. I approached the man and introduced myself and Deputy Cook and told him I needed to speak with him. He said that was fine, but he would like to keep working on the deer if I didn't mind. I told him that would be fine; however, I did want to ask him some questions, so I needed to advise him of his rights. I read him the Miranda warning, and he stated he understood. I asked him to tell me about killing the deer. He said he had not killed a deer all season and needed some meat, so he went onto his relative's land and shot the doe. I asked if he had a hunting license, and he said he didn't think he needed one on private property. I asked who owned the property, and he said it belonged to his granddad's cousin. I advised him that unless he or his parents owned the property, he needed a license. He simply shrugged his shoulders and kept working on the deer. I asked if he thought he might have gotten off onto his neighbor's land, and he said he didn't think so. Before I could ask another question, he stated that he had dragged the deer out across their property and loaded it on his truck that was parked on their property. As he placed the last piece of deer meat into a cooler, I asked if he would be willing to take me and show me where he had shot the deer. Soon we were walking through the dark woods. We hadn't gone far when I realized he either wasn't sure where he was or was trying to get me disoriented. After we had made a circle and come back to where we had started, the fellow admitted to me he wasn't sure where he had shot the deer. I asked if he knew where the property line was, and he said he wasn't sure.

We continued to look through the area, and Deputy Cook eventually located some blood. While we did not definitely find where the deer had been shot, we did establish that the deer and the hunter had been on the posted property at least part of the time. As we walked back to the hunter's property, I explained that he had a few violations we needed to discuss. I explained he was definitely in violation by not having a hunting license or a harvest record, which was also required. In addition, I told him I had a feeling the deer was killed on the neighboring property and, at the least, he had entered the adjacent property to retrieve the deer without first obtaining permission.

Alabama Regulation 220-2-.13 is entitled "Reasonable Effort Must Be Made to Retrieve Crippled Birds, Animals and Fish." It says, "It shall be illegal for any person, firm, or corporation to kill or cripple any species of game bird, game animal or game fish without making a reasonable effort to retrieve same and include it in his daily bag or creel limit."

Unfortunately, many folks fail to read the entire regulation, and this leads to problems. The second segment of the regulation states, "Nothing in this regulation permits or requires a person to enter upon the land or waters of another for the purpose of retrieving game or fish without the permission of the landowner." I have encountered several people on property where they have no permission to be who have attempted to use this regulation to justify their actions. It doesn't fly.

I told the hunter that I would continue the investigation into the incident, but I felt certain I would be contacting him soon with a warrant or warrants for his arrest. I assured him his cooperation would play a major part in the charges he would receive. I obtained his phone number and we shook hands and I left the scene.

Further investigation revealed the suspect had not had a hunting license for the past couple of years. I knew early on I would be charging him with hunting without a license and no harvest record. I found myself torn as to whether or not to charge him with hunting on the land of another without permission. Whether he was on the property of his relative or that of his neighbor, he did not possess written permission from either one. While I felt he was guilty of this, the minimum fine for this violation was $1,000. I decided that instead of bringing that charge, I would charge him with a violation of the retrieval regulation. If the judge would take my recommendation for a minimum fine on all charges, this would result in a total penalty of around $400.

I obtained the warrants and phoned the defendant. He advised he could meet me that evening. We met in Stewartville at five thirty in the afternoon. I explained the charges and completed bonds for each. While filling out the paperwork I explained his good attitude had gone a long way in determining his charges. It also had been the reason he had been allowed to keep the deer and was allowed to sign his own appearance bond instead of being processed through the jail. He thanked me and was on his way.

The next month, I stood in the front of the courtroom, scanning the faces of those in attendance. Many times, it is difficult to recognize folks, even though it may have only been a few weeks since you arrested them. I finally spotted the young man. Unfortunately, the names were on the docket in alphabetical order, which meant this fellow would be near the end of the list.

Probably ninety minutes later, the man's name was called, and we approached the judge's bench. The man was wearing leather and carried a motorcycle helmet in his hand. The judge asked the man if he wanted the court to appoint him an attorney, and replied he did not. The judge had him sign an attorney waiver and then read the charges and asked how he pled. "I'm guilty," was his reply. The judge told him his fines and court costs would total $400 and asked if he could pay that or if he needed some time. The judge asked how much he could pay today, and he replied, "Forty dollars." The judge advised him he would give him three months to pay the remainder and that he was free to go.

About three months later, I was watching the nightly news when a story caught my attention. Sheriff's deputies in a nearby county had been involved in a high-speed pursuit of an individual on a motorcycle. While that type thing was pretty routine, when they gave the name of the motorcyclist, I immediately recognized it as the same name as the fellow I had had in court months earlier. Unfortunately, during the pursuit, the rider had hit a car head-on and had died at the scene. It was the same young man I had encountered. He was twenty-nine years old.

You may have noticed the title of this story is "Another Divine Appointment." The last story in my first book was entitled "Divine Appointment." It was the story of a fellow I had arrested who was killed in a motorcycle accident prior to appearing in court. I stated I felt certain the fellow had every intention of making it to his court date; however, he did not know there had been a divine appointment scheduled for him. We all have a divine appointment scheduled for us. We don't know the day, but we can rest assured it's coming. Unless the Lord returns first, we will all die.

It may occur like it did for these two men. Fast, quick, and in a hurry—and not at all expected. I hope they were ready to meet the Lord. Are you? Many stories in this book ended asking you that question. There is no question that is more important. We will all spend eternity in either heaven or hell. Our choice now will make that determination. God sent his only son, Jesus, who lived a sinless life and died on a cruel cross so that we could be forgiven. He is ready to forgive you today. Today is *the* day to move from a position of *no* hope and move to one of eternal life. The Bible says, "If you confess with your mouth, 'Jesus is Lord,' and believe in your heart that God raised him from the dead, you will be saved. For it is with your heart that you believe and are justified, and it is with your mouth that you confess and are saved" (Romans 10:9–10).

"For God so loved the world that He gave His one and only Son, that whoever believes in Him shall not perish, but have eternal life" (John 3:16).

To receive the free pardon of sin and accept Jesus as your Savior you need to:
- Admit you are a sinner.
- Believe Jesus died for your sins and God raised Jesus from the dead.
- Confess Jesus as your Lord and Savior.

If you have questions or concerns you would like help with, seek out your local Bible-based church. You can also go to the rickandbubba.com website and click on the "Faith" tab.

Remember, we will all die, and it may be sooner than we think.

I pray God will richly bless you. He has me.

EPILOGUE

As you can tell, I've lived a charmed life. It was at times not easy wearing green; however, it was a great life. I didn't have a great life because of my job; the Lord gave me a great life. I was blessed with Christian parents who loved each other and loved me. My sister loved me and supported me 100 percent. My wife supported me in every endeavor and loves me despite my faults. I was blessed with two sons and had many good people in my life. I thank my Uncle Reed for instilling in me a love of the outdoors that led me to my career.

I have been truly blessed.

I would like to thank my high school ag teacher, Greg Hamner, for appointing me the reporter for the Future Farmers of America and making me write a column in the school newspaper. I thank Mrs. Marcia Nesbitt, my tenth-grade English teacher, for providing me the essentials of writing and speaking. I thank Mr. Gary Green, my all-time favorite college professor, for being a good example of a man of character. I thank my dear friend and fellow wildlife biologist Dr. Jeanne Jones for supporting me and being a good friend. I thank CEOs who helped me along the way. These are just a few of the folks who shaped me along the way. There are many others, and I thank you all.

God bless.

www.ingramcontent.com/pod-product-compliance
Lightning Source LLC
Chambersburg PA
CBHW050618300426
44112CB00012B/1561